RELAY ™

VOLUME 1

REALITY DENIED

ZAC THOMPSON
ANDY CLARKE
DALIBOR TALAJIĆ
ERIC BROMBERG
DONNY CATES

R E L A Y
V O L U M E 1
R E A L I T Y D E N I E D

ZAC THOMPSON writer

ANDY CLARKE & **DALIBOR TALAJIC** artists

ERIC BROMBERG, DONNY CATES & **ZAC THOMPSON** story

JOSE VILLARRUBIA (#1-5) & **DAN BROWN** (#0-1) colorists

CHARLES PRITCHETT letterer

ANDY CLARKE w/ **DAN BROWN** & **JOSE VILLARRUBIA** front cover & original covers

ANDY CLARKE, KAEL NGU, LUCIO PARILLO, HAYDEN SHERMAN & **CHRISTIAN WARD** variant covers

JOHN J. HILL logo designer

COREY BREEN book designer

MIKE MARTS editor

AFTERSHOCK™

MIKE MARTS - Editor-in-Chief • **JOE PRUETT** - Publisher/CCO • **LEE KRAMER** - President • **JON KRAMER** - Chief Executive Officer
STEVE ROTTERDAM - SVP, Sales & Marketing • **DAN SHIRES** - VP, Film & Television UK • **CHRISTINA HARRINGTON** - Managing Editor
MARC HAMMOND - Sr. Retail Sales Development Manager • **RUTHANN THOMPSON** - Sr. Retailer Relations Manager • **BLAKE STOCKER** - Chief Financial Officer
AARON MARION - Publicist • **LISA MOODY** - Finance • **RYAN CARROLL** - Development Coordinator • **CHARLES PRITCHETT** - Comics Production
COREY BREEN - Collections Production • **TEDDY LEO** - Editorial Assistant • **STEPHANIE CASEBIER** & **SARAH PRUETT** - Publishing Assistants

AfterShock Logo Design by **COMICRAFT**
Publicity: contact **AARON MARION** (aaron@publichausagency.com) & **RYAN CROY** (ryan@publichausagency.com) at **PUBLICHAUS**
Special thanks to: **IRA KURGAN, MARINE KSADZHIKYAN, ANTONIA LIANOS, STEPHAN NILSON** & **JULIE PIFHER**

I N T R O D U C T I O N

In RELAY, Zac Thompson asks the big questions.

Against the backdrop of this cosmos-spanning comic, Zac questions the core of our shared humanity. Does unity eventually lead to uniformity? What is the best way to govern—the greatest good for the greatest number, or are there natural tiers of humankind? What is the path to happiness—stable and fulfilling, or risky and exciting? These big questions are inspired by the works of sci-fi master Philip K. Dick, who often seeks the objective truths within our subjective "reality".

He inspires those like Zac.

I am thrilled to have taken part in this grand endeavor called RELAY, and I hope readers continue to love it as much as we've loved seeing it come to life. I, too, am inspired by Philip K. Dick. In fact, I'm inspired and intrigued by the entire genre of science fiction—for, oftentimes, a potential scenario can tell us more about humanity than an actual one. Yet as machine-based decisions continue to shape our society, we are increasingly living in a science fiction world, one where the potentials are suddenly becoming the actuals. It is, in many ways, precarious progress.

I only hope we keep asking the big questions about tomorrow, so that we can make better decisions—our own decisions, channeling our own humanity—today.

ERIC BROMBERG
April 2019

THE FARMER AND THE FIRST WORLD

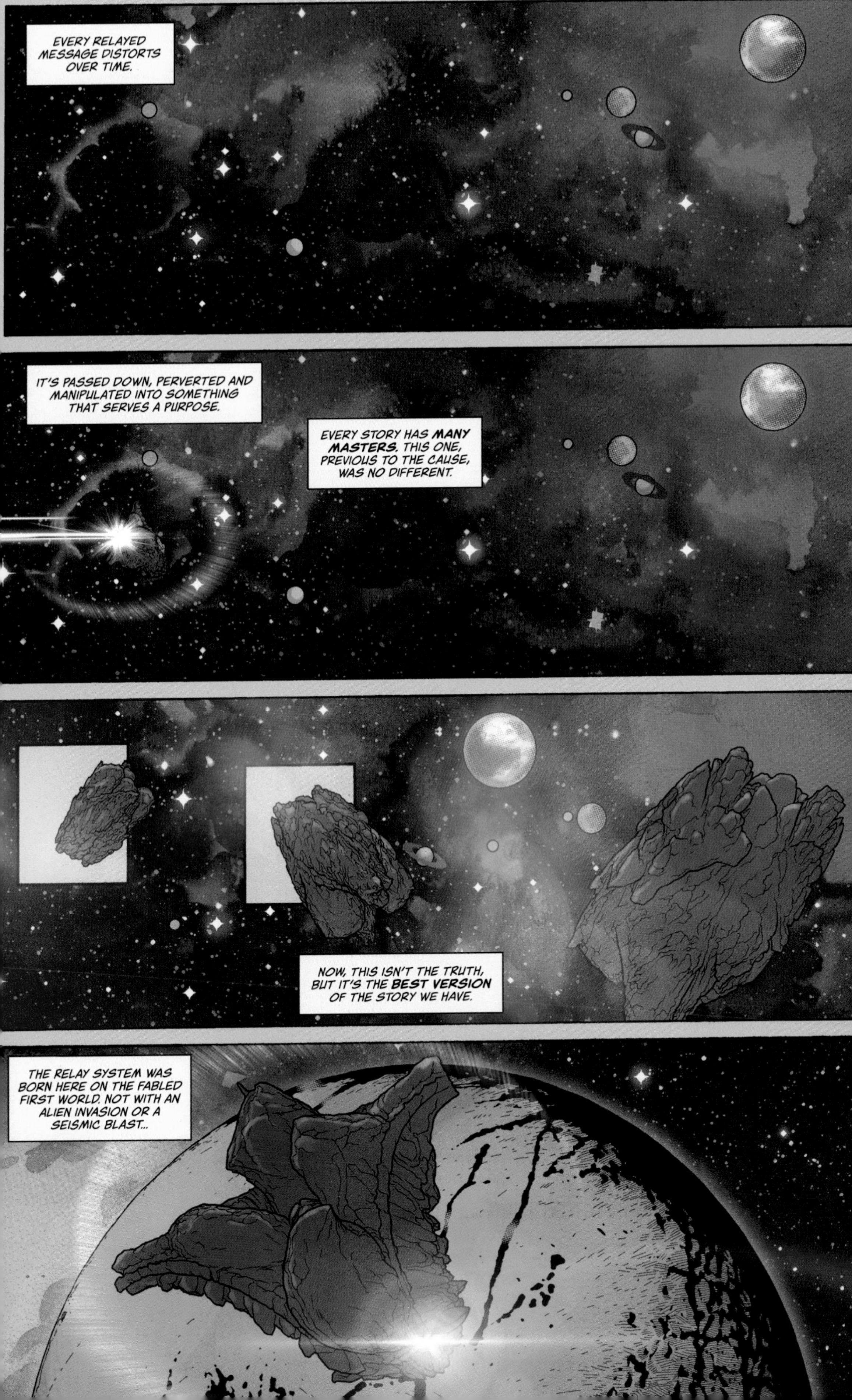
EVERY RELAYED MESSAGE DISTORTS OVER TIME.
IT'S PASSED DOWN, PERVERTED AND MANIPULATED INTO SOMETHING THAT SERVES A PURPOSE.
EVERY STORY HAS **MANY MASTERS.** THIS ONE, PREVIOUS TO THE CAUSE, WAS NO DIFFERENT.
NOW, THIS ISN'T THE TRUTH, BUT IT'S THE **BEST VERSION** OF THE STORY WE HAVE.
THE RELAY SYSTEM WAS BORN HERE ON THE FABLED FIRST WORLD. NOT WITH AN ALIEN INVASION OR A SEISMIC BLAST...

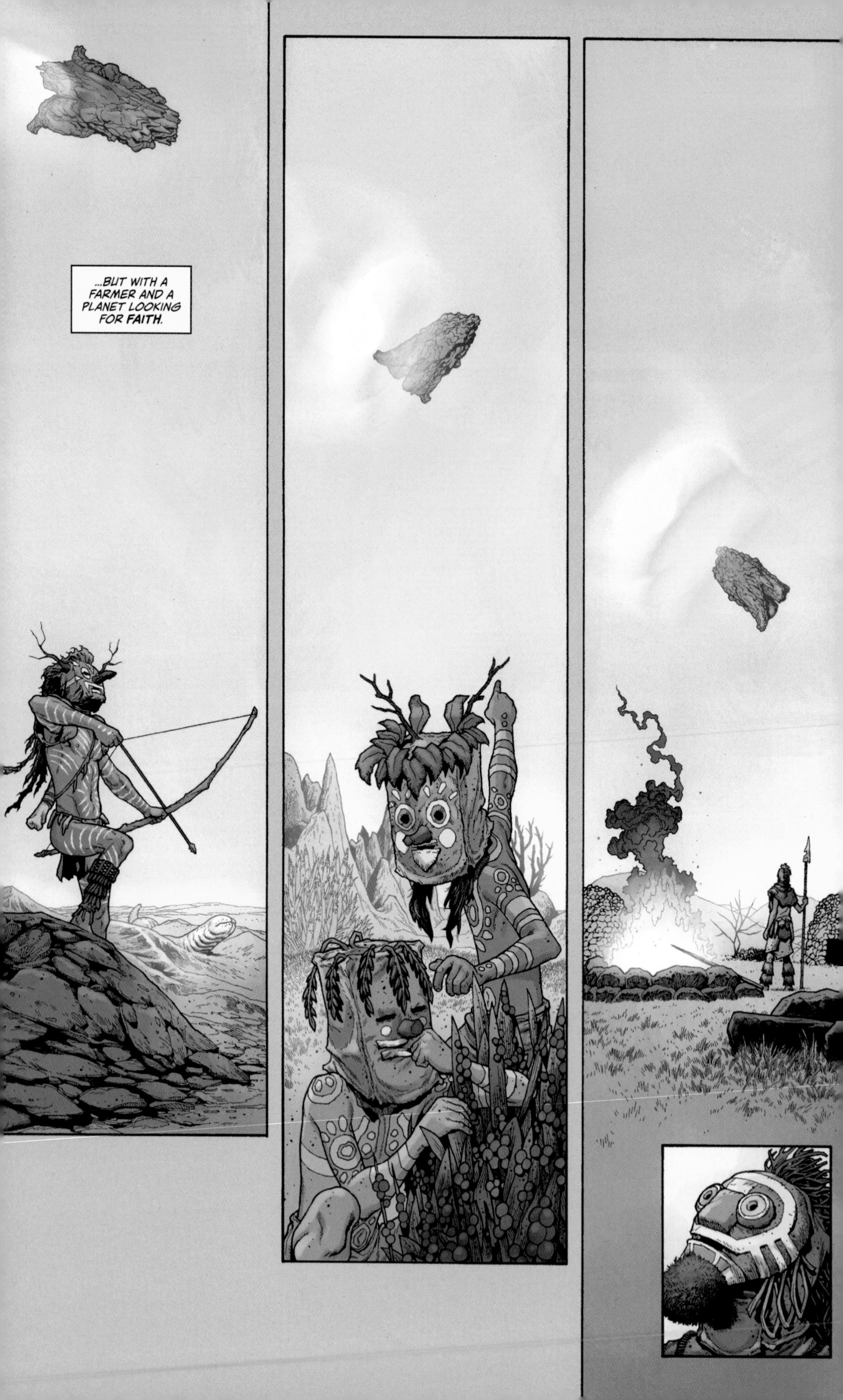
...BUT WITH A
FARMER AND A
PLANET LOOKING
FOR FAITH.

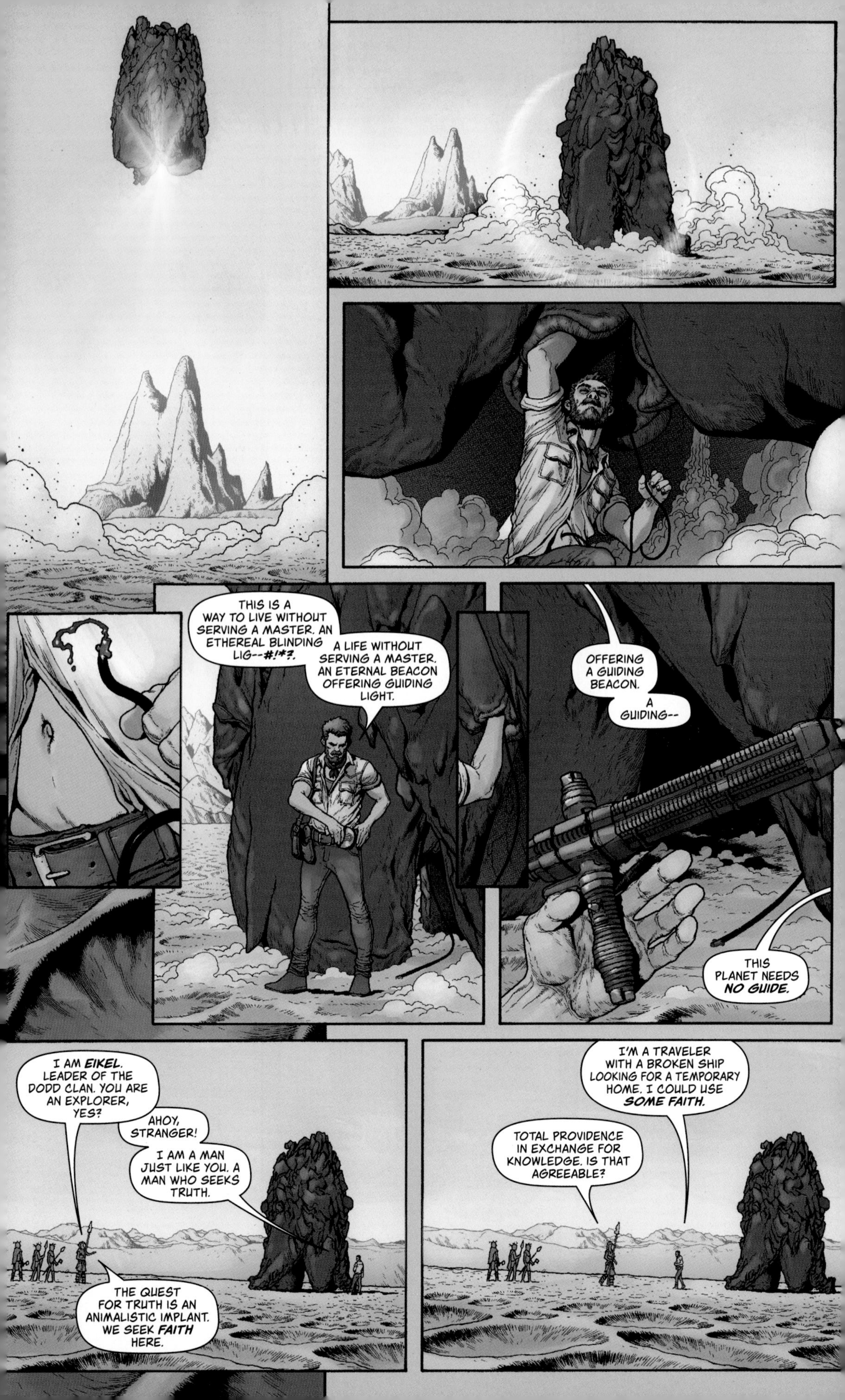
THIS IS A WAY TO LIVE WITHOUT SERVING A MASTER. AN ETHEREAL BLINDING LIG--#!*?.
A LIFE WITHOUT SERVING A MASTER. AN ETERNAL BEACON OFFERING GUIDING LIGHT.
OFFERING A GUIDING BEACON.
A GUIDING--
THIS PLANET NEEDS NO GUIDE.
I AM EIKEL. LEADER OF THE DODD CLAN. YOU ARE AN EXPLORER, YES?
AHOY, STRANGER!
I AM A MAN JUST LIKE YOU. A MAN WHO SEEKS TRUTH.
THE QUEST FOR TRUTH IS AN ANIMALISTIC IMPLANT. WE SEEK FAITH HERE.
I'M A TRAVELER WITH A BROKEN SHIP LOOKING FOR A TEMPORARY HOME. I COULD USE SOME FAITH.
TOTAL PROVIDENCE IN EXCHANGE FOR KNOWLEDGE. IS THAT AGREEABLE?

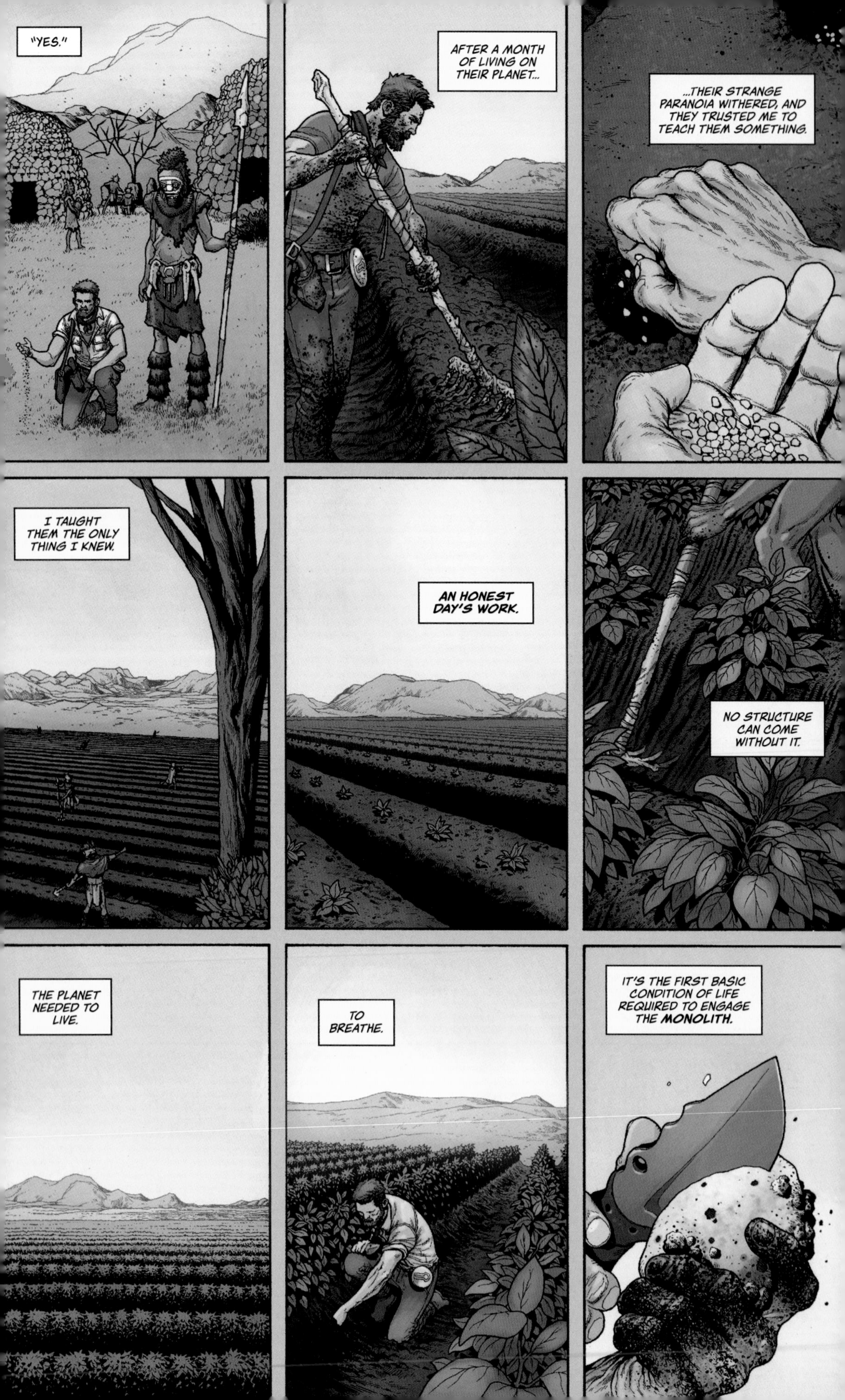
"YES."
AFTER A MONTH OF LIVING ON THEIR PLANET...
...THEIR STRANGE PARANOIA WITHERED, AND THEY TRUSTED ME TO TEACH THEM SOMETHING.
I TAUGHT THEM THE ONLY THING I KNEW.
AN HONEST DAY'S WORK.
NO STRUCTURE CAN COME WITHOUT IT.
THE PLANET NEEDED TO LIVE.
TO BREATHE.
IT'S THE FIRST BASIC CONDITION OF LIFE REQUIRED TO ENGAGE THE MONOLITH.

IT TOOK US EIGHT WEEKS TO GROPE OUR WAY TO SOME EFFECTUAL PLACE.

TO CREATE A SUSTAINABLE ENTERPRISE.

WHERE I TANGLED THESE PEOPLE IN THE STRINGS OF PROGRESS.

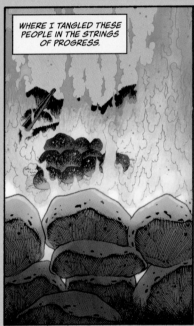

I HOPED TO OFFER THEM **SOMETHING MORE.** A BETTER LIFE. A MORE COMPLETE TYPE OF EXISTENCE.

IT MAY SEEM A LITTLE BACKWARDS, I KNOW. BUT THE WAY FORWARD IS A REFLECTION OF OUR OWN WORLD. AN OFFER OF PROSPERITY THROUGH SHARING.

MANIPULATING KNOWLEDGE TO CREATE AN ECOSYSTEM RIPE FOR EVOLUTION. THAT'S THE WAY I SOLD IT.

SOMETHING THAT'S PERFECT ON THE DAY OF ITS INCEPTION BUT DISTORTS TOWARD **PERVERSION** WITH EACH SUBSEQUENT MOMENT.

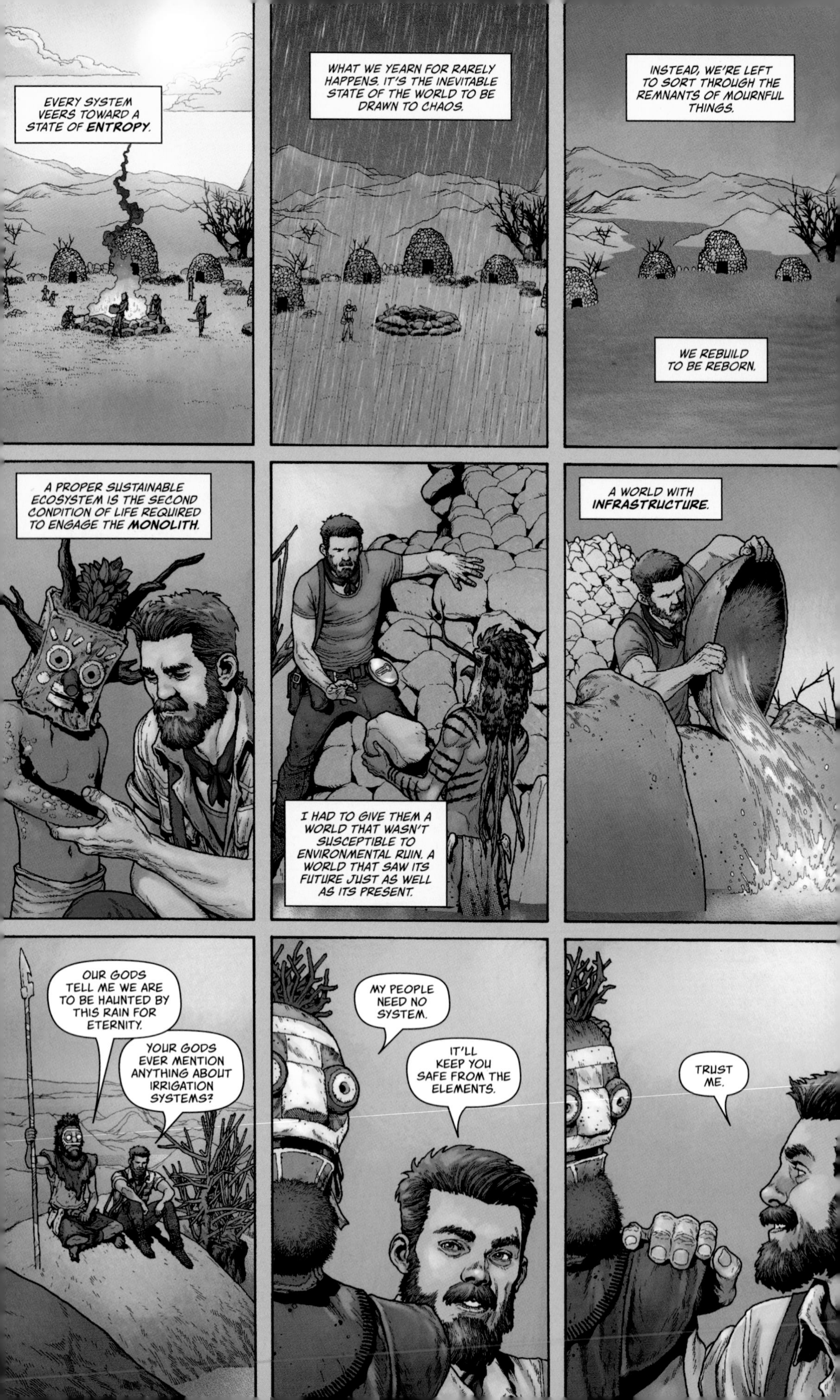
EVERY SYSTEM VEERS TOWARD A STATE OF ENTROPY.
WHAT WE YEARN FOR RARELY HAPPENS. IT'S THE INEVITABLE STATE OF THE WORLD TO BE DRAWN TO CHAOS.
INSTEAD, WE'RE LEFT TO SORT THROUGH THE REMNANTS OF MOURNFUL THINGS.
WE REBUILD TO BE REBORN.
A PROPER SUSTAINABLE ECOSYSTEM IS THE SECOND CONDITION OF LIFE REQUIRED TO ENGAGE THE MONOLITH.
I HAD TO GIVE THEM A WORLD THAT WASN'T SUSCEPTIBLE TO ENVIRONMENTAL RUIN. A WORLD THAT SAW ITS FUTURE JUST AS WELL AS ITS PRESENT.
A WORLD WITH INFRASTRUCTURE.
OUR GODS TELL ME WE ARE TO BE HAUNTED BY THIS RAIN FOR ETERNITY.
YOUR GODS EVER MENTION ANYTHING ABOUT IRRIGATION SYSTEMS?
MY PEOPLE NEED NO SYSTEM.
IT'LL KEEP YOU SAFE FROM THE ELEMENTS.
TRUST ME.

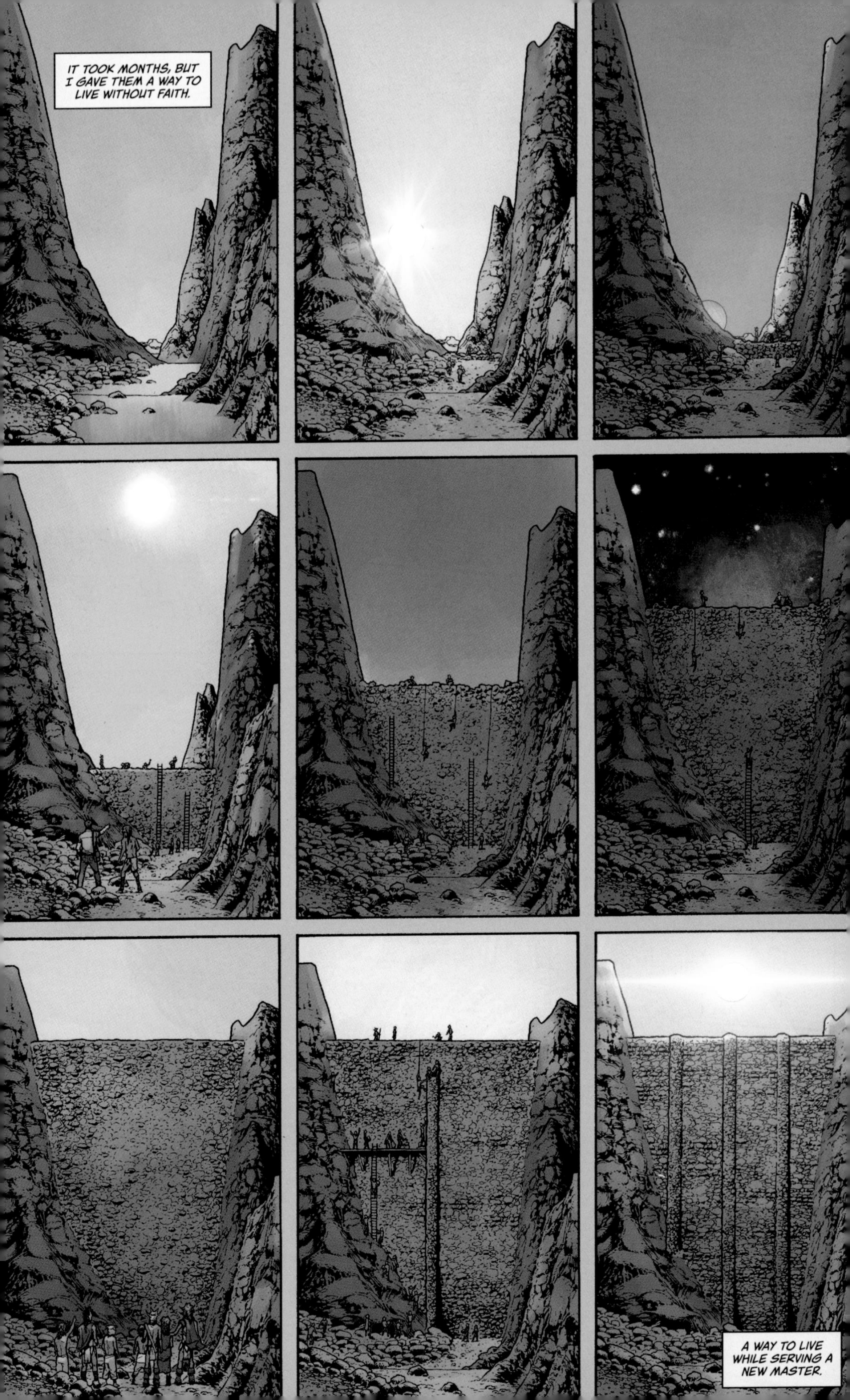
IT TOOK MONTHS, BUT I GAVE THEM A WAY TO LIVE WITHOUT FAITH.
A WAY TO LIVE WHILE SERVING A NEW MASTER.

IF YOU LEAVE US NOW, WE WILL BE FOREVER INDEBTED TO YOU. IN THE NEXT LIFE, YOU WILL BE OUR *SWORN GOD.*

IT'S JUST SURVIVAL, AND I'M HAPPY TO HELP.

"WE FEED OUR MINDS TONIGHT, IN CELEBRATION."

EAT THIS, *DERANGE* YOURSELF.

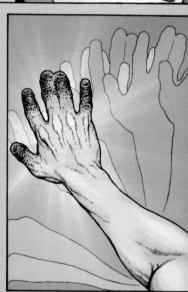

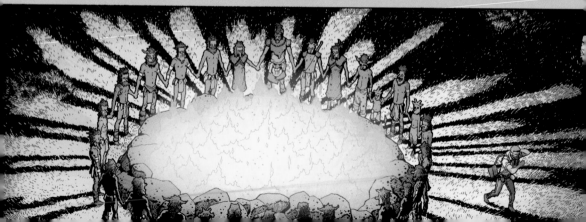

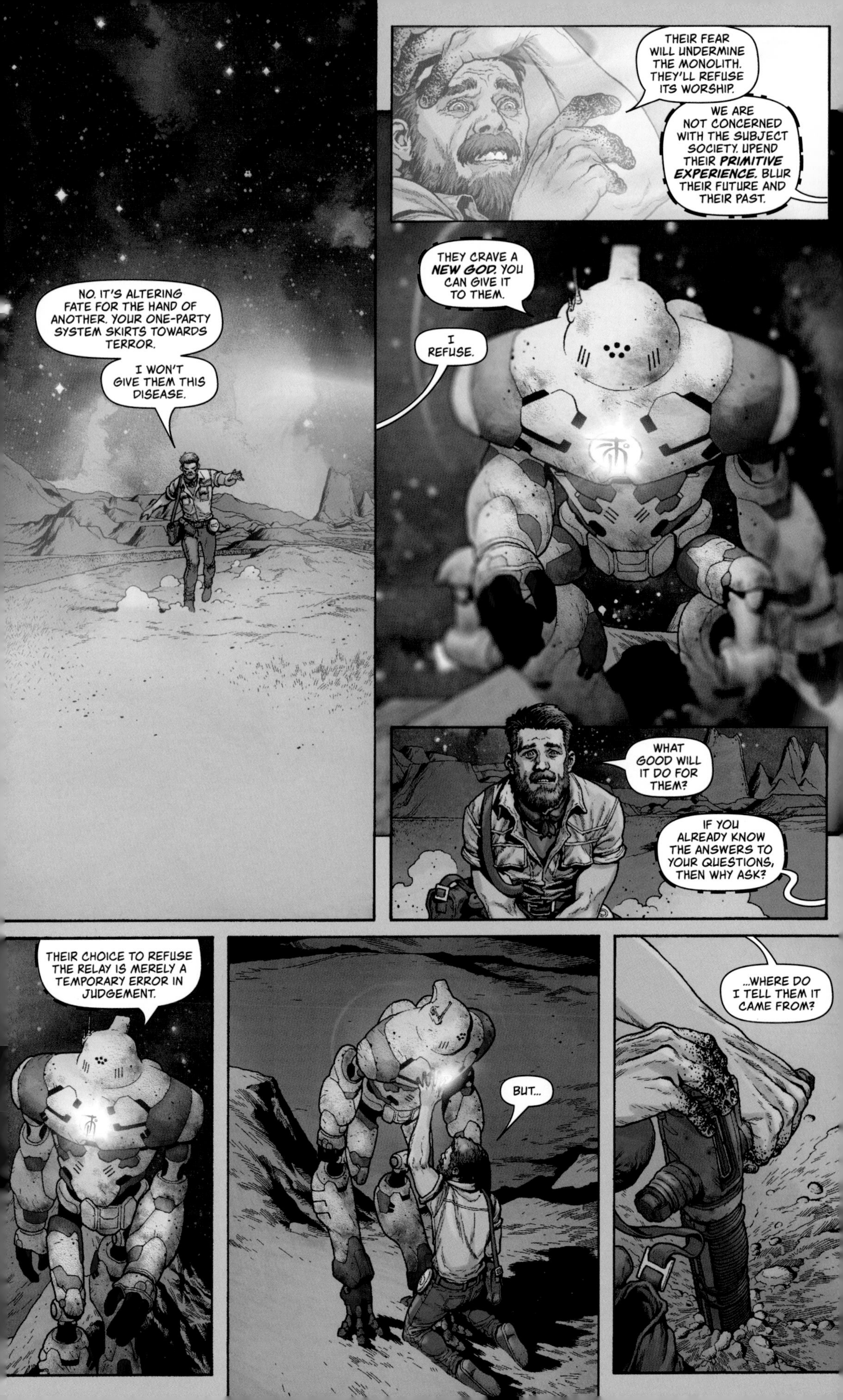
NO. IT'S ALTERING FATE FOR THE HAND OF ANOTHER. YOUR ONE-PARTY SYSTEM SKIRTS TOWARDS TERROR.
I WON'T GIVE THEM THIS DISEASE.
THEIR FEAR WILL UNDERMINE THE MONOLITH. THEY'LL REFUSE ITS WORSHIP.
WE ARE NOT CONCERNED WITH THE SUBJECT SOCIETY. UPEND THEIR PRIMITIVE EXPERIENCE. BLUR THEIR FUTURE AND THEIR PAST.
THEY CRAVE A NEW GOD. YOU CAN GIVE IT TO THEM.
I REFUSE.
WHAT GOOD WILL IT DO FOR THEM?
IF YOU ALREADY KNOW THE ANSWERS TO YOUR QUESTIONS, THEN WHY ASK?
THEIR CHOICE TO REFUSE THE RELAY IS MERELY A TEMPORARY ERROR IN JUDGEMENT.
BUT...
...WHERE DO I TELL THEM IT CAME FROM?

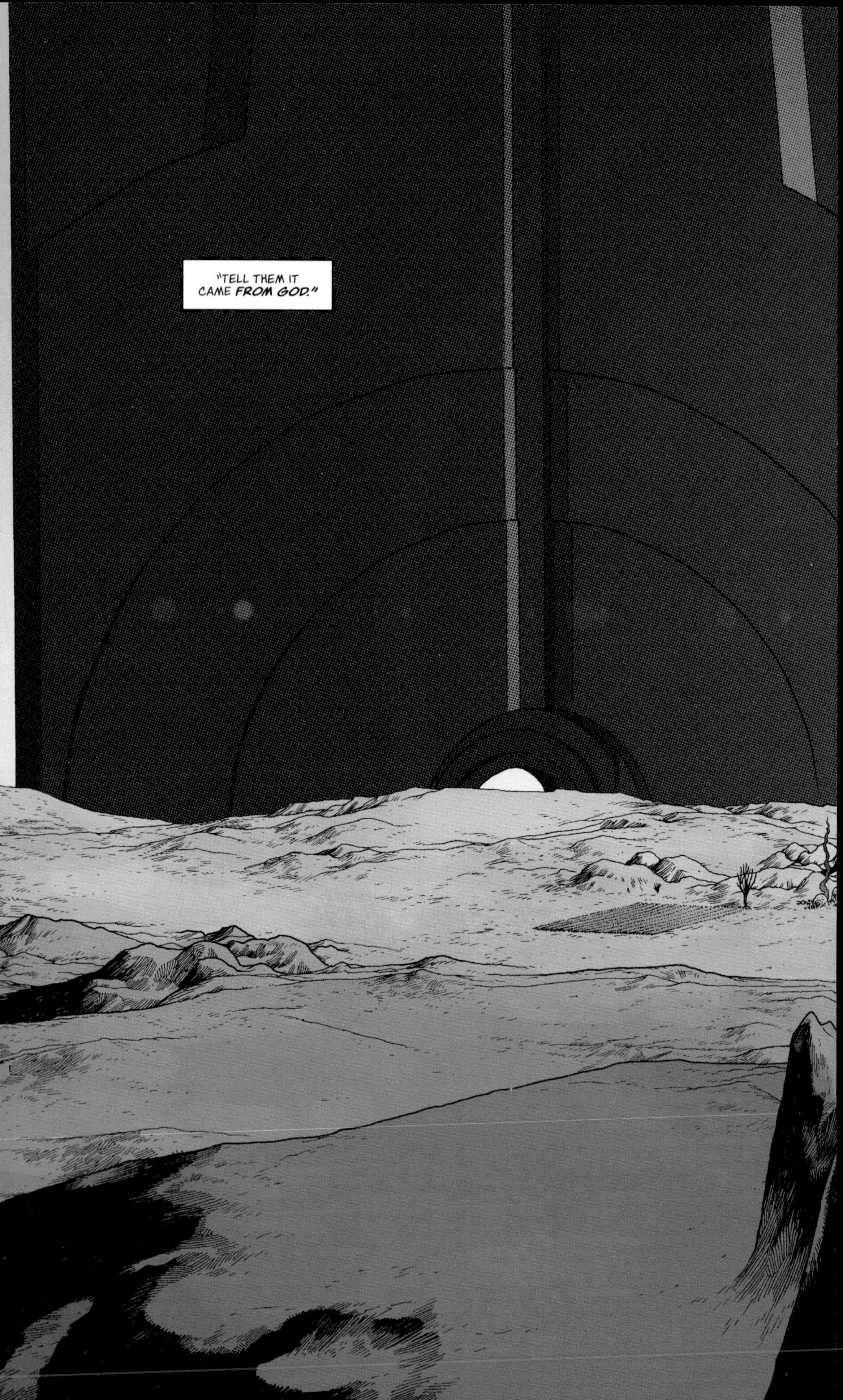
"TELL THEM IT CAME FROM GOD."

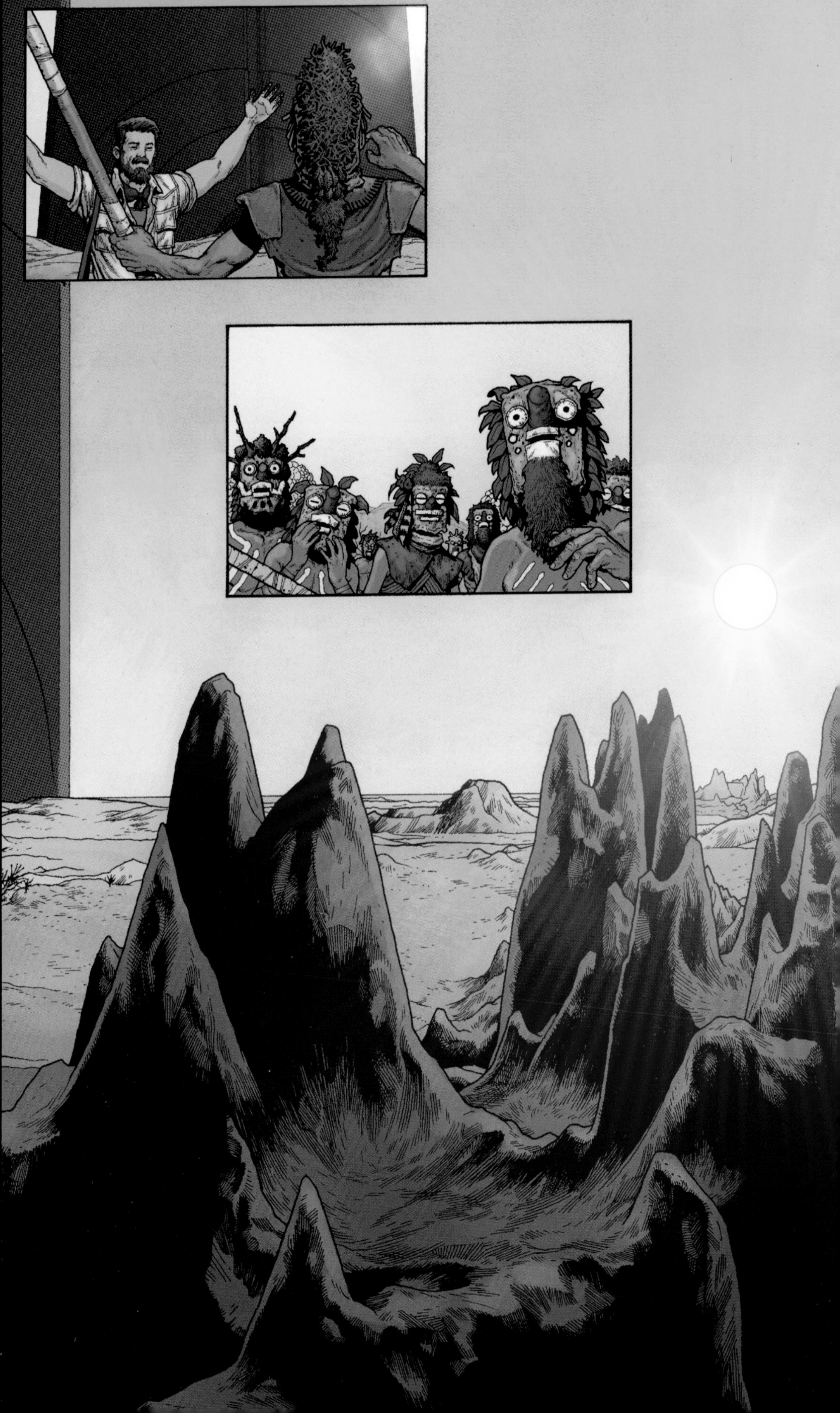

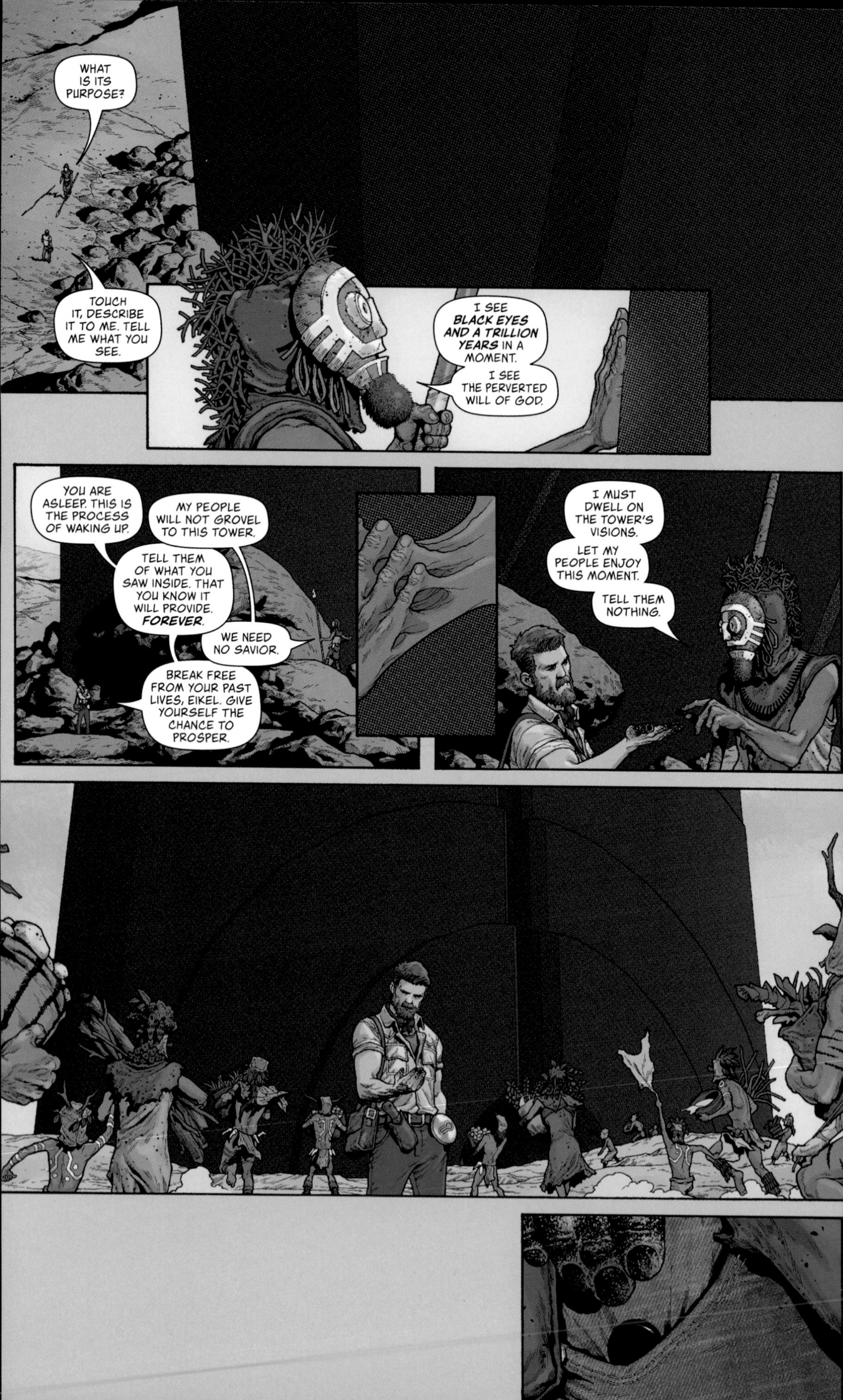
WHAT IS ITS PURPOSE?
TOUCH IT, DESCRIBE IT TO ME. TELL ME WHAT YOU SEE.
I SEE BLACK EYES AND A TRILLION YEARS IN A MOMENT.
I SEE THE PERVERTED WILL OF GOD.
YOU ARE ASLEEP. THIS IS THE PROCESS OF WAKING UP.
MY PEOPLE WILL NOT GROVEL TO THIS TOWER.
TELL THEM OF WHAT YOU SAW INSIDE. THAT YOU KNOW IT WILL PROVIDE. FOREVER.
WE NEED NO SAVIOR.
BREAK FREE FROM YOUR PAST LIVES, EIKEL. GIVE YOURSELF THE CHANCE TO PROSPER.
I MUST DWELL ON THE TOWER'S VISIONS.
LET MY PEOPLE ENJOY THIS MOMENT.
TELL THEM NOTHING.

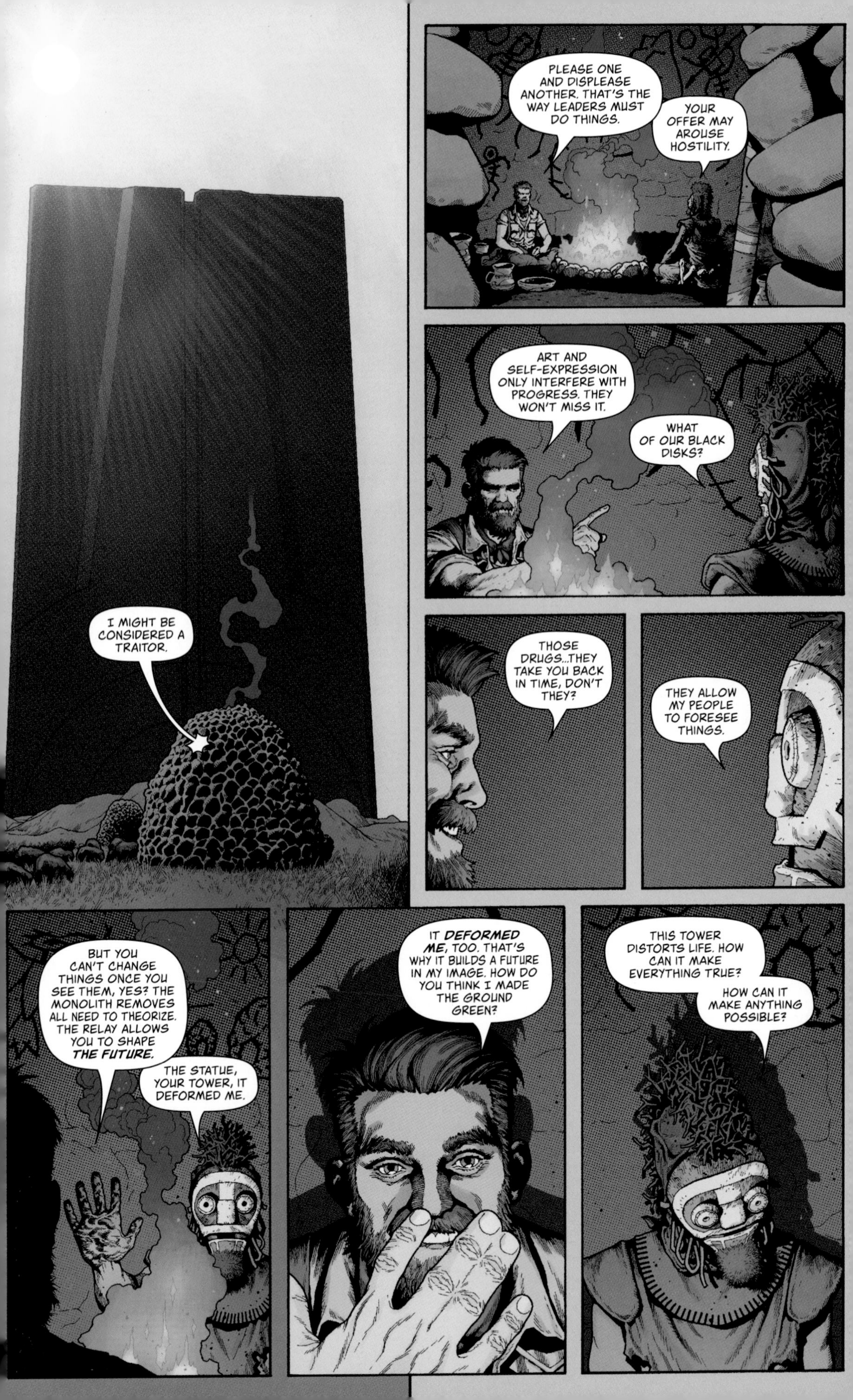
I MIGHT BE CONSIDERED A TRAITOR.
PLEASE ONE AND DISPLEASE ANOTHER. THAT'S THE WAY LEADERS MUST DO THINGS.
YOUR OFFER MAY AROUSE HOSTILITY.
ART AND SELF-EXPRESSION ONLY INTERFERE WITH PROGRESS. THEY WON'T MISS IT.
WHAT OF OUR BLACK DISKS?
THOSE DRUGS...THEY TAKE YOU BACK IN TIME, DON'T THEY?
THEY ALLOW MY PEOPLE TO FORESEE THINGS.
BUT YOU CAN'T CHANGE THINGS ONCE YOU SEE THEM, YES? THE MONOLITH REMOVES ALL NEED TO THEORIZE. THE RELAY ALLOWS YOU TO SHAPE ***THE FUTURE.***
THE STATUE, YOUR TOWER, IT DEFORMED ME.
IT ***DEFORMED ME,*** TOO. THAT'S WHY IT BUILDS A FUTURE IN MY IMAGE. HOW DO YOU THINK I MADE THE GROUND GREEN?
THIS TOWER DISTORTS LIFE. HOW CAN IT MAKE EVERYTHING TRUE?
HOW CAN IT MAKE ANYTHING POSSIBLE?

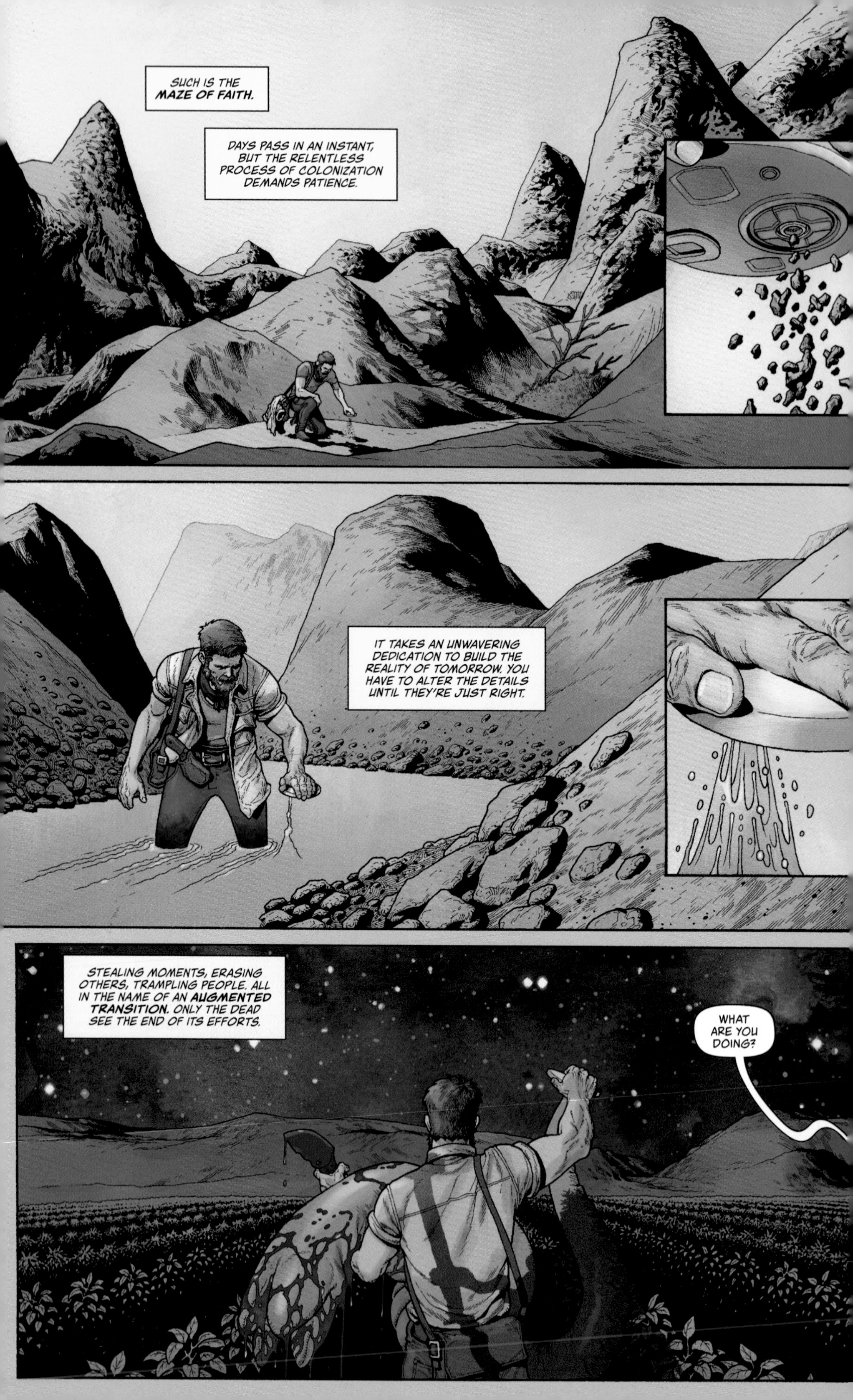
SUCH IS THE MAZE OF FAITH.
DAYS PASS IN AN INSTANT, BUT THE RELENTLESS PROCESS OF COLONIZATION DEMANDS PATIENCE.
IT TAKES AN UNWAVERING DEDICATION TO BUILD THE REALITY OF TOMORROW. YOU HAVE TO ALTER THE DETAILS UNTIL THEY'RE JUST RIGHT.
STEALING MOMENTS, ERASING OTHERS, TRAMPLING PEOPLE. ALL IN THE NAME OF AN AUGMENTED TRANSITION. ONLY THE DEAD SEE THE END OF ITS EFFORTS.
WHAT ARE YOU DOING?

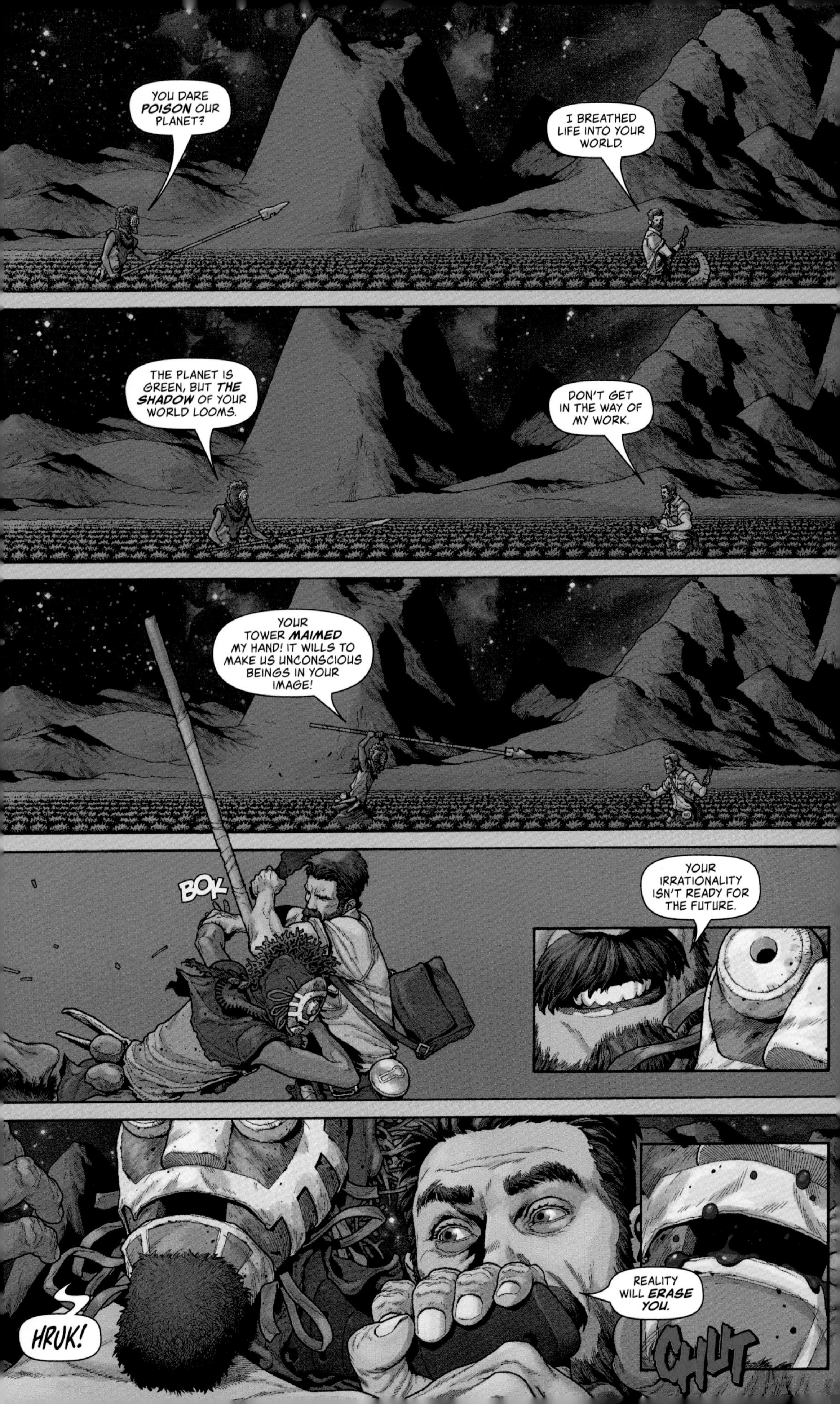
YOU DARE **POISON** OUR PLANET?
I BREATHED LIFE INTO YOUR WORLD.
THE PLANET IS GREEN, BUT **THE SHADOW** OF YOUR WORLD LOOMS.
DON'T GET IN THE WAY OF MY WORK.
YOUR TOWER **MAIMED** MY HAND! IT WILLS TO MAKE US UNCONSCIOUS BEINGS IN YOUR IMAGE!
BOK
YOUR IRRATIONALITY ISN'T READY FOR THE FUTURE.
HRUK!
REALITY WILL **ERASE YOU.**
CHLIT

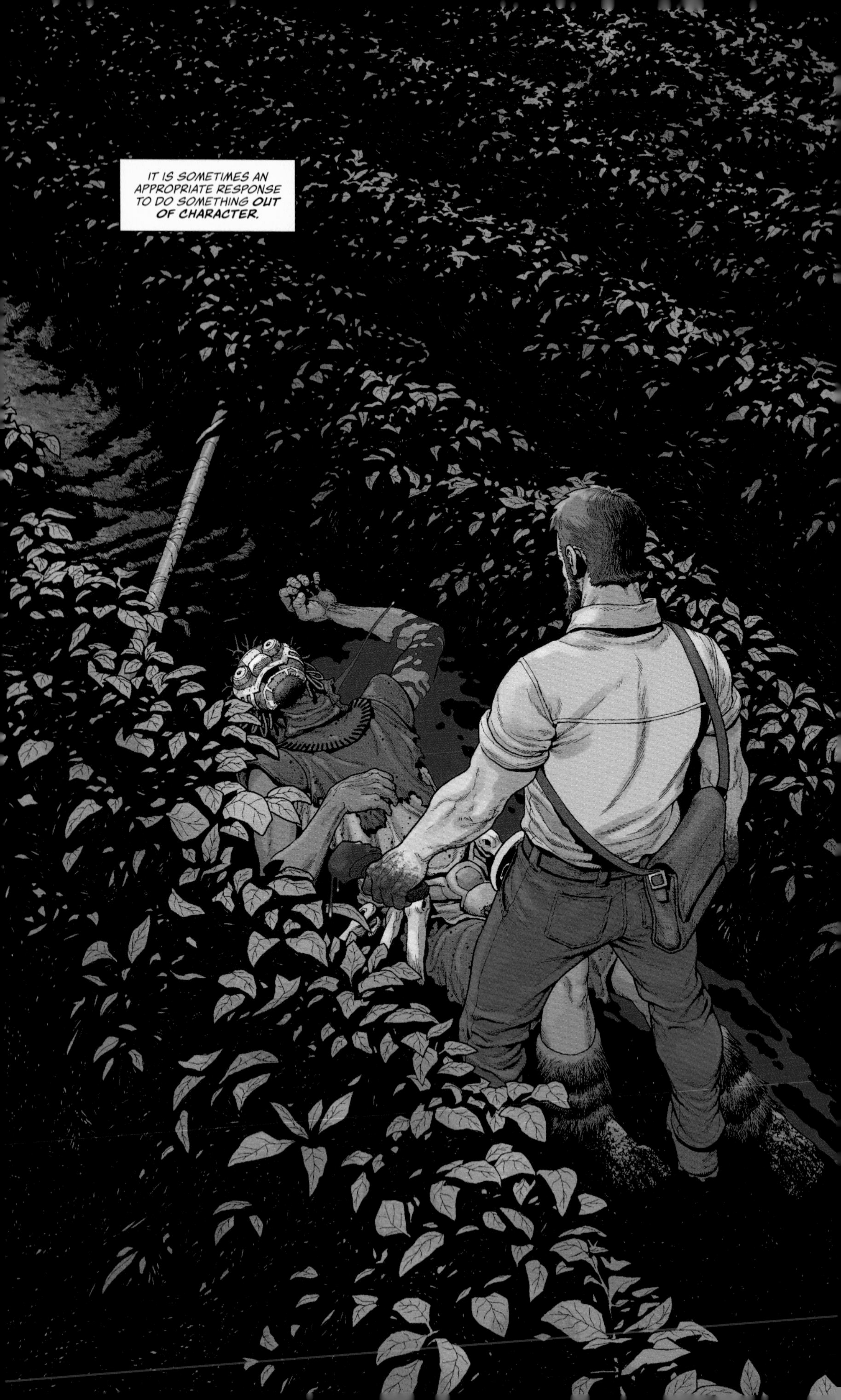
IT IS SOMETIMES AN APPROPRIATE RESPONSE TO DO SOMETHING OUT OF CHARACTER.

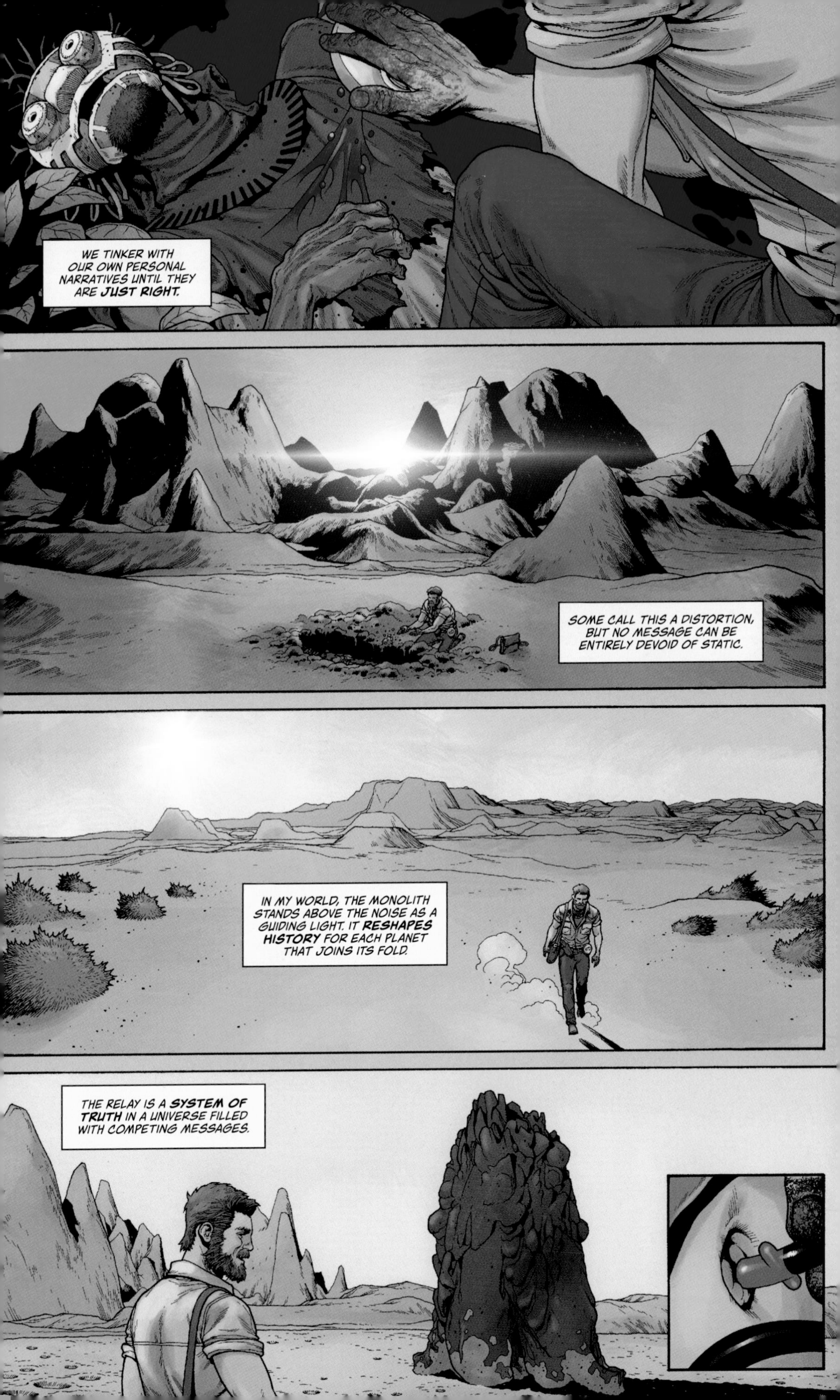
WE TINKER WITH OUR OWN PERSONAL NARRATIVES UNTIL THEY ARE JUST RIGHT.
SOME CALL THIS A DISTORTION, BUT NO MESSAGE CAN BE ENTIRELY DEVOID OF STATIC.
IN MY WORLD, THE MONOLITH STANDS ABOVE THE NOISE AS A GUIDING LIGHT. IT RESHAPES HISTORY FOR EACH PLANET THAT JOINS ITS FOLD.
THE RELAY IS A SYSTEM OF TRUTH IN A UNIVERSE FILLED WITH COMPETING MESSAGES.

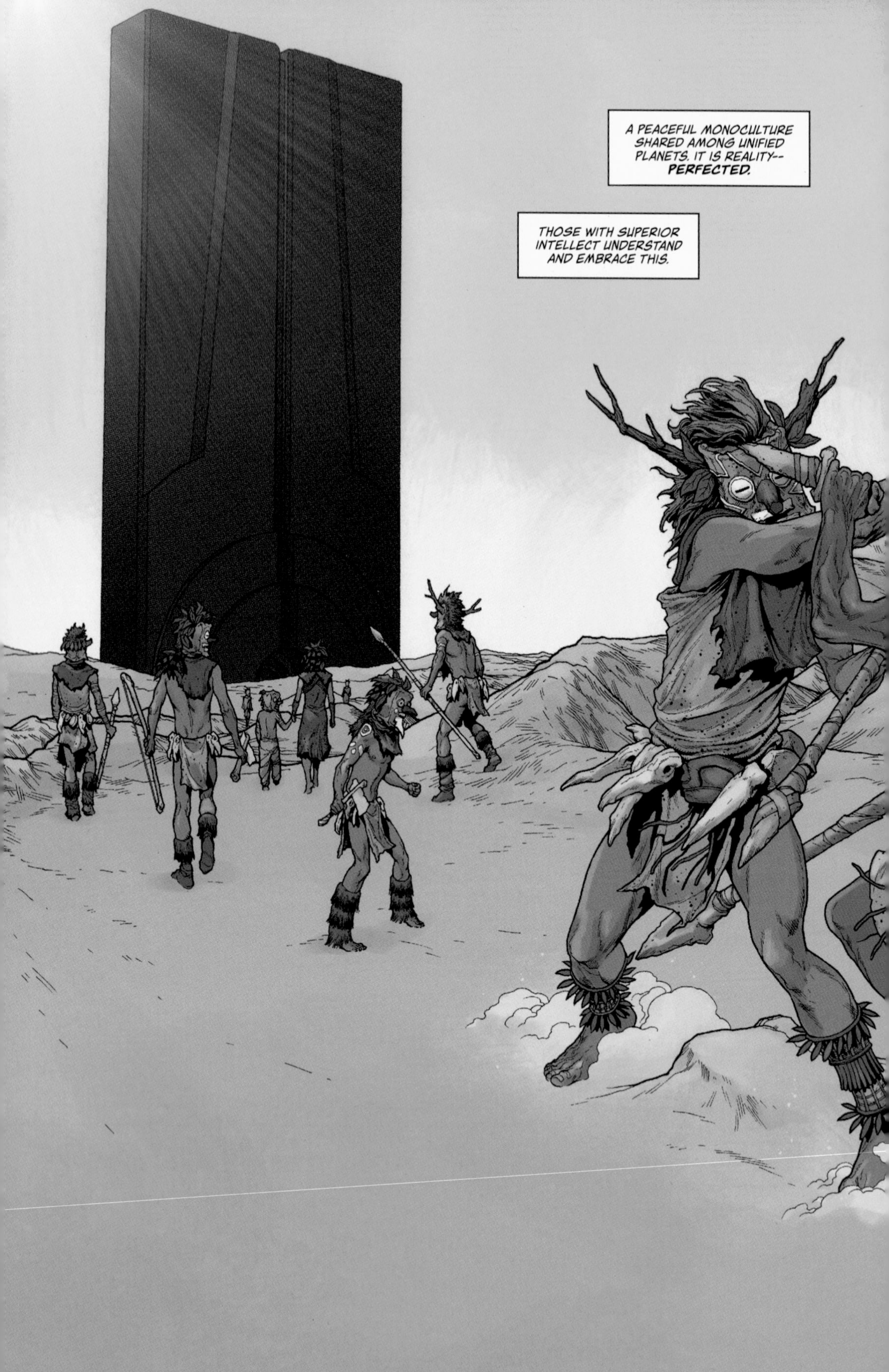
A PEACEFUL MONOCULTURE SHARED AMONG UNIFIED PLANETS. IT IS REALITY-- **PERFECTED.**
THOSE WITH SUPERIOR INTELLECT UNDERSTAND AND EMBRACE THIS.

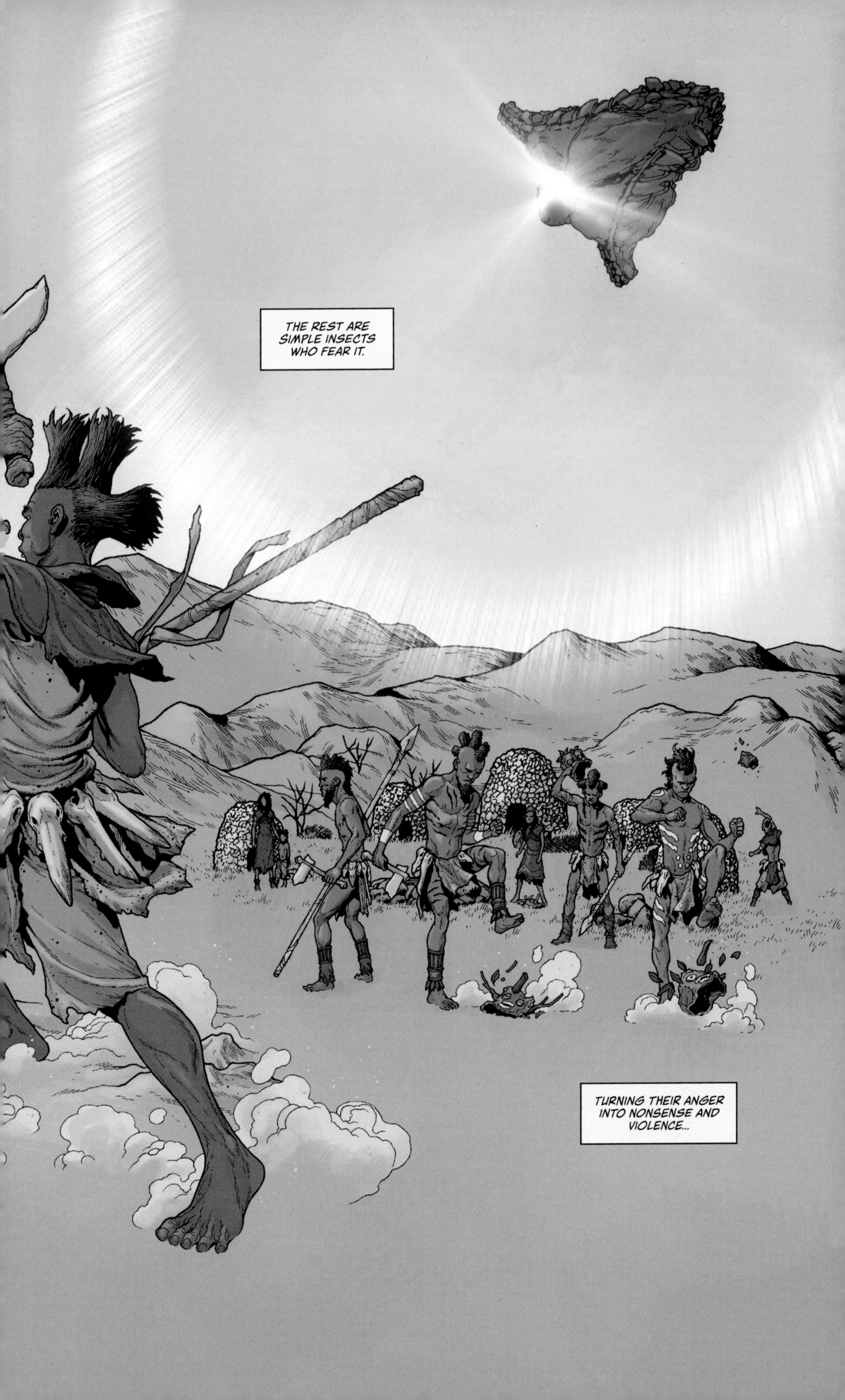
THE REST ARE SIMPLE INSECTS WHO FEAR IT.
TURNING THEIR ANGER INTO NONSENSE AND VIOLENCE...

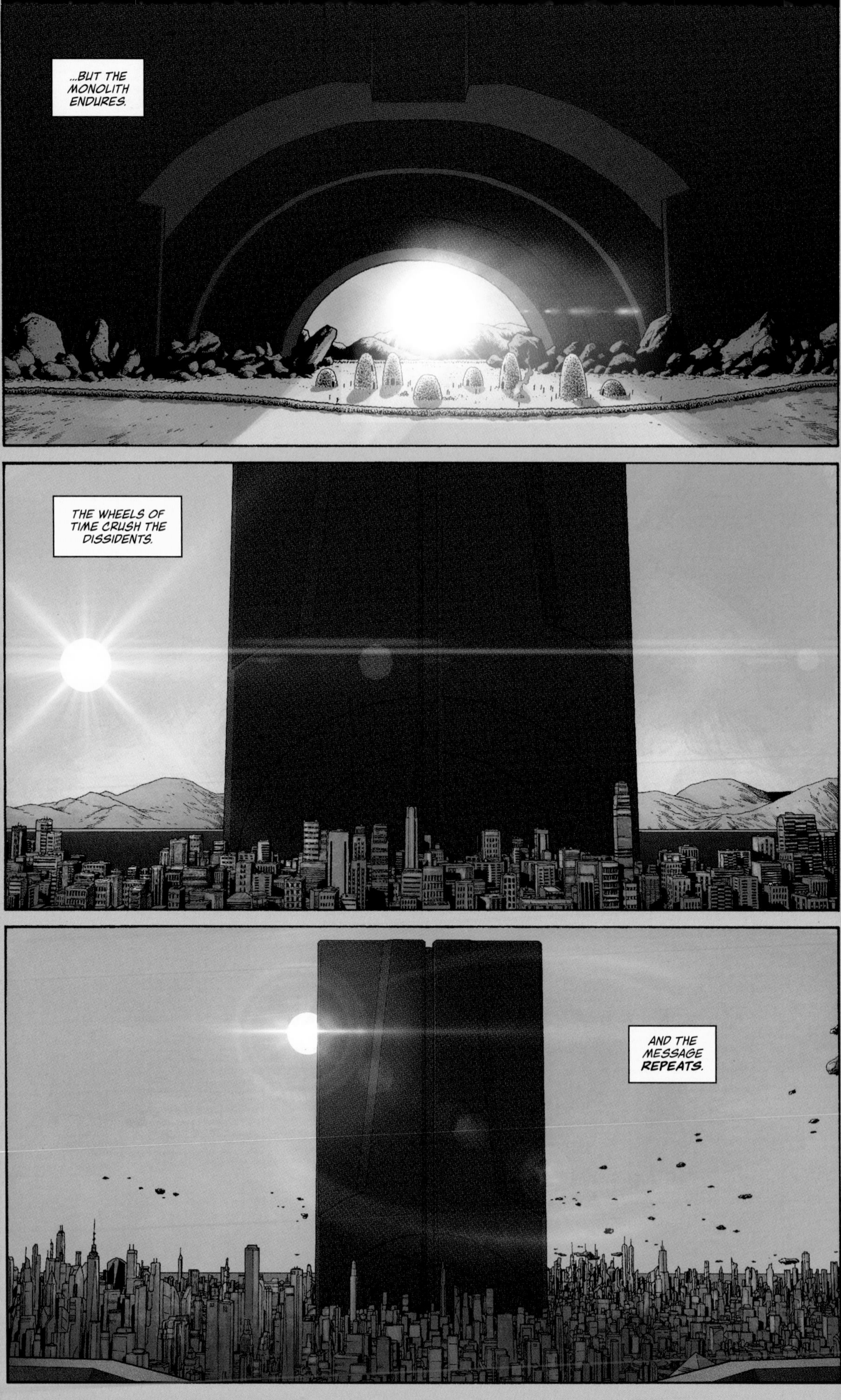
...BUT THE MONOLITH ENDURES.
THE WHEELS OF TIME CRUSH THE DISSIDENTS.
AND THE MESSAGE REPEATS.

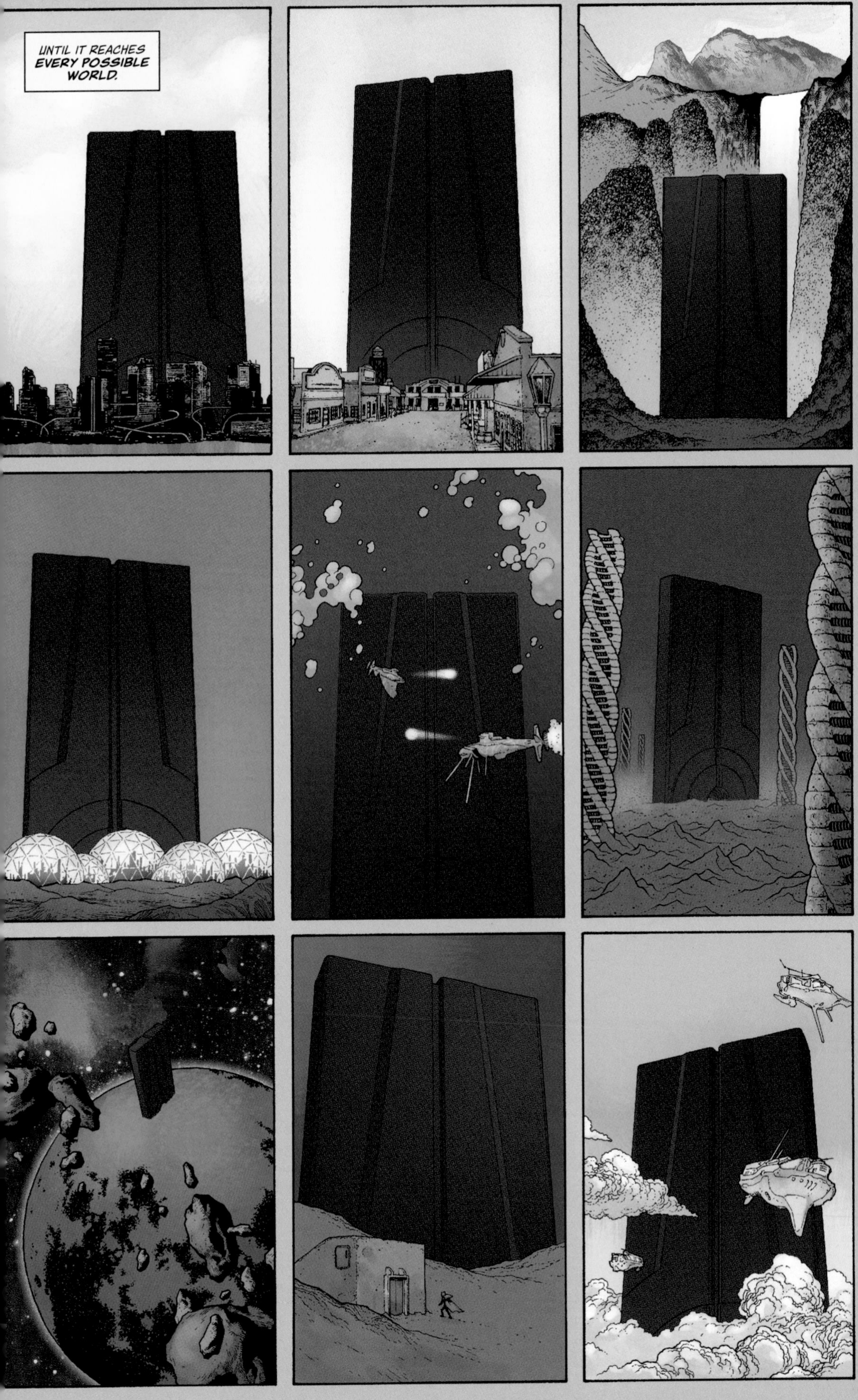
UNTIL IT REACHES EVERY POSSIBLE WORLD.

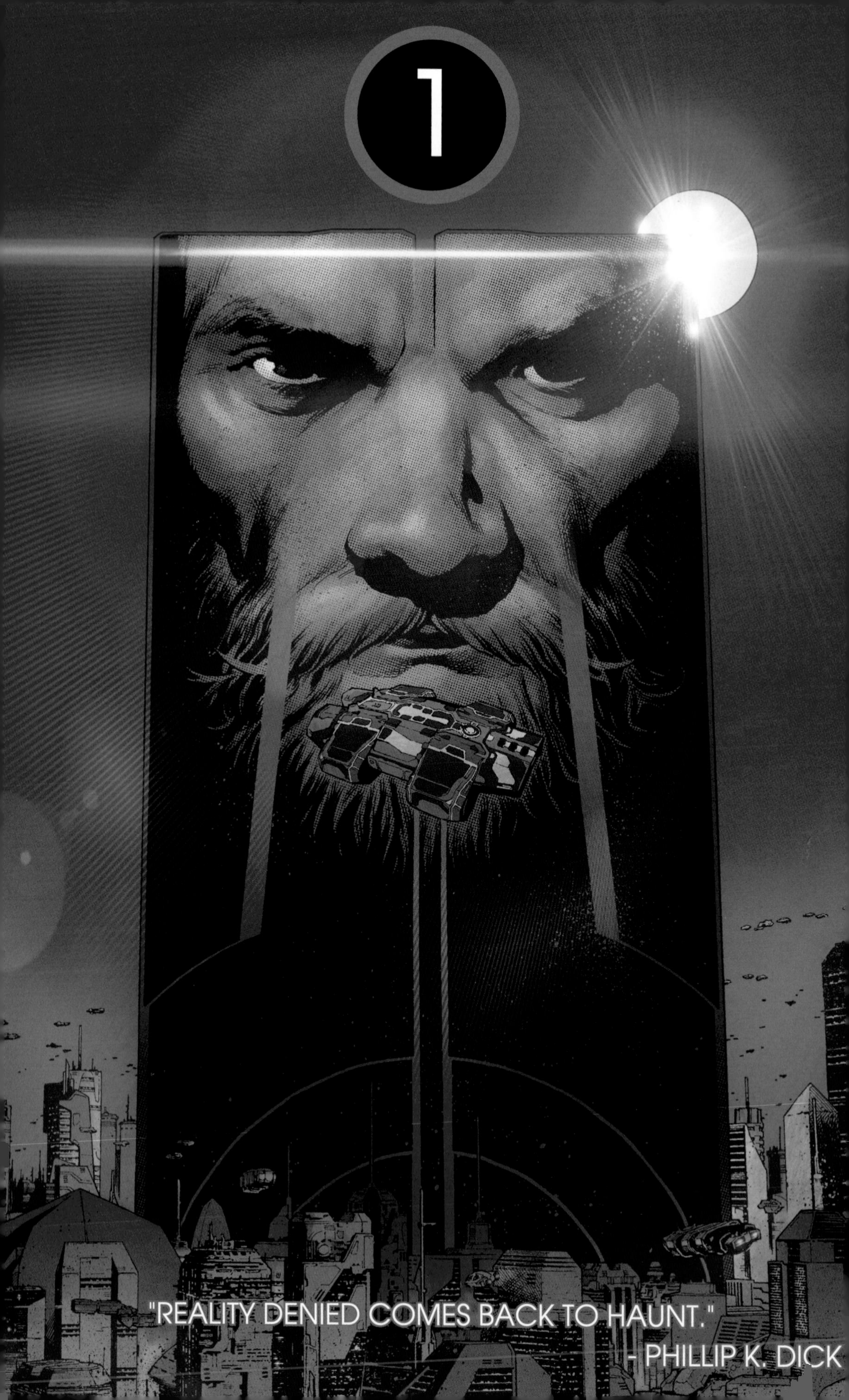
1
"REALITY DENIED COMES BACK TO HAUNT."
- PHILLIP K. DICK

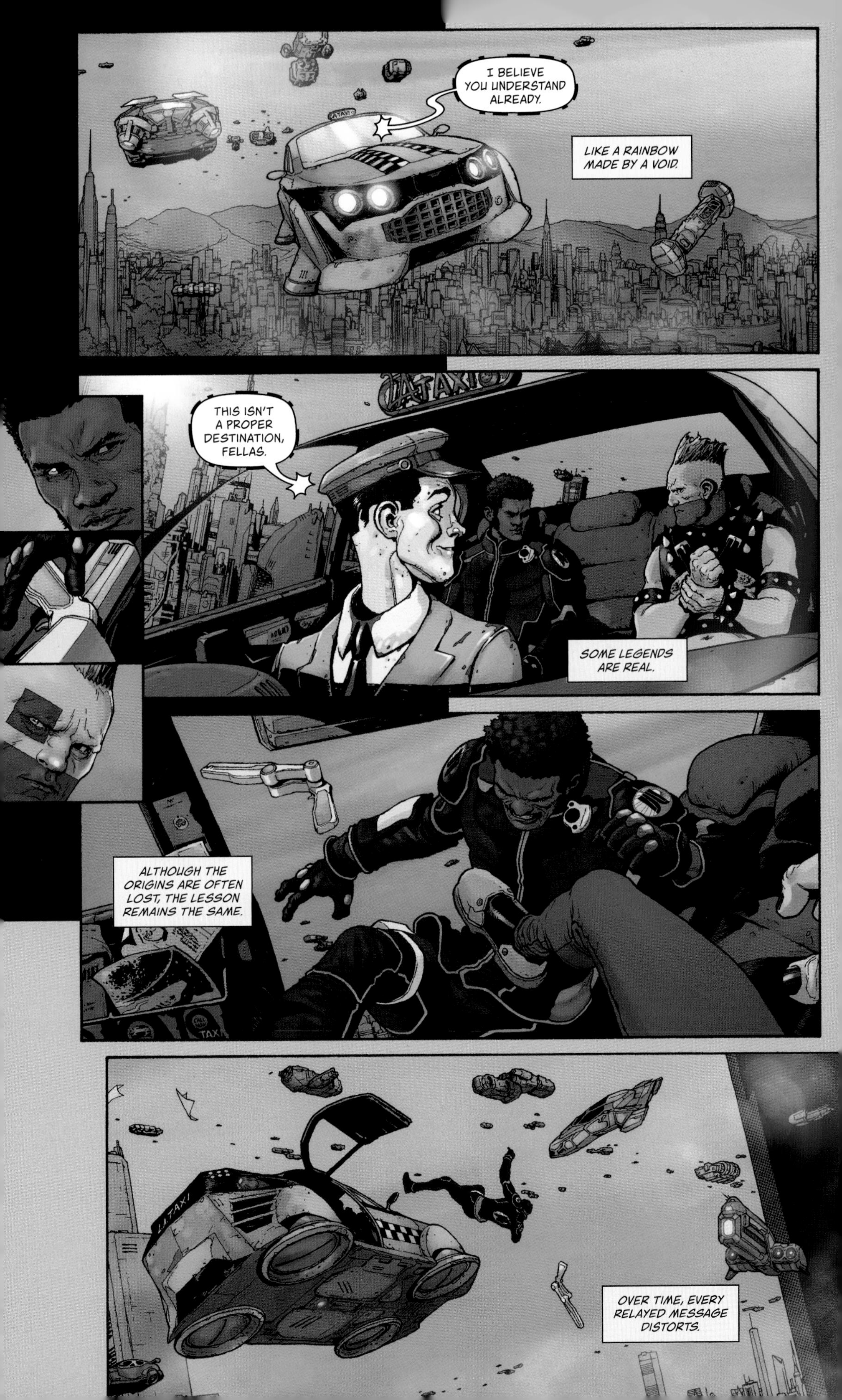
I BELIEVE YOU UNDERSTAND ALREADY.
LIKE A RAINBOW MADE BY A VOID.
THIS ISN'T A PROPER DESTINATION, FELLAS.
SOME LEGENDS ARE REAL.
ALTHOUGH THE ORIGINS ARE OFTEN LOST, THE LESSON REMAINS THE SAME.
OVER TIME, EVERY RELAYED MESSAGE DISTORTS.

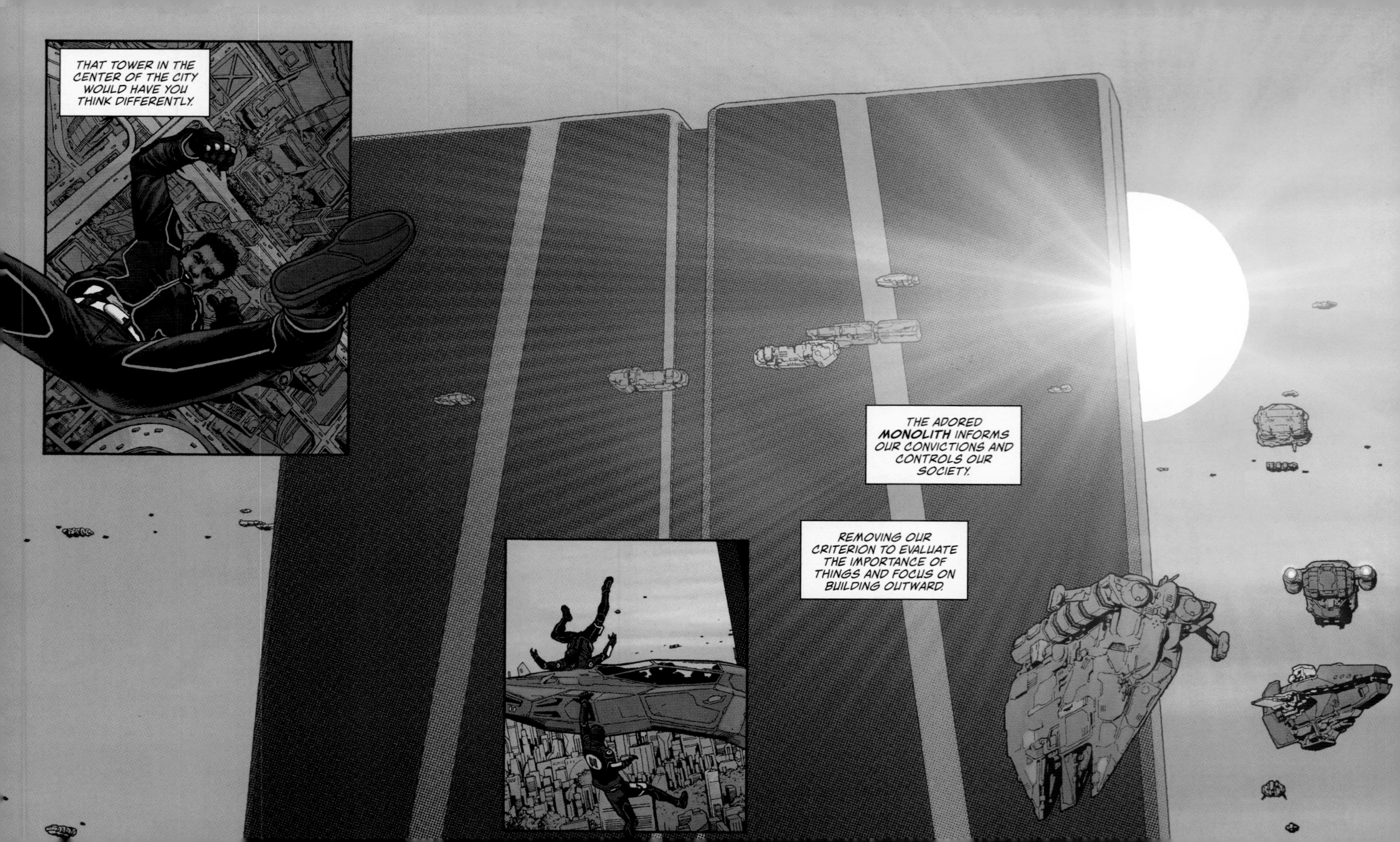
THAT TOWER IN THE CENTER OF THE CITY WOULD HAVE YOU THINK DIFFERENTLY.
THE ADORED **MONOLITH** INFORMS OUR CONVICTIONS AND CONTROLS OUR SOCIETY.
REMOVING OUR CRITERION TO EVALUATE THE IMPORTANCE OF THINGS AND FOCUS ON BUILDING OUTWARD.

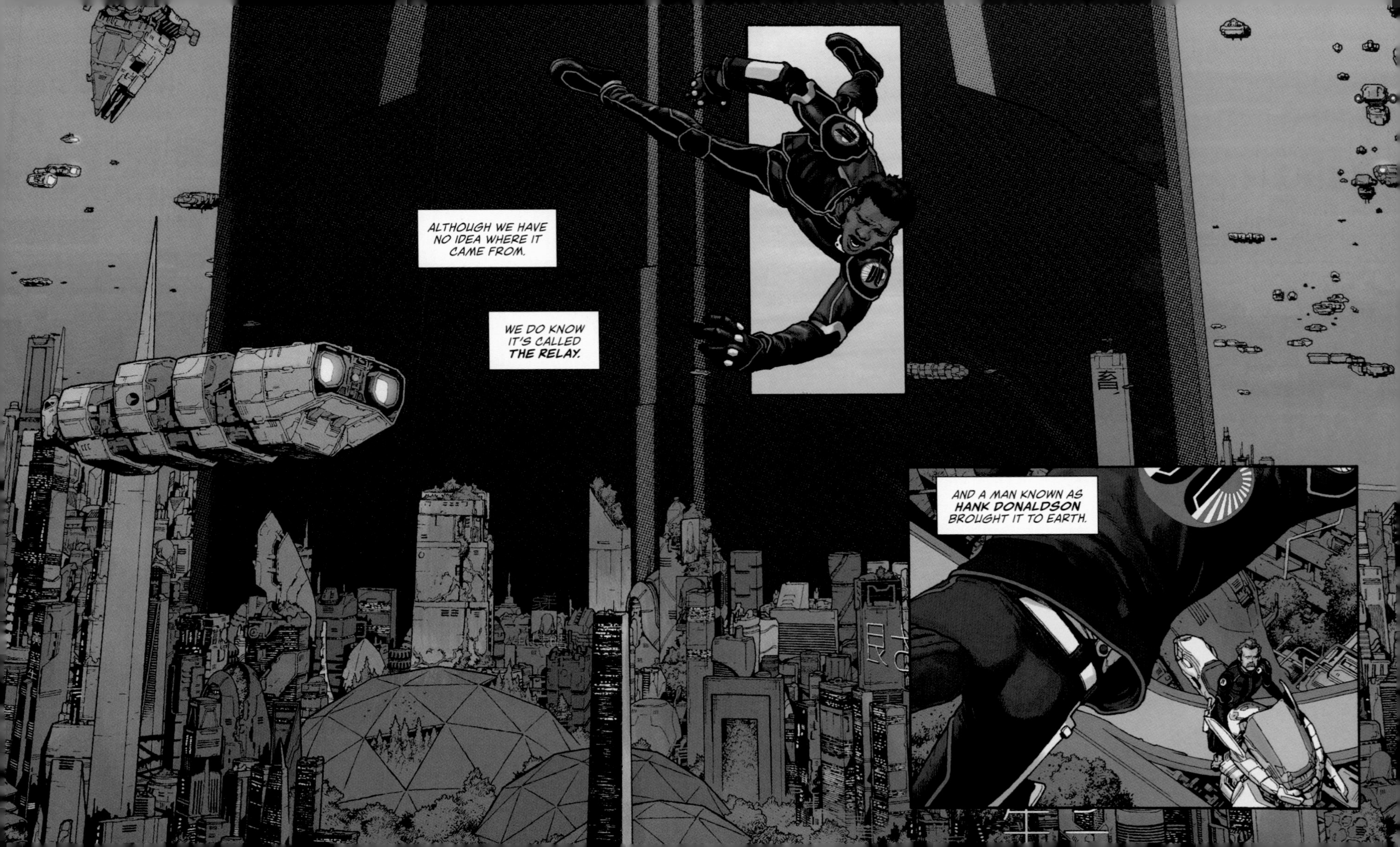
ALTHOUGH WE HAVE NO IDEA WHERE IT CAME FROM.
WE DO KNOW IT'S CALLED **THE RELAY.**
AND A MAN KNOWN AS **HANK DONALDSON** BROUGHT IT TO EARTH.

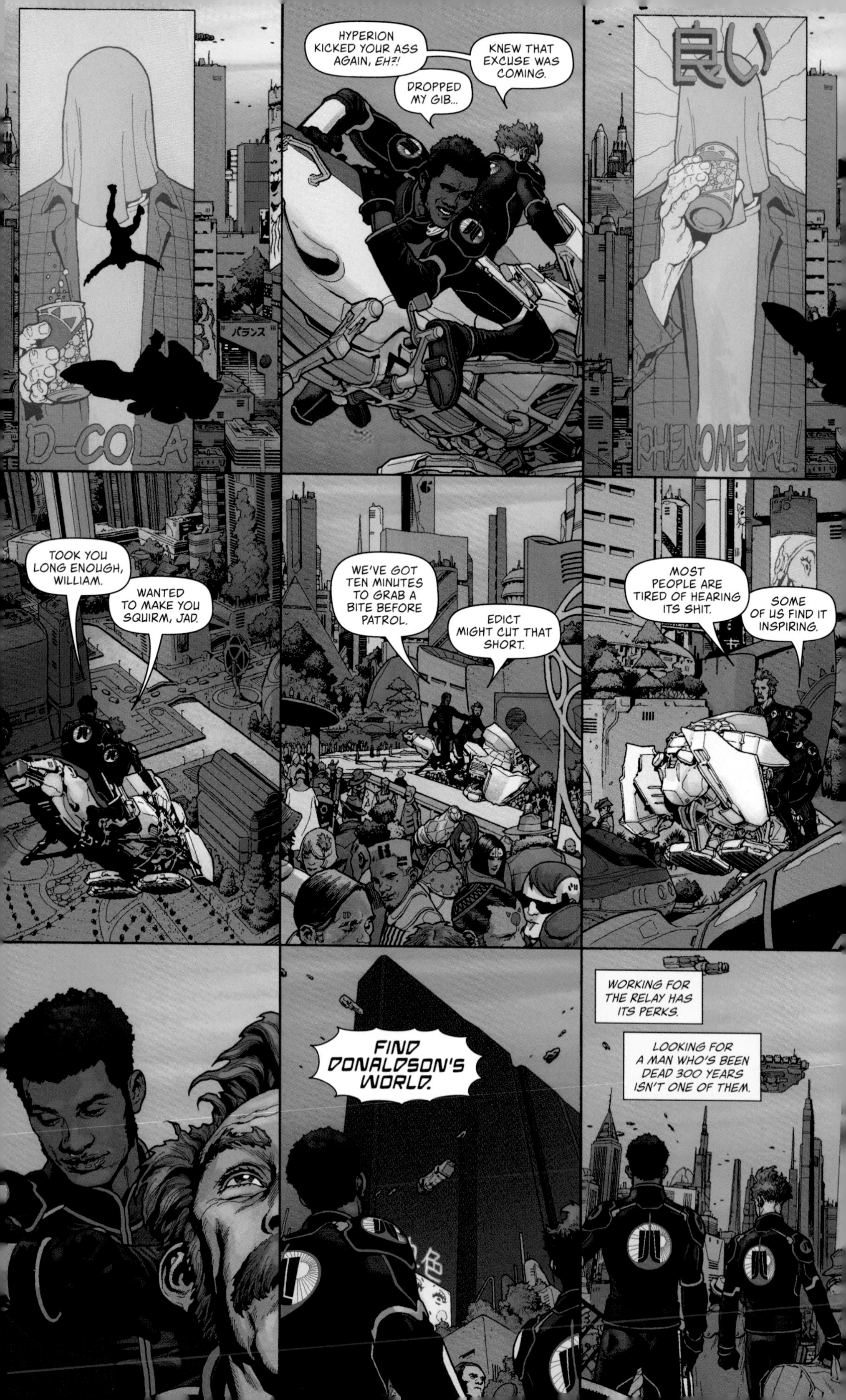
D-COLA
HYPERION KICKED YOUR ASS AGAIN, EH?!
DROPPED MY GIB...
KNEW THAT EXCUSE WAS COMING.
良い
PHENOMENAL!
TOOK YOU LONG ENOUGH, WILLIAM.
WANTED TO MAKE YOU SQUIRM, JAD.
WE'VE GOT TEN MINUTES TO GRAB A BITE BEFORE PATROL.
EDICT MIGHT CUT THAT SHORT.
MOST PEOPLE ARE TIRED OF HEARING ITS SHIT.
SOME OF US FIND IT INSPIRING.
FIND DONALDSON'S WORLD.
WORKING FOR THE RELAY HAS ITS PERKS.
LOOKING FOR A MAN WHO'S BEEN DEAD 300 YEARS ISN'T ONE OF THEM.

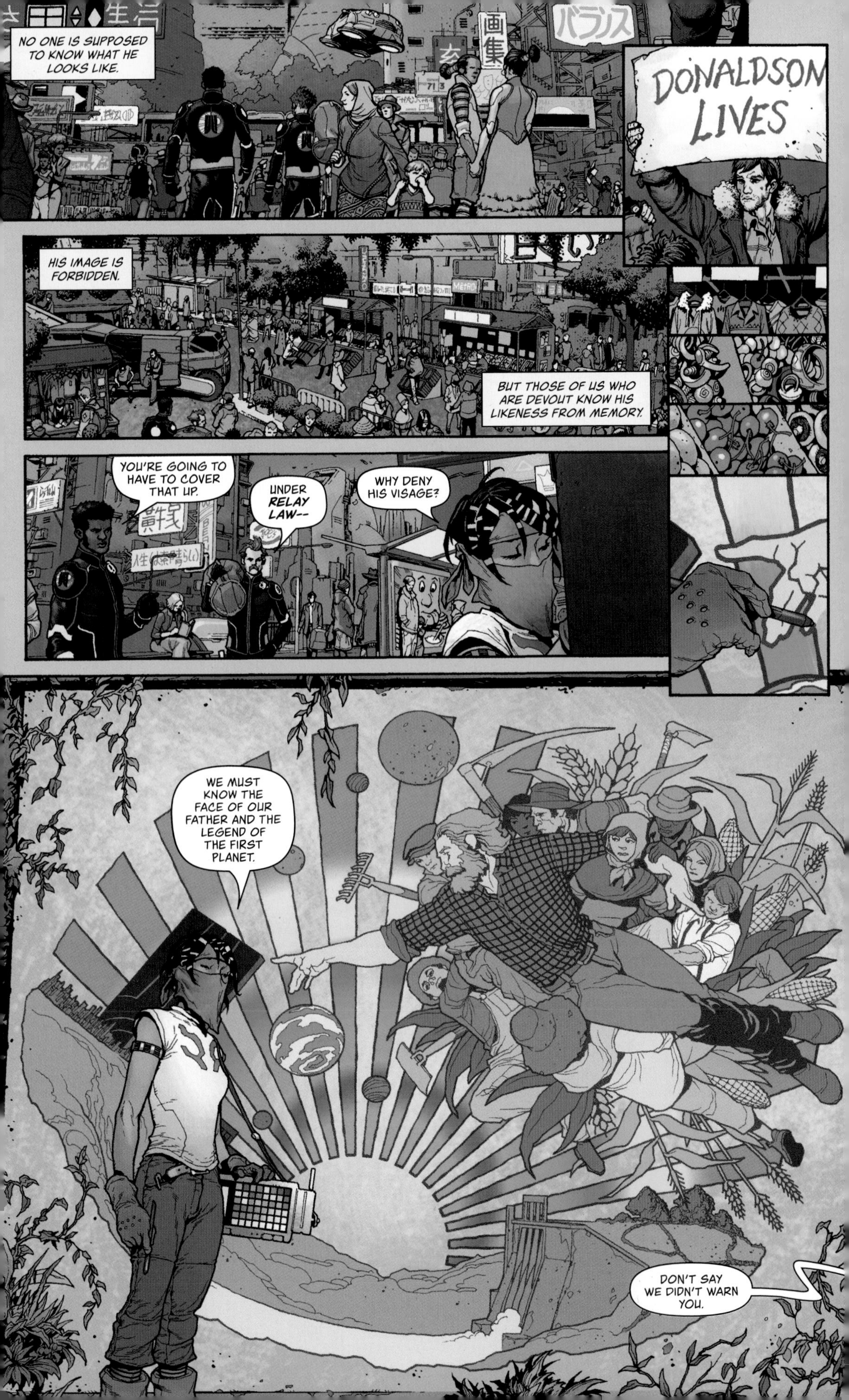
NO ONE IS SUPPOSED TO KNOW WHAT HE LOOKS LIKE.
DONALDSON LIVES
HIS IMAGE IS FORBIDDEN.
BUT THOSE OF US WHO ARE DEVOUT KNOW HIS LIKENESS FROM MEMORY.
YOU'RE GOING TO HAVE TO COVER THAT UP.
UNDER RELAY LAW--
WHY DENY HIS VISAGE?
WE MUST KNOW THE FACE OF OUR FATHER AND THE LEGEND OF THE FIRST PLANET.
DON'T SAY WE DIDN'T WARN YOU.

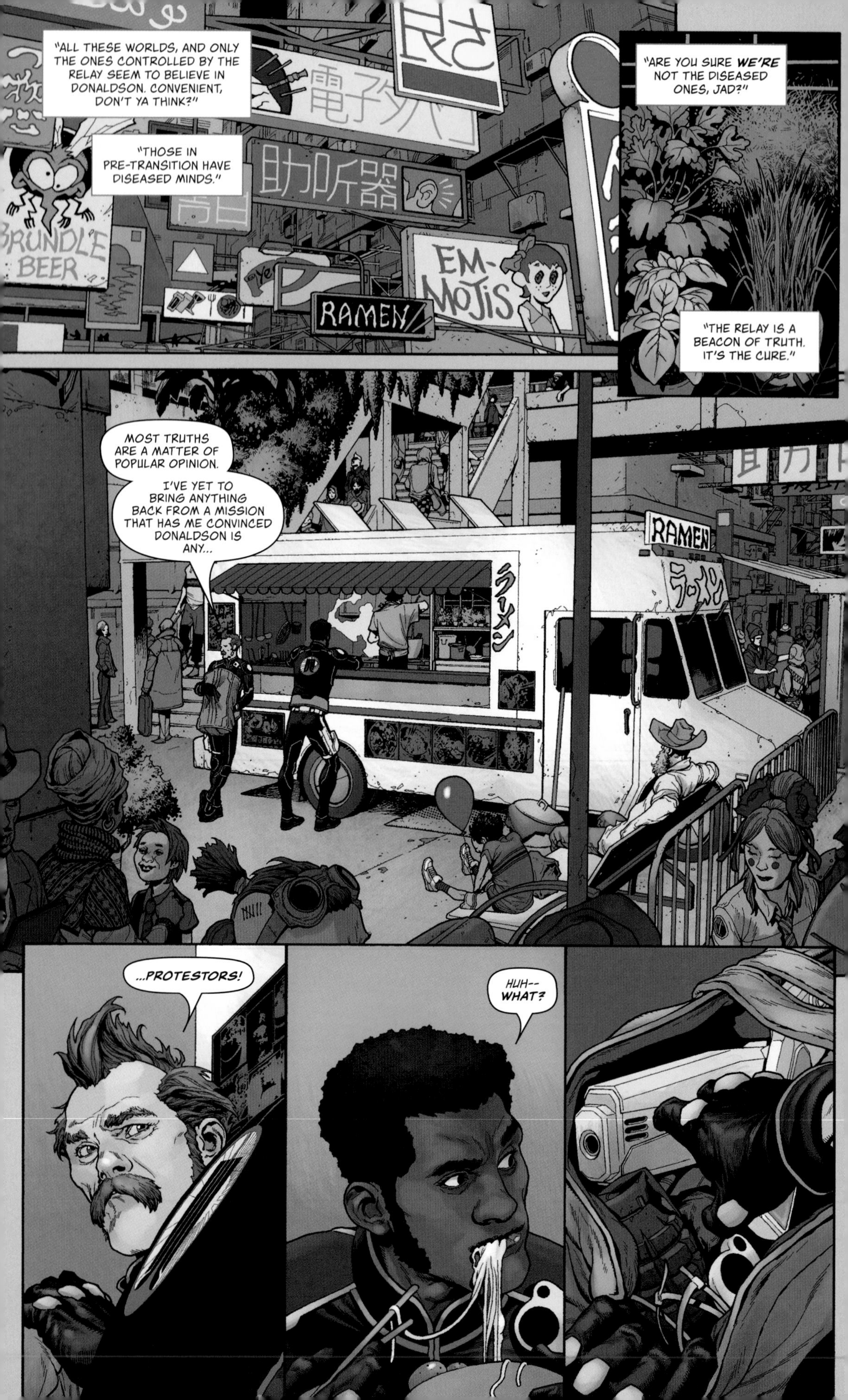
"ALL THESE WORLDS, AND ONLY THE ONES CONTROLLED BY THE RELAY SEEM TO BELIEVE IN DONALDSON. CONVENIENT, DON'T YA THINK?"
"THOSE IN PRE-TRANSITION HAVE DISEASED MINDS."
BRUNDLE BEER
EM-MOJIS
RAMEN
"ARE YOU SURE ***WE'RE*** NOT THE DISEASED ONES, JAD?"
"THE RELAY IS A BEACON OF TRUTH. IT'S THE CURE."
MOST TRUTHS ARE A MATTER OF POPULAR OPINION.
I'VE YET TO BRING ANYTHING BACK FROM A MISSION THAT HAS ME CONVINCED DONALDSON IS ANY...
RAMEN
ラーメン
...PROTESTORS!
HUH-- ***WHAT?***

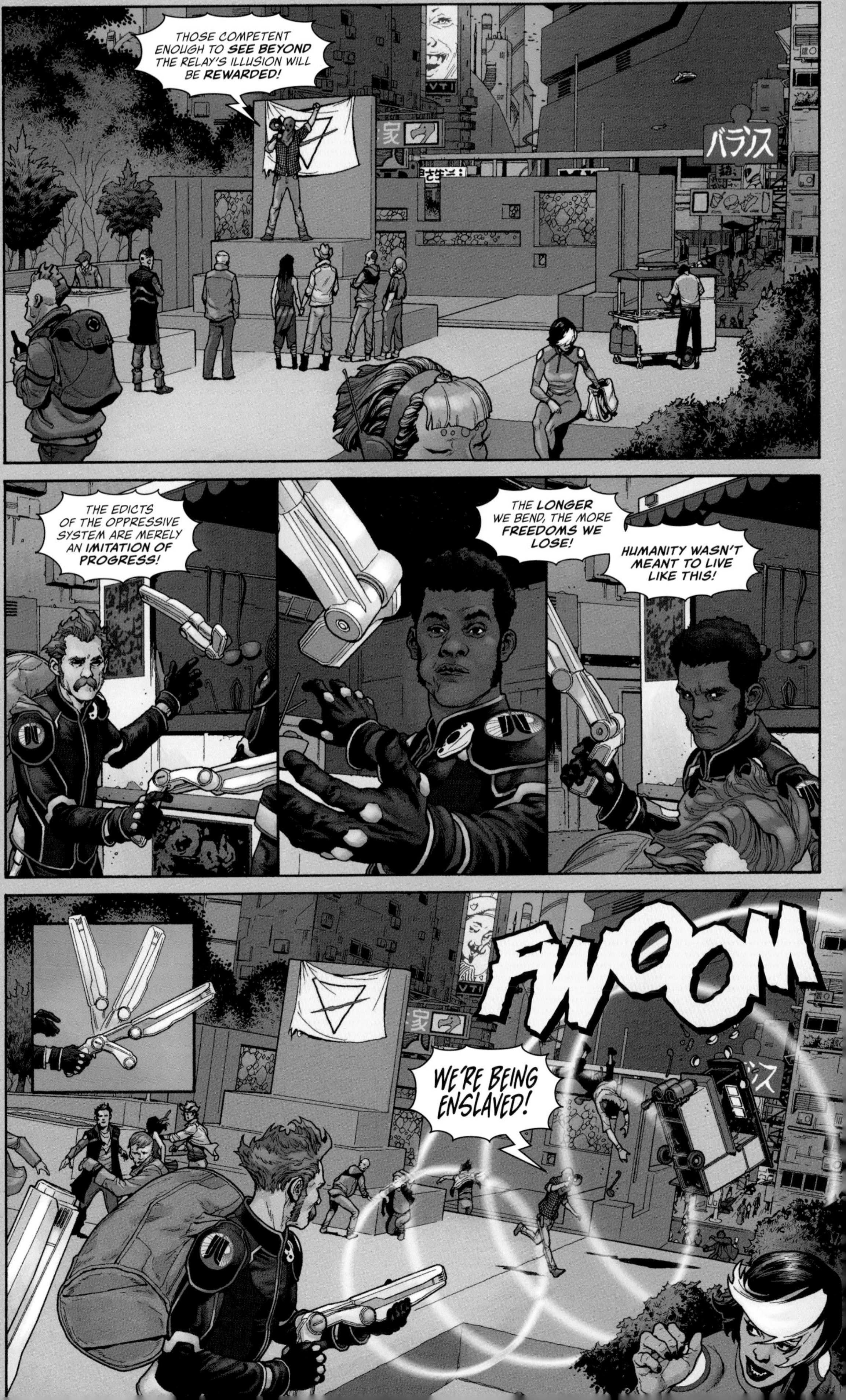
THOSE COMPETENT ENOUGH TO SEE BEYOND THE RELAY'S ILLUSION WILL BE REWARDED!
バランス
THE EDICTS OF THE OPPRESSIVE SYSTEM ARE MERELY AN IMITATION OF PROGRESS!
THE LONGER WE BEND, THE MORE FREEDOMS WE LOSE!
HUMANITY WASN'T MEANT TO LIVE LIKE THIS!
FWOOM
WE'RE BEING ENSLAVED!

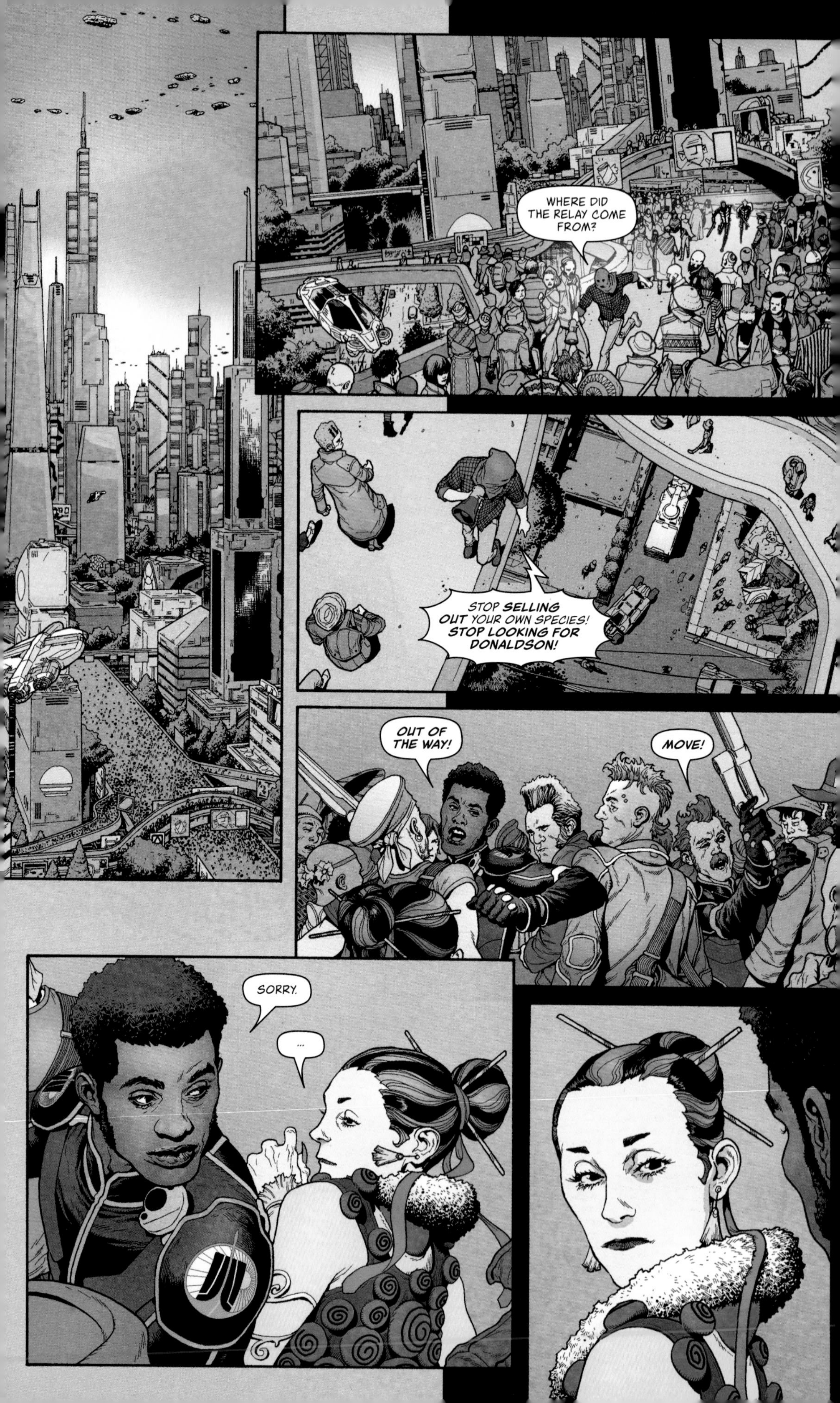
WHERE DID THE RELAY COME FROM?
STOP SELLING OUT YOUR OWN SPECIES! STOP LOOKING FOR DONALDSON!
OUT OF THE WAY!
MOVE!
SORRY.
...

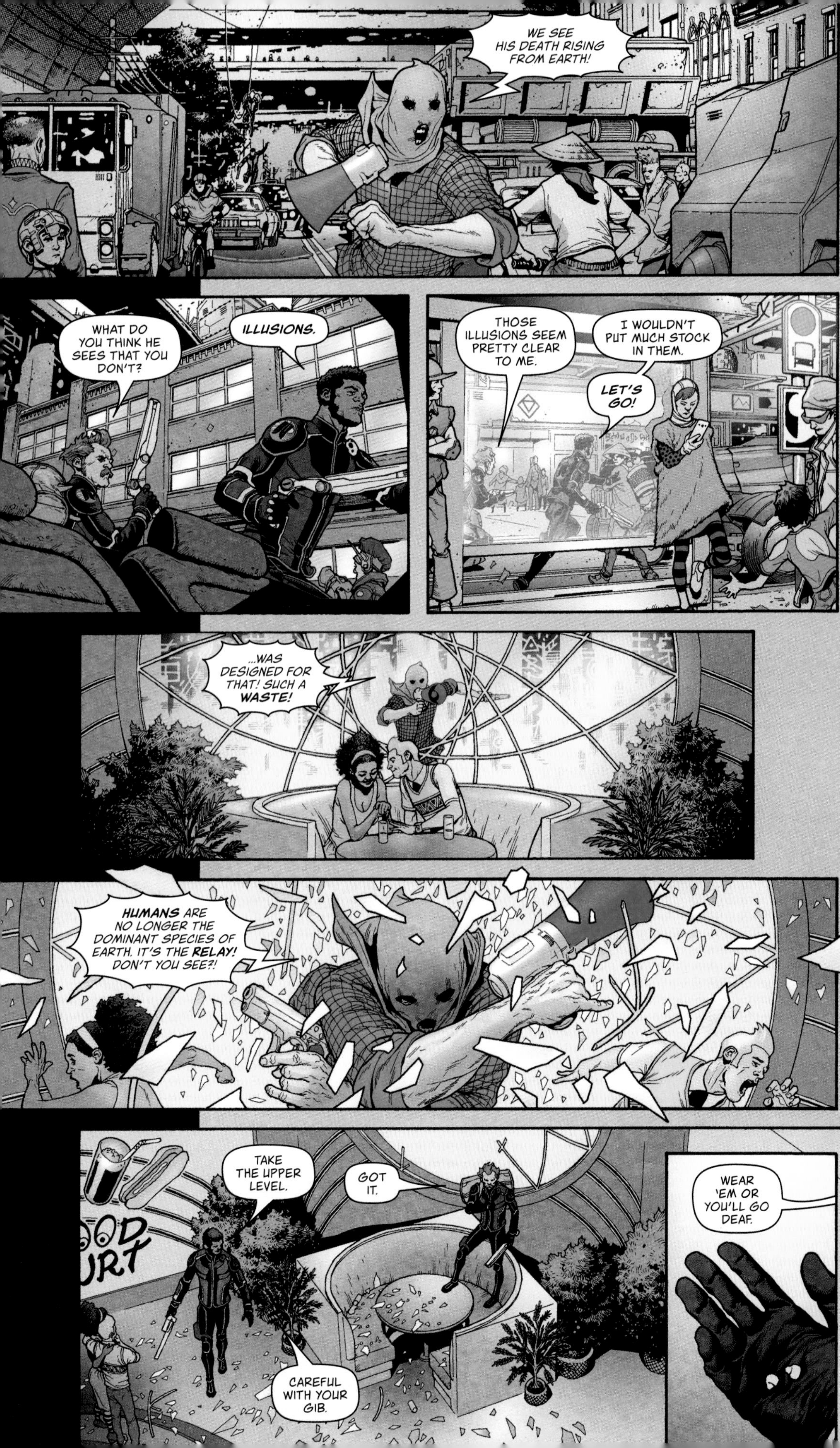
WE SEE HIS DEATH RISING FROM EARTH!
WHAT DO YOU THINK HE SEES THAT YOU DON'T?
ILLUSIONS.
THOSE ILLUSIONS SEEM PRETTY CLEAR TO ME.
I WOULDN'T PUT MUCH STOCK IN THEM.
LET'S GO!
...WAS DESIGNED FOR THAT! SUCH A WASTE!
HUMANS ARE NO LONGER THE DOMINANT SPECIES OF EARTH. IT'S THE RELAY! DON'T YOU SEE?!
TAKE THE UPPER LEVEL.
GOT IT.
CAREFUL WITH YOUR GIB.
WEAR 'EM OR YOU'LL GO DEAF.

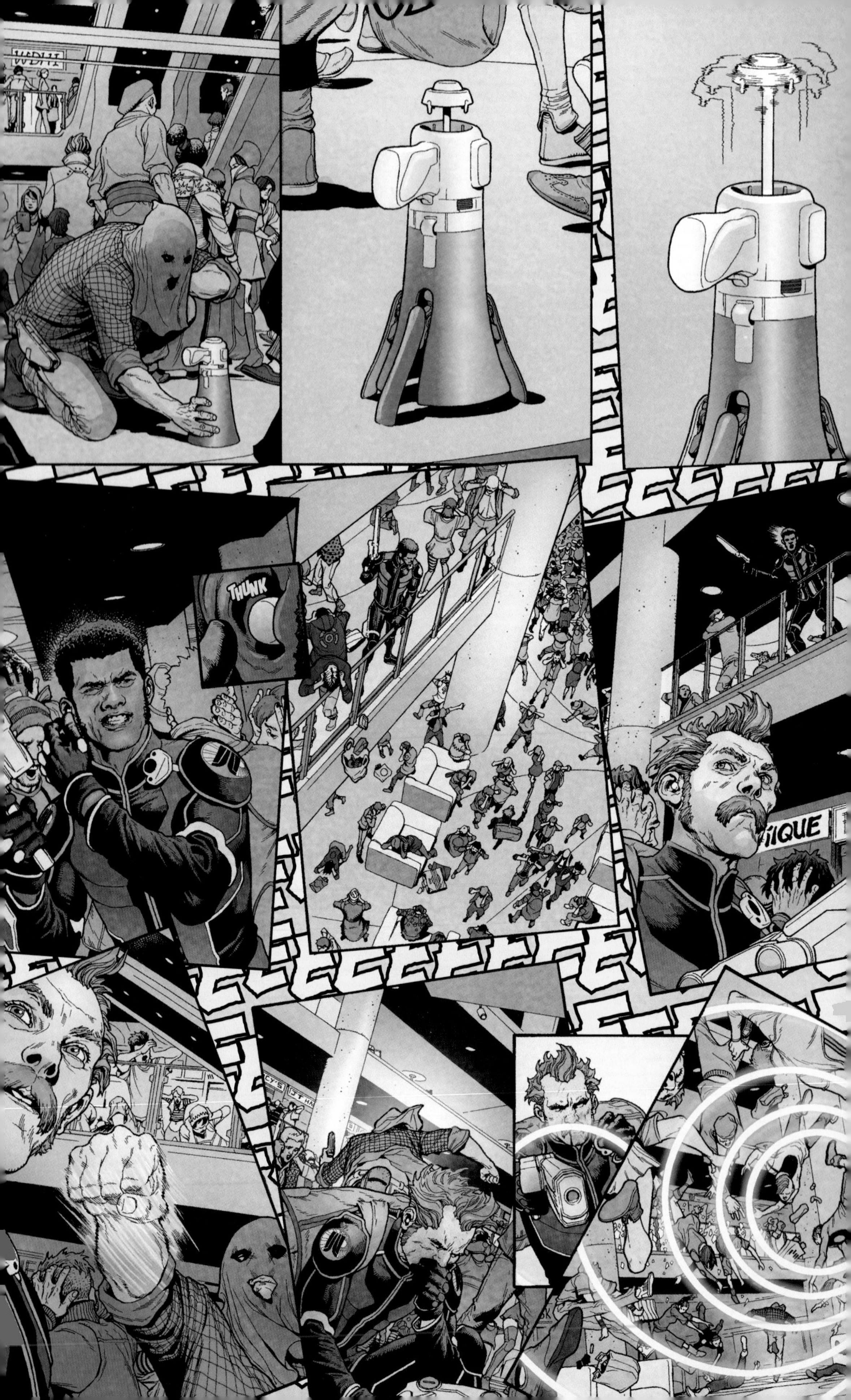
THUNK

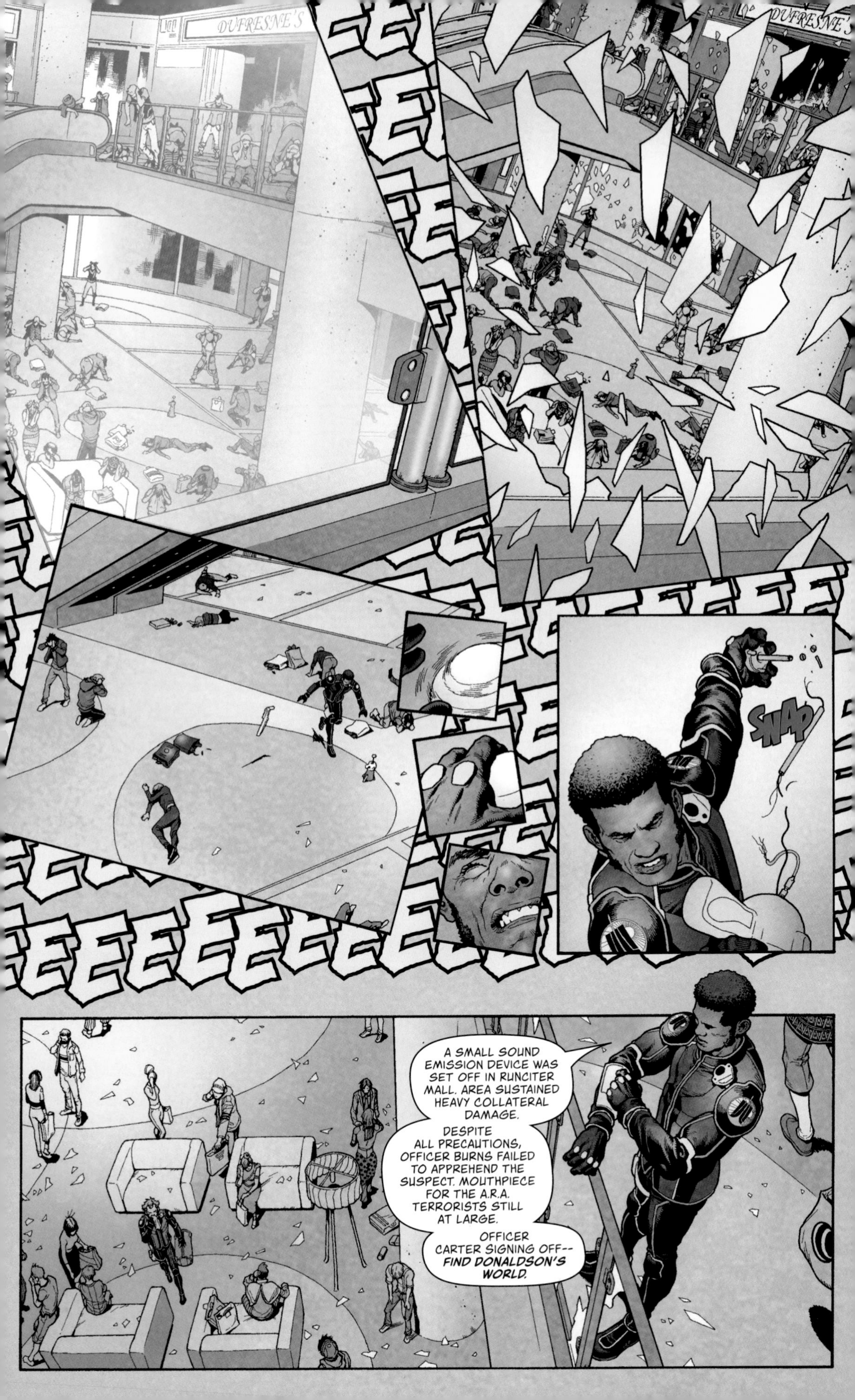
DUFRESNE'S
DUFRESNE'S
SNAP
A SMALL SOUND EMISSION DEVICE WAS SET OFF IN RUNCITER MALL. AREA SUSTAINED HEAVY COLLATERAL DAMAGE.
DESPITE ALL PRECAUTIONS, OFFICER BURNS FAILED TO APPREHEND THE SUSPECT. MOUTHPIECE FOR THE A.R.A. TERRORISTS STILL AT LARGE.
OFFICER CARTER SIGNING OFF-- *FIND DONALDSON'S WORLD.*

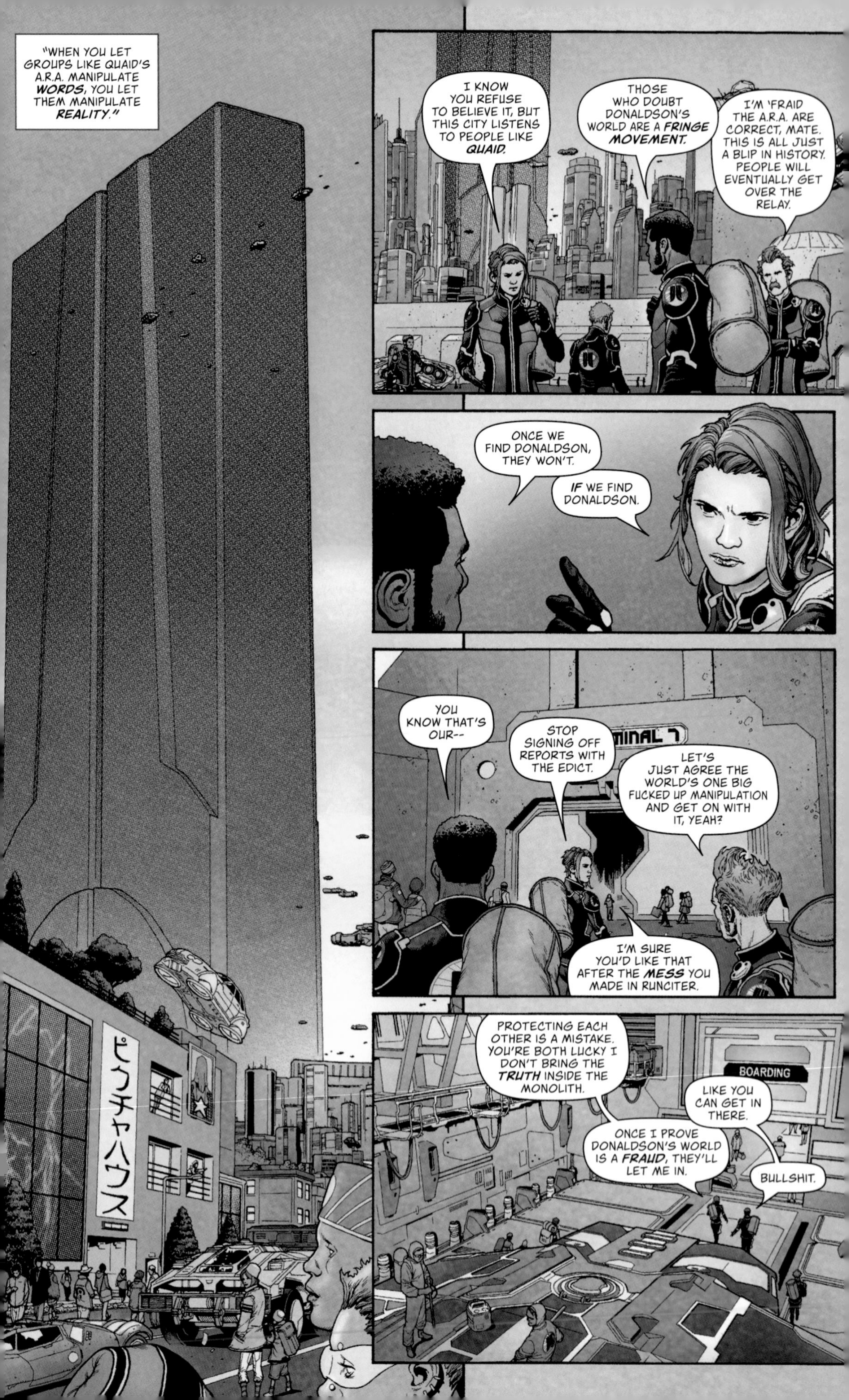

"WHEN YOU LET GROUPS LIKE QUAID'S A.R.A. MANIPULATE WORDS, YOU LET THEM MANIPULATE REALITY."
I KNOW YOU REFUSE TO BELIEVE IT, BUT THIS CITY LISTENS TO PEOPLE LIKE QUAID.
THOSE WHO DOUBT DONALDSON'S WORLD ARE A FRINGE MOVEMENT.
I'M 'FRAID THE A.R.A. ARE CORRECT, MATE. THIS IS ALL JUST A BLIP IN HISTORY. PEOPLE WILL EVENTUALLY GET OVER THE RELAY.
ONCE WE FIND DONALDSON, THEY WON'T.
IF WE FIND DONALDSON.
YOU KNOW THAT'S OUR--
STOP SIGNING OFF REPORTS WITH THE EDICT.
LET'S JUST AGREE THE WORLD'S ONE BIG FUCKED UP MANIPULATION AND GET ON WITH IT, YEAH?
I'M SURE YOU'D LIKE THAT AFTER THE MESS YOU MADE IN RUNCITER.
PROTECTING EACH OTHER IS A MISTAKE. YOU'RE BOTH LUCKY I DON'T BRING THE TRUTH INSIDE THE MONOLITH.
LIKE YOU CAN GET IN THERE.
ONCE I PROVE DONALDSON'S WORLD IS A FRAUD, THEY'LL LET ME IN.
BULLSHIT.

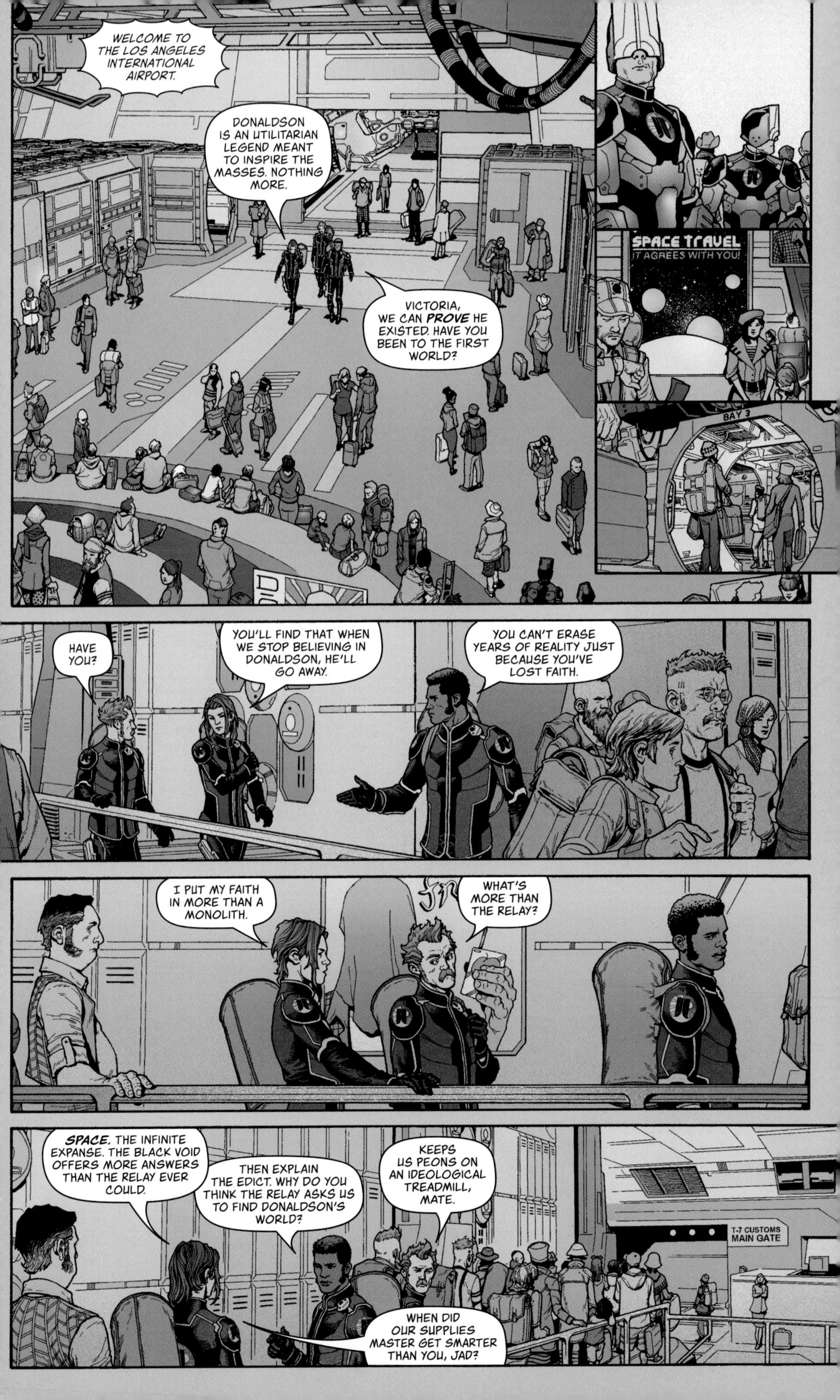
WELCOME TO THE LOS ANGELES INTERNATIONAL AIRPORT.
DONALDSON IS AN UTILITARIAN LEGEND MEANT TO INSPIRE THE MASSES. NOTHING MORE.
VICTORIA, WE CAN PROVE HE EXISTED. HAVE YOU BEEN TO THE FIRST WORLD?
SPACE TRAVEL
IT AGREES WITH YOU!
BAY 3
HAVE YOU?
YOU'LL FIND THAT WHEN WE STOP BELIEVING IN DONALDSON, HE'LL GO AWAY.
YOU CAN'T ERASE YEARS OF REALITY JUST BECAUSE YOU'VE LOST FAITH.
I PUT MY FAITH IN MORE THAN A MONOLITH.
WHAT'S MORE THAN THE RELAY?
SPACE. THE INFINITE EXPANSE. THE BLACK VOID OFFERS MORE ANSWERS THAN THE RELAY EVER COULD.
THEN EXPLAIN THE EDICT. WHY DO YOU THINK THE RELAY ASKS US TO FIND DONALDSON'S WORLD?
KEEPS US PEONS ON AN IDEOLOGICAL TREADMILL, MATE.
T-7 CUSTOMS
MAIN GATE
WHEN DID OUR SUPPLIES MASTER GET SMARTER THAN YOU, JAD?

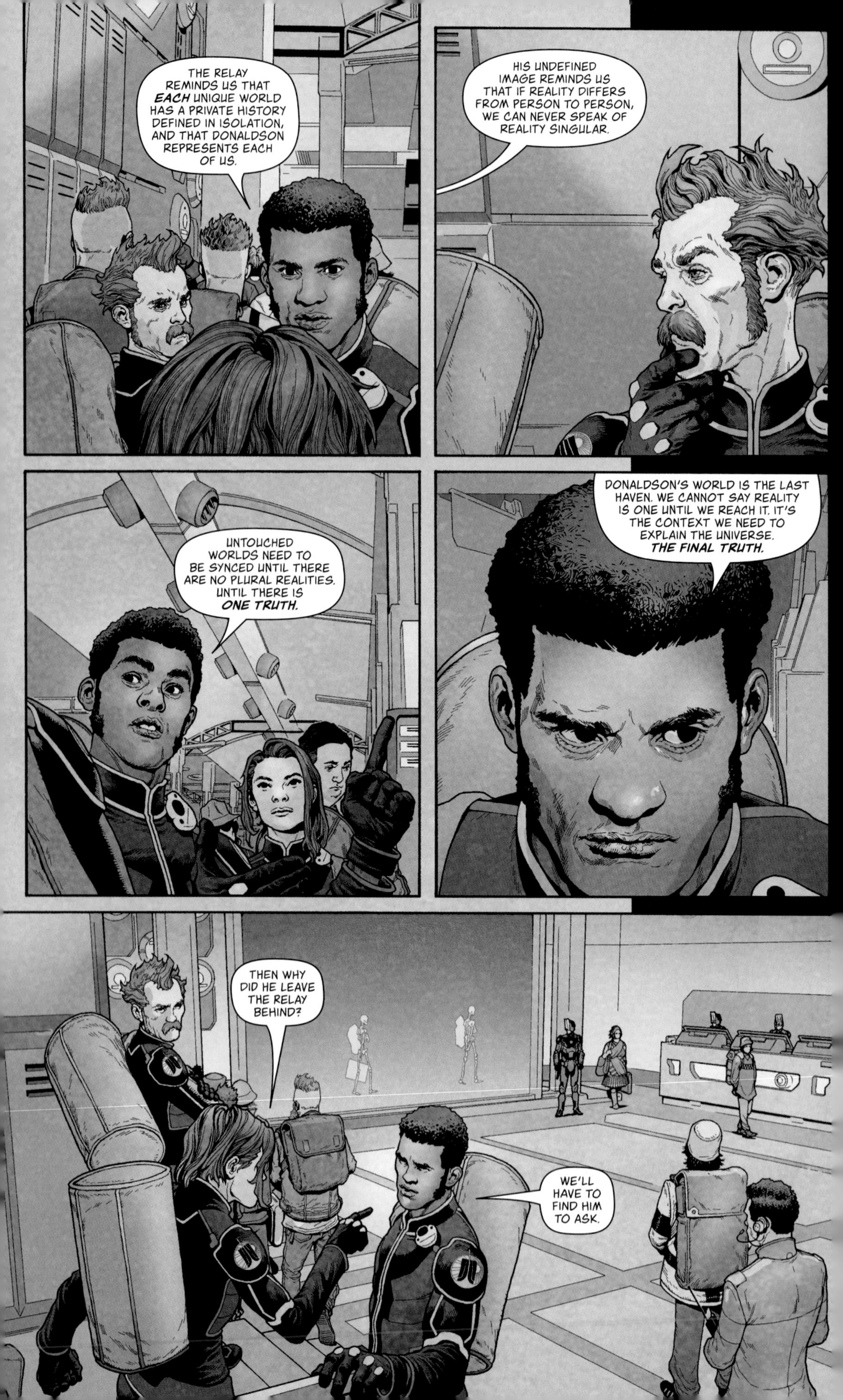
THE RELAY REMINDS US THAT *EACH* UNIQUE WORLD HAS A PRIVATE HISTORY DEFINED IN ISOLATION, AND THAT DONALDSON REPRESENTS EACH OF US.
HIS UNDEFINED IMAGE REMINDS US THAT IF REALITY DIFFERS FROM PERSON TO PERSON, WE CAN NEVER SPEAK OF REALITY SINGULAR.
UNTOUCHED WORLDS NEED TO BE SYNCED UNTIL THERE ARE NO PLURAL REALITIES. UNTIL THERE IS *ONE TRUTH.*
DONALDSON'S WORLD IS THE LAST HAVEN. WE CANNOT SAY REALITY IS ONE UNTIL WE REACH IT. IT'S THE CONTEXT WE NEED TO EXPLAIN THE UNIVERSE. *THE FINAL TRUTH.*
THEN WHY DID HE LEAVE THE RELAY BEHIND?
WE'LL HAVE TO FIND HIM TO ASK.

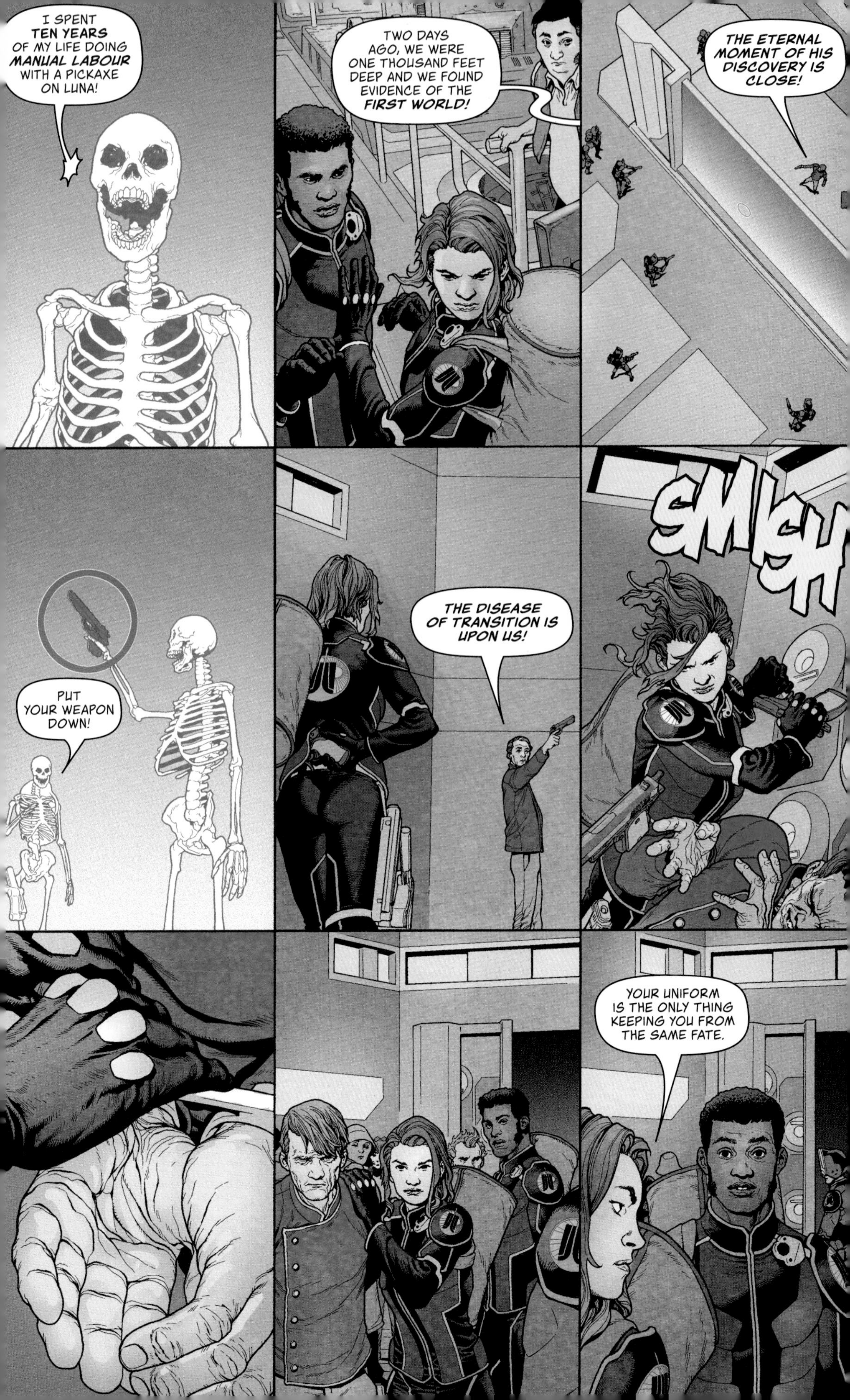
I SPENT TEN YEARS OF MY LIFE DOING MANUAL LABOUR WITH A PICKAXE ON LUNA!
TWO DAYS AGO, WE WERE ONE THOUSAND FEET DEEP AND WE FOUND EVIDENCE OF THE FIRST WORLD!
THE ETERNAL MOMENT OF HIS DISCOVERY IS CLOSE!
PUT YOUR WEAPON DOWN!
THE DISEASE OF TRANSITION IS UPON US!
SMISH
YOUR UNIFORM IS THE ONLY THING KEEPING YOU FROM THE SAME FATE.

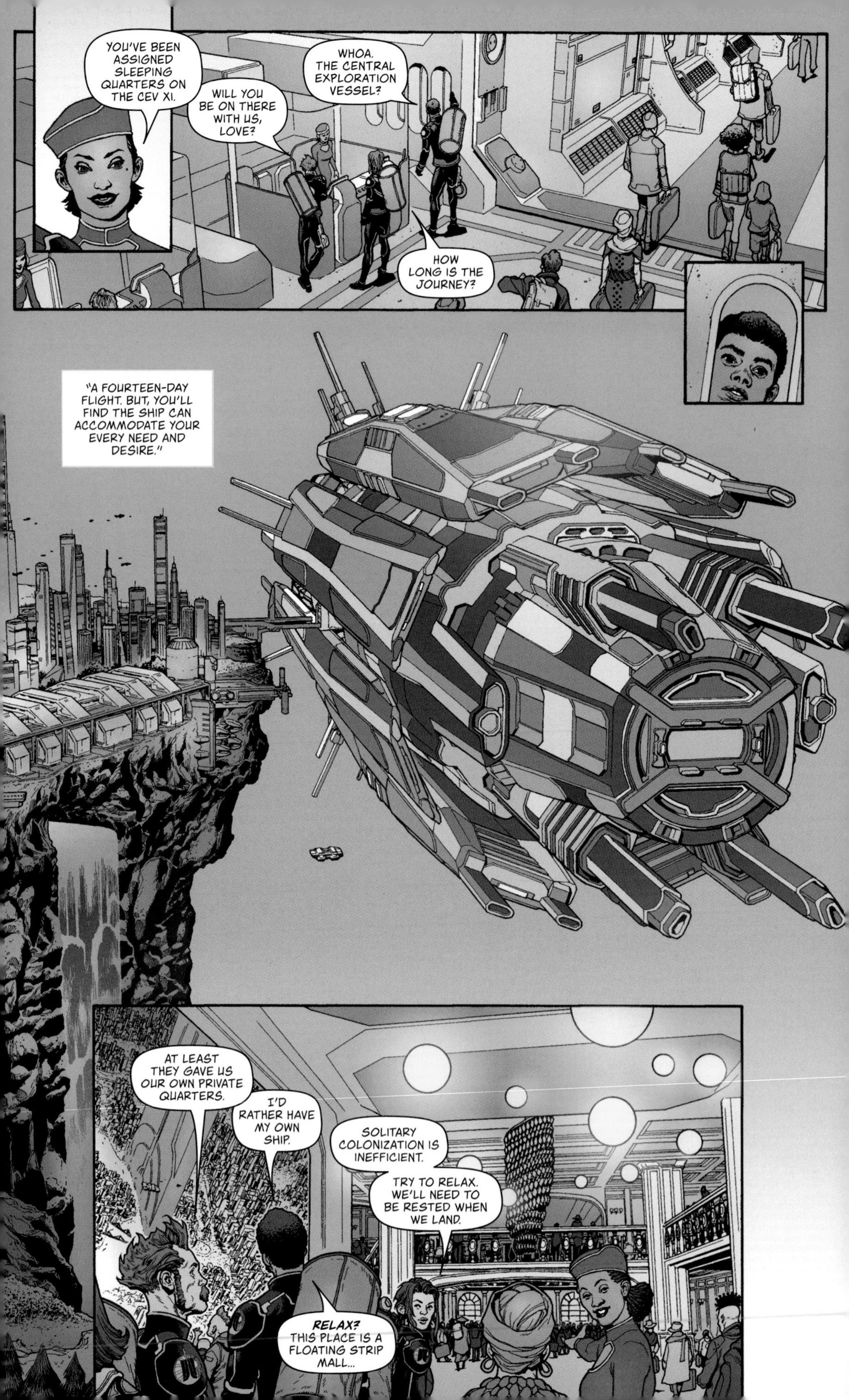
YOU'VE BEEN ASSIGNED SLEEPING QUARTERS ON THE CEV XI.
WILL YOU BE ON THERE WITH US, LOVE?
WHOA. THE CENTRAL EXPLORATION VESSEL?
HOW LONG IS THE JOURNEY?
"A FOURTEEN-DAY FLIGHT. BUT, YOU'LL FIND THE SHIP CAN ACCOMMODATE YOUR EVERY NEED AND DESIRE."
AT LEAST THEY GAVE US OUR OWN PRIVATE QUARTERS.
I'D RATHER HAVE MY OWN SHIP.
SOLITARY COLONIZATION IS INEFFICIENT.
TRY TO RELAX. WE'LL NEED TO BE RESTED WHEN WE LAND.
RELAX? THIS PLACE IS A FLOATING STRIP MALL...

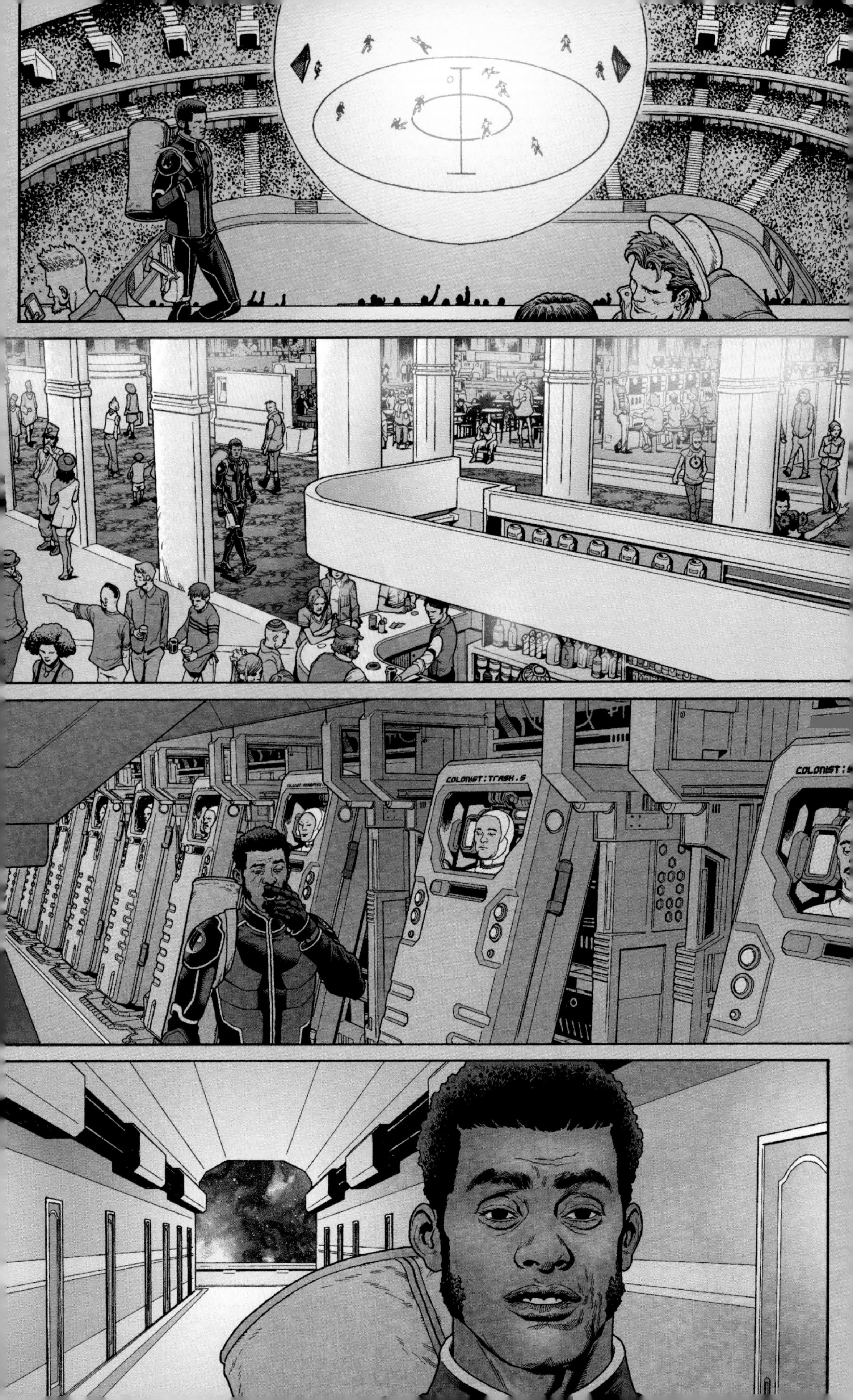
COLONIST:TRASH.5
COLONIST:

MOST KNOWN PLANETS HAVE ALREADY JOINED THE RELAY SYSTEM.

WE'RE COOPED UP IN THESE ROOMS FOR WEEKS UNTIL WE FIND NEW UNCOLONIZED WORLDS.

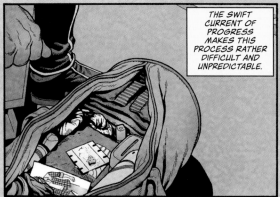

THE SWIFT CURRENT OF PROGRESS MAKES THIS PROCESS RATHER DIFFICULT AND UNPREDICTABLE.

AS PART OF THE BOARDING PARTY, WE NEVER KNOW WHERE WE'RE GOING OR HOW LONG WE'LL BE GONE.

THE DESTINATION ULTIMATELY DOESN'T MATTER. WE LAND AND DEFINE MORALS. WE CREATE HOPE.

WE ACCELERATE PROGRESS BY OFFERING THE MONOLITH.

DONALDSON and the FIRST WORLD

WE OFFER A REDEFINITION OF REALITY.

JAD

THE PLANETS WHO REFUSE FACE **SWIFT** ANNIHILATION.

IF A PLANET WILLINGLY JOINS THE RELAY, THEIR CUSTOMS, CULTURE AND LEARNINGS ARE TRADED FOR OUR OWN VASTLY INTELLIGENT SYSTEM.

A MOURNFUL BUT NECESSARY ACT IN THE FACE OF AN INSANE WORLD.

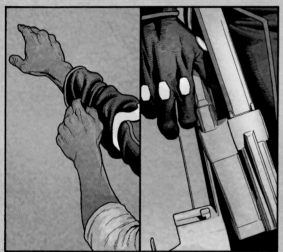

AN ALL KNOWING, ALL ACCOMMODATING DIVINE INTERVENTION.

WITH ONE UNFULFILLED WISH.

the TRANSCENDENT TRADE

BUT WE HAVEN'T FOUND ANY EVIDENCE OF HIS WORLD...

FIND DONALDSON'S WORLD

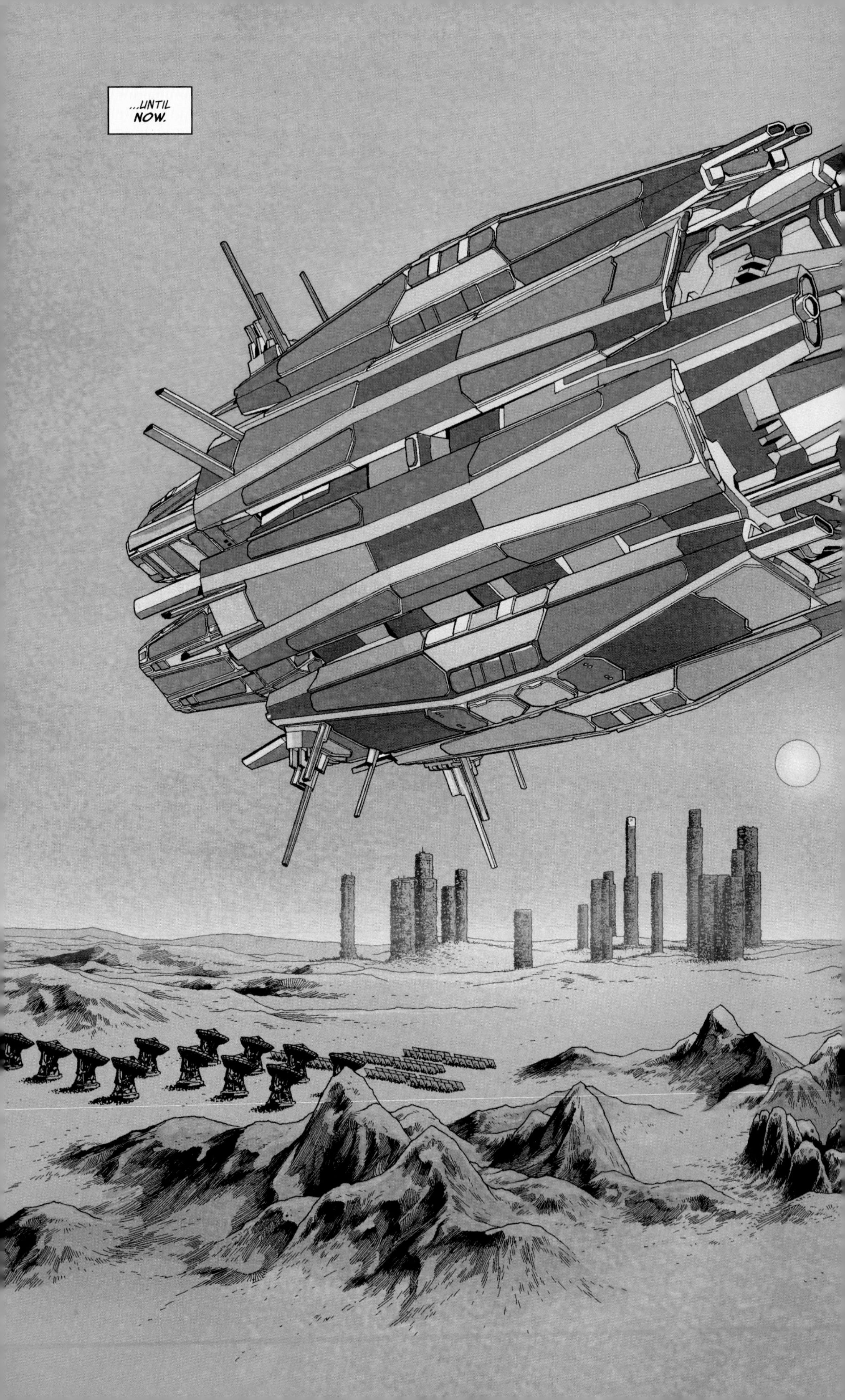
...UNTIL
NOW.

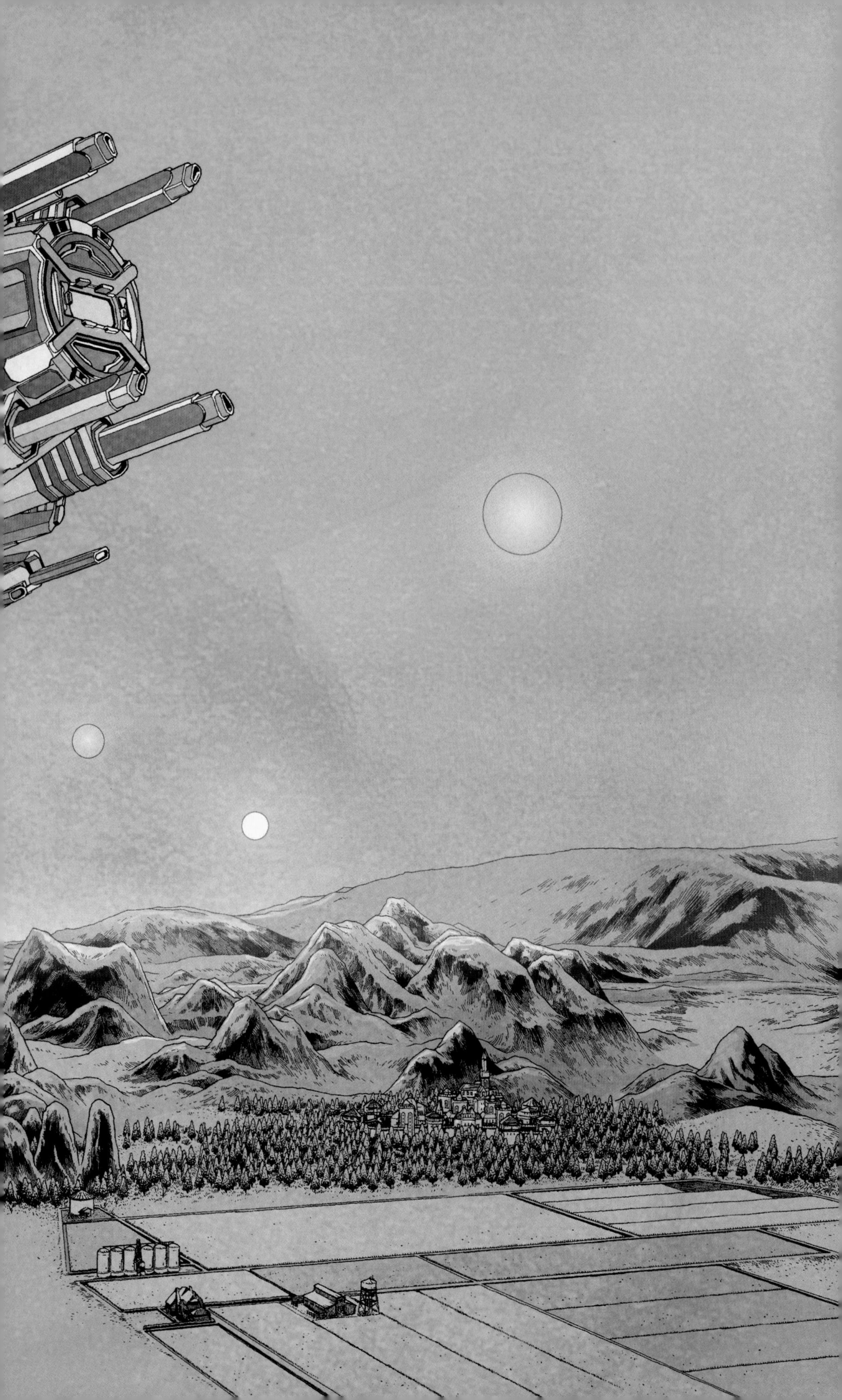

2

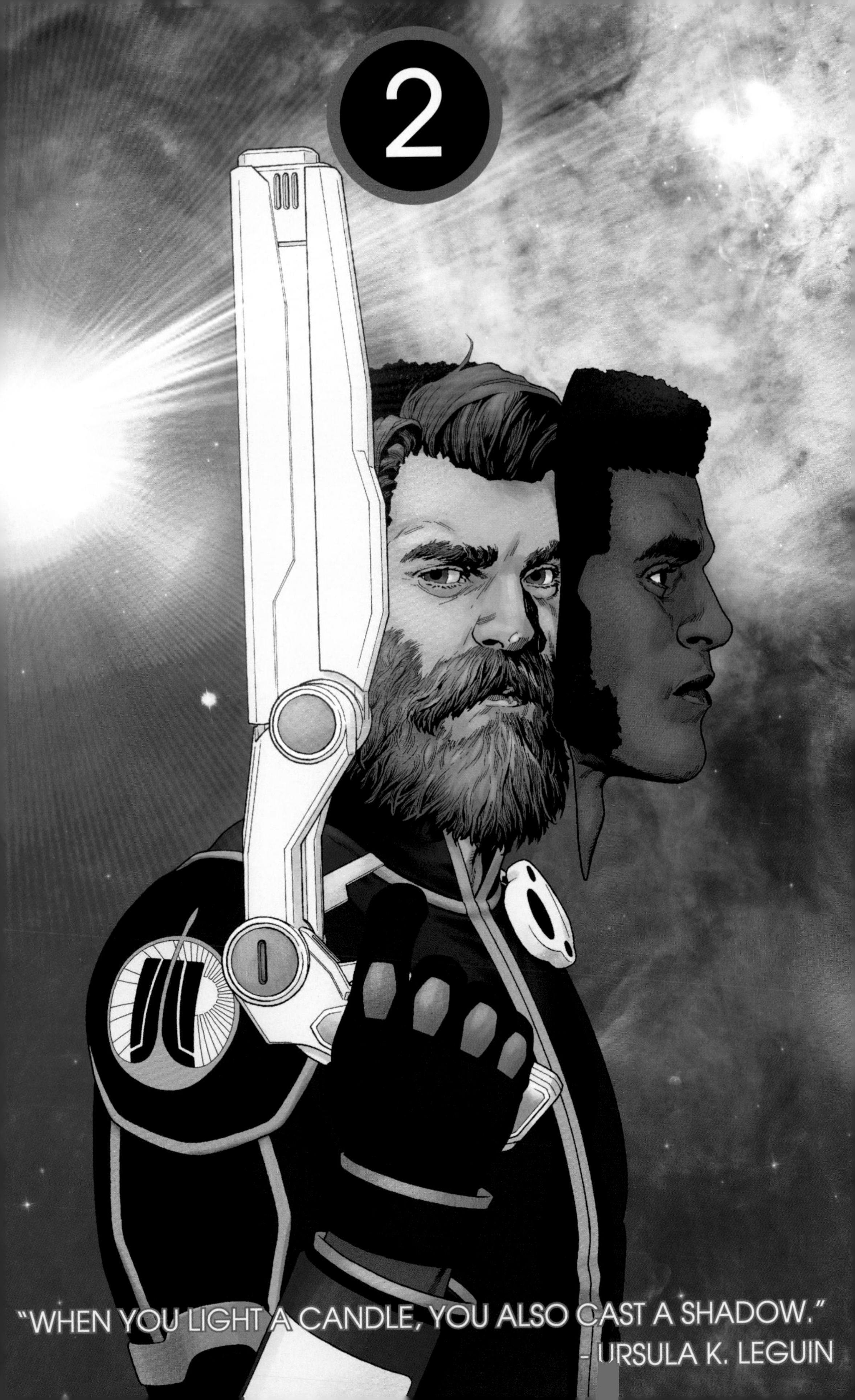

"WHEN YOU LIGHT A CANDLE, YOU ALSO CAST A SHADOW."
- URSULA K. LEGUIN

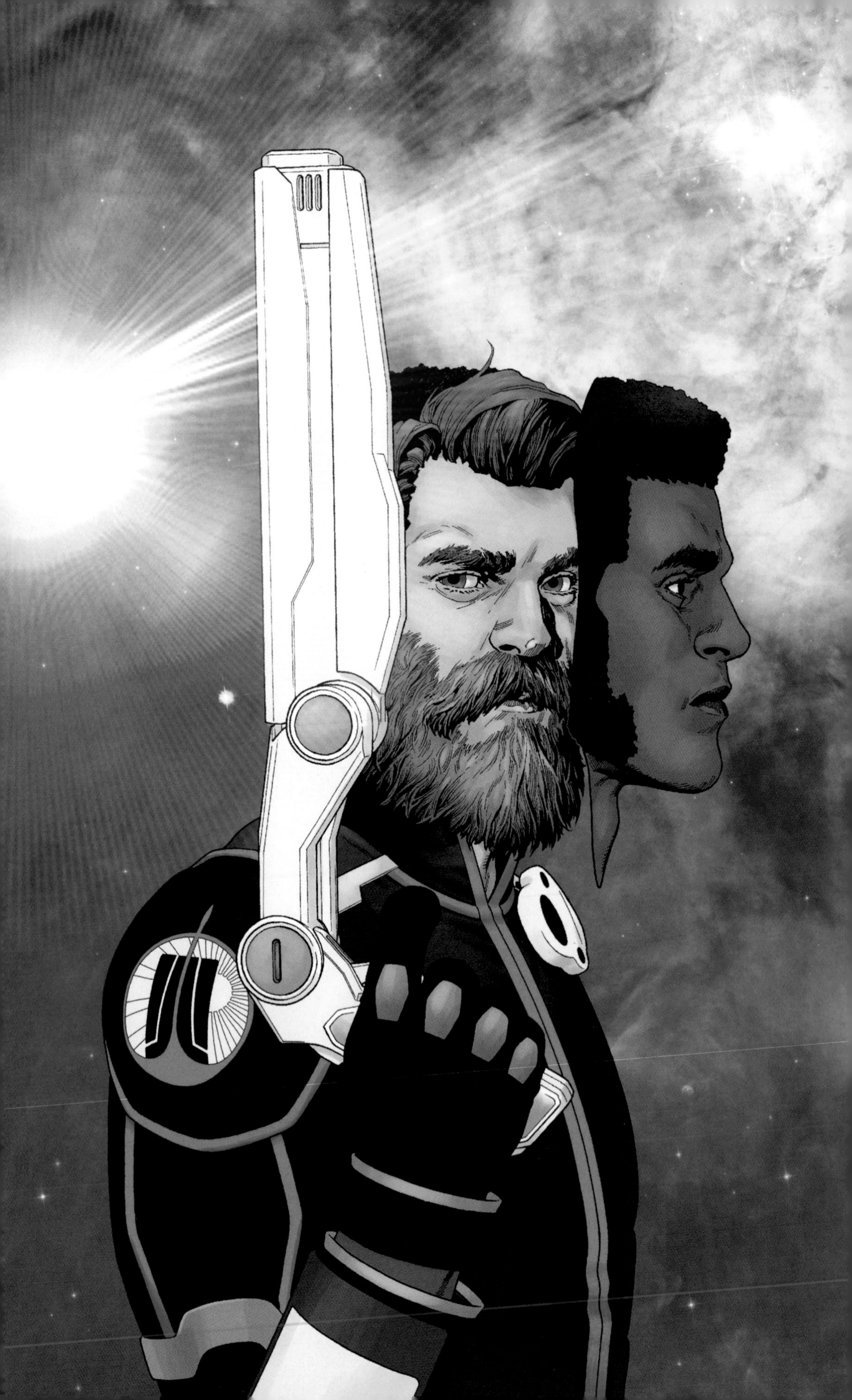

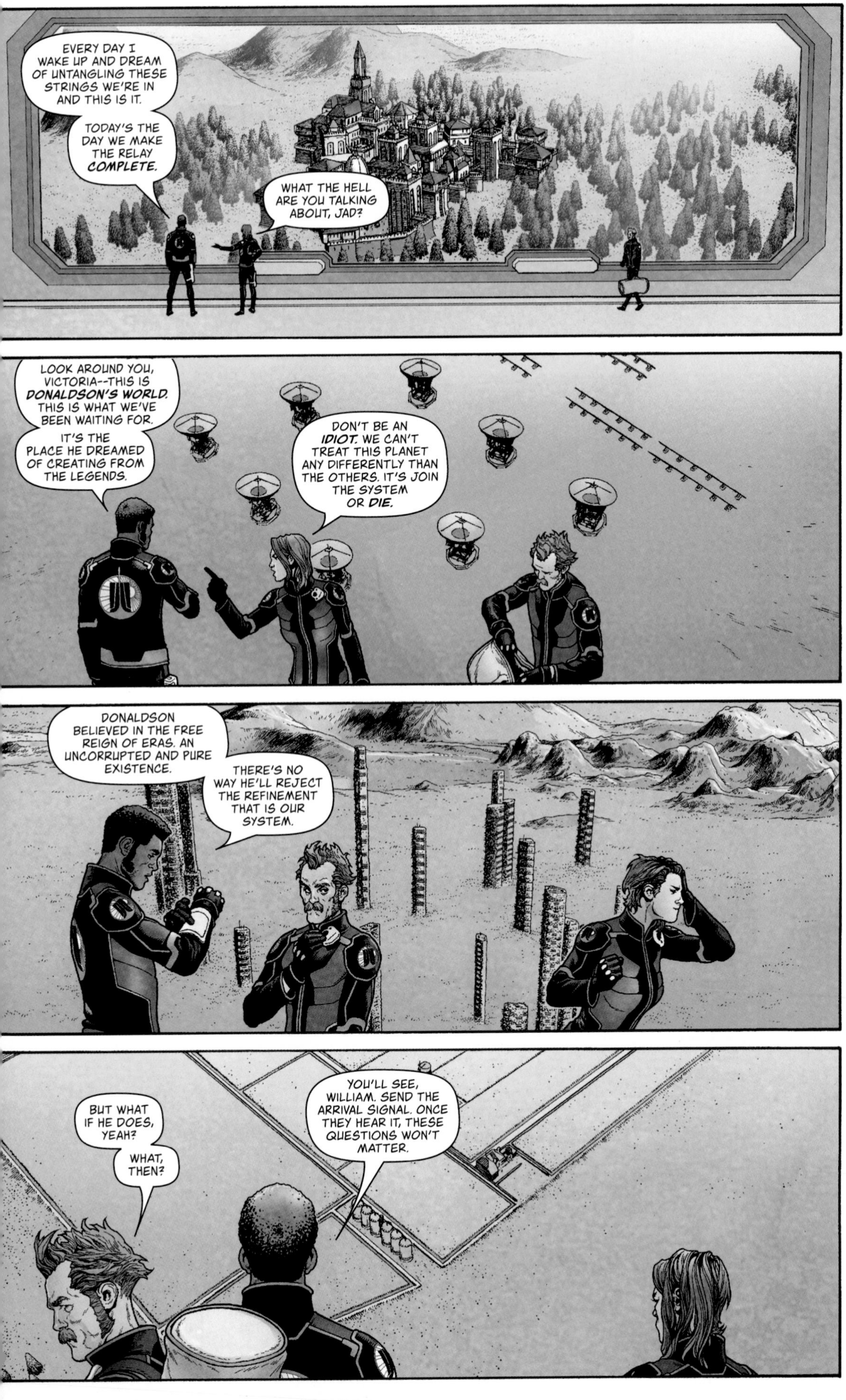
EVERY DAY I WAKE UP AND DREAM OF UNTANGLING THESE STRINGS WE'RE IN AND THIS IS IT.
TODAY'S THE DAY WE MAKE THE RELAY *COMPLETE.*
WHAT THE HELL ARE YOU TALKING ABOUT, JAD?
LOOK AROUND YOU, VICTORIA--THIS IS *DONALDSON'S WORLD.* THIS IS WHAT WE'VE BEEN WAITING FOR.
IT'S THE PLACE HE DREAMED OF CREATING FROM THE LEGENDS.
DON'T BE AN *IDIOT.* WE CAN'T TREAT THIS PLANET ANY DIFFERENTLY THAN THE OTHERS. IT'S JOIN THE SYSTEM OR *DIE.*
DONALDSON BELIEVED IN THE FREE REIGN OF ERAS. AN UNCORRUPTED AND PURE EXISTENCE.
THERE'S NO WAY HE'LL REJECT THE REFINEMENT THAT IS OUR SYSTEM.
BUT WHAT IF HE DOES, YEAH?
WHAT, THEN?
YOU'LL SEE, WILLIAM. SEND THE ARRIVAL SIGNAL. ONCE THEY HEAR IT, THESE QUESTIONS WON'T MATTER.

YOUR
TRUTH...

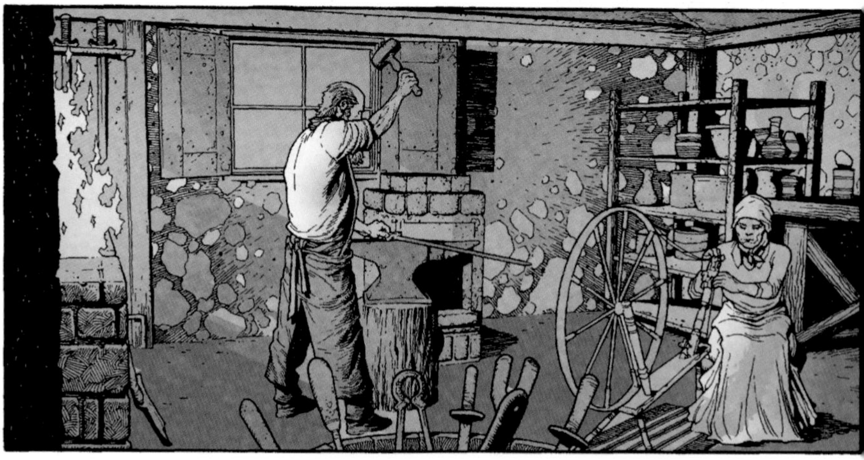

...IS A
MATTER OF
OPINION.

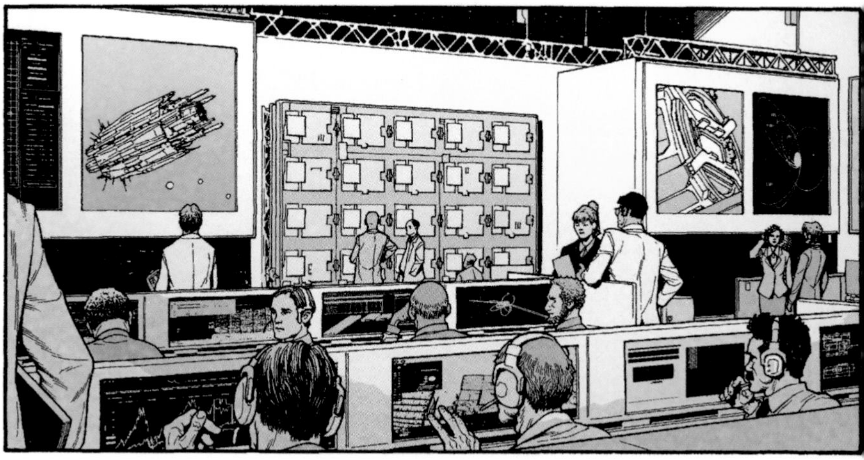

WE'VE COME
TO LIBERATE
YOU WITH AN
OFFER OF
OBJECTIVE
TRUTH.

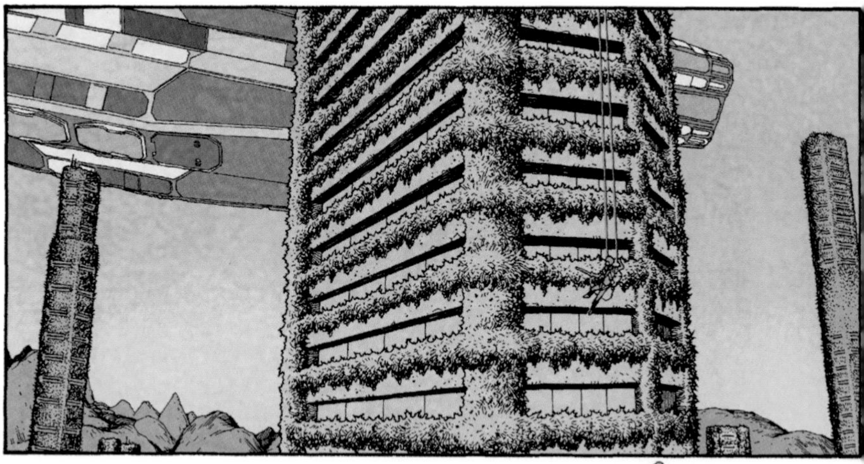

WE ARE THE
INEVITABLE
EVOLUTION OF
YOUR PLANET.

WE ARE
THE RELAY.

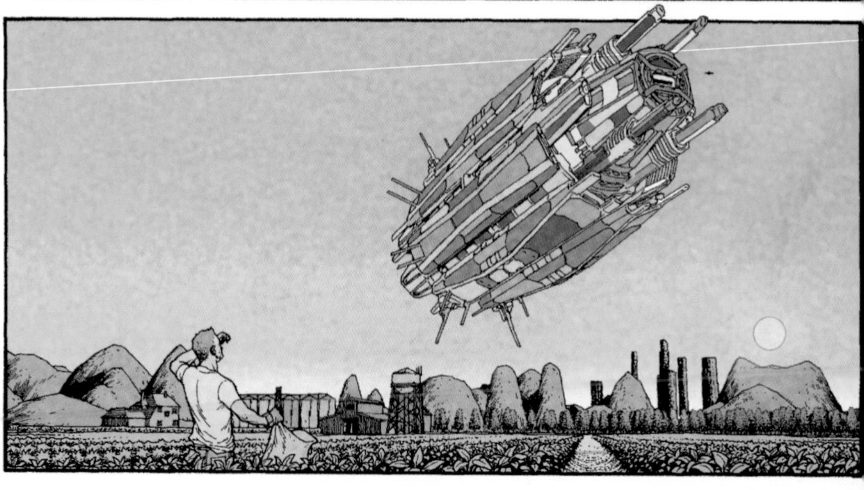

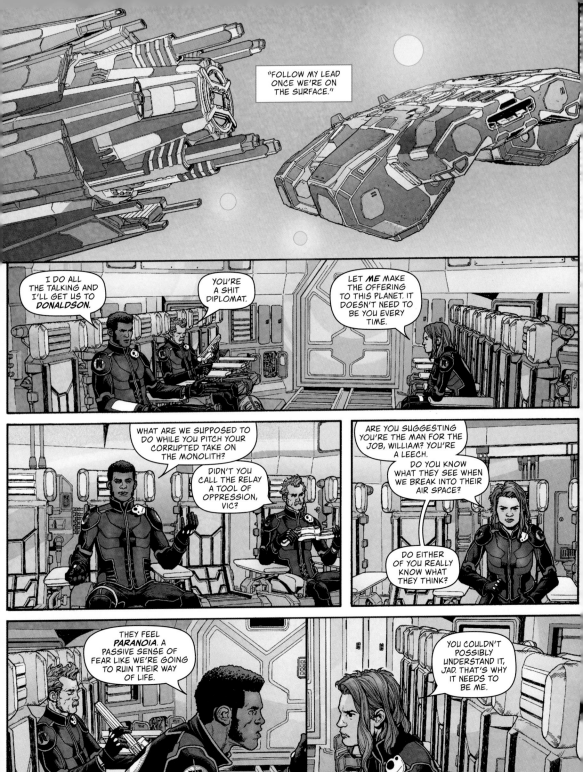

"FOLLOW MY LEAD ONCE WE'RE ON THE SURFACE."

I DO ALL THE TALKING AND I'LL GET US TO **DONALDSON**.

YOU'RE A SHIT DIPLOMAT.

LET *ME* MAKE THE OFFERING TO THIS PLANET. IT DOESN'T NEED TO BE YOU EVERY TIME.

WHAT ARE WE SUPPOSED TO DO WHILE YOU PITCH YOUR CORRUPTED TAKE ON THE MONOLITH?

DIDN'T YOU CALL THE RELAY A TOOL OF OPPRESSION, VIC?

ARE YOU SUGGESTING YOU'RE THE MAN FOR THE JOB, WILLIAM? YOU'RE A LEECH.

DO YOU KNOW WHAT THEY SEE WHEN WE BREAK INTO THEIR AIR SPACE?

DO EITHER OF YOU REALLY KNOW WHAT THEY THINK?

THEY FEEL *PARANOIA*. A PASSIVE SENSE OF FEAR LIKE WE'RE GOING TO RUIN THEIR WAY OF LIFE.

YOU COULDN'T POSSIBLY UNDERSTAND IT, JAD. THAT'S WHY IT NEEDS TO BE ME.

I CAN EMPATHIZE WITH IT. THAT'S ENOUGH TO OFFER AN ENLIGHTENED WAY OUT OF THEIR MAZE.

YOU TWO CALM THE CITIZENS AND COLLECT THE NECESSARY ENVIRONMENTAL AND TECHNOLOGICAL DATA.

I'LL TALK TO DONALDSON.

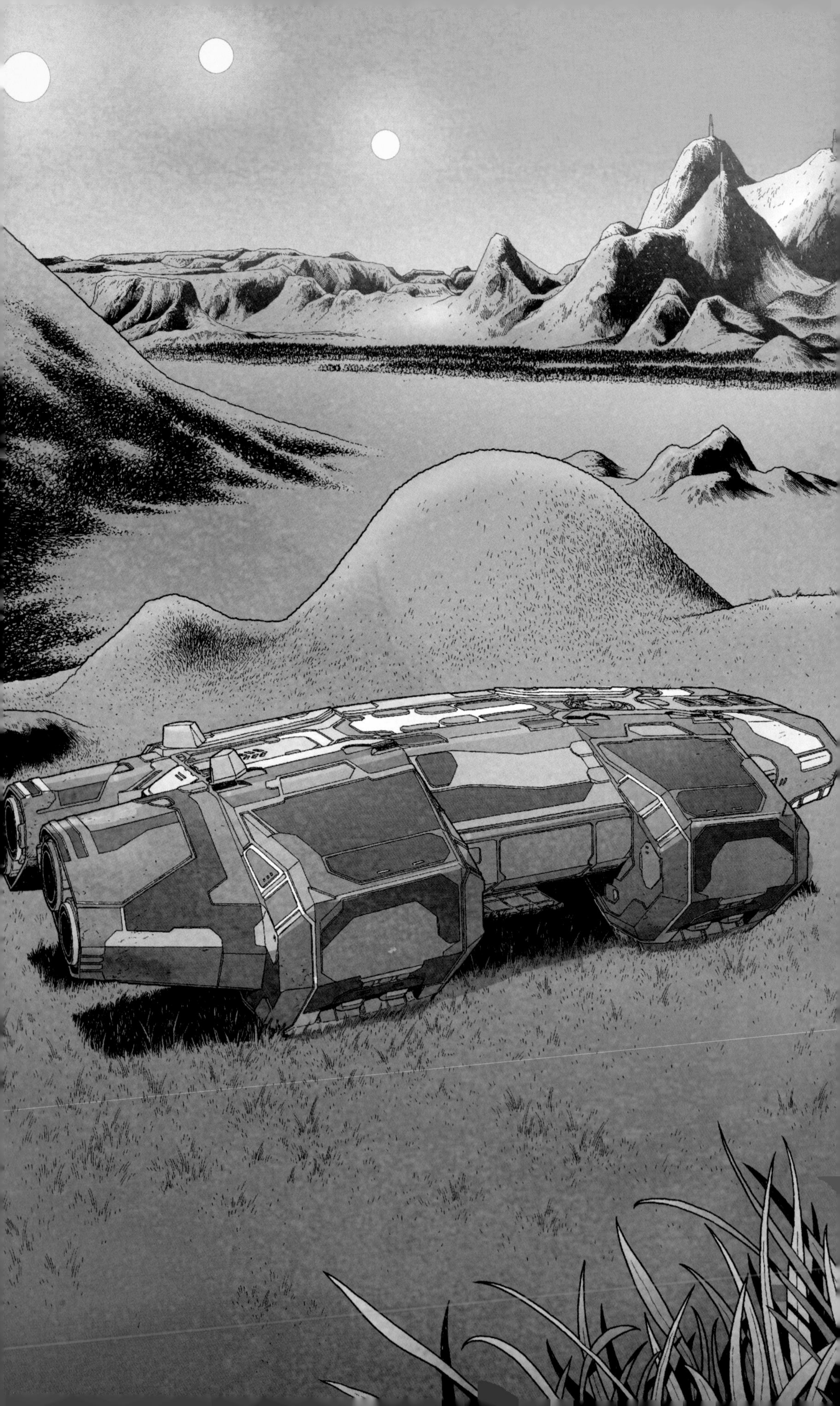

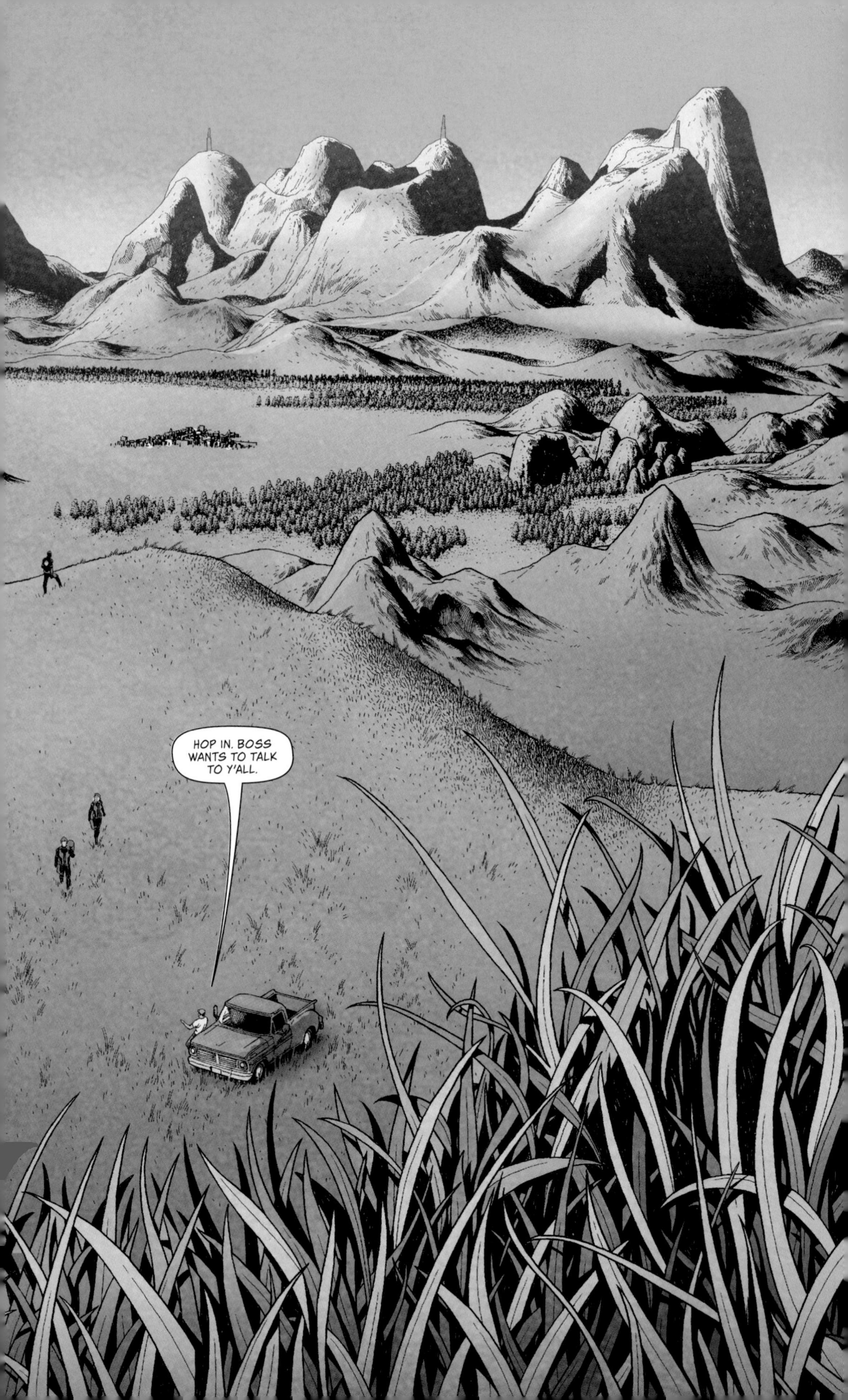
HOP IN. BOSS WANTS TO TALK TO Y'ALL.

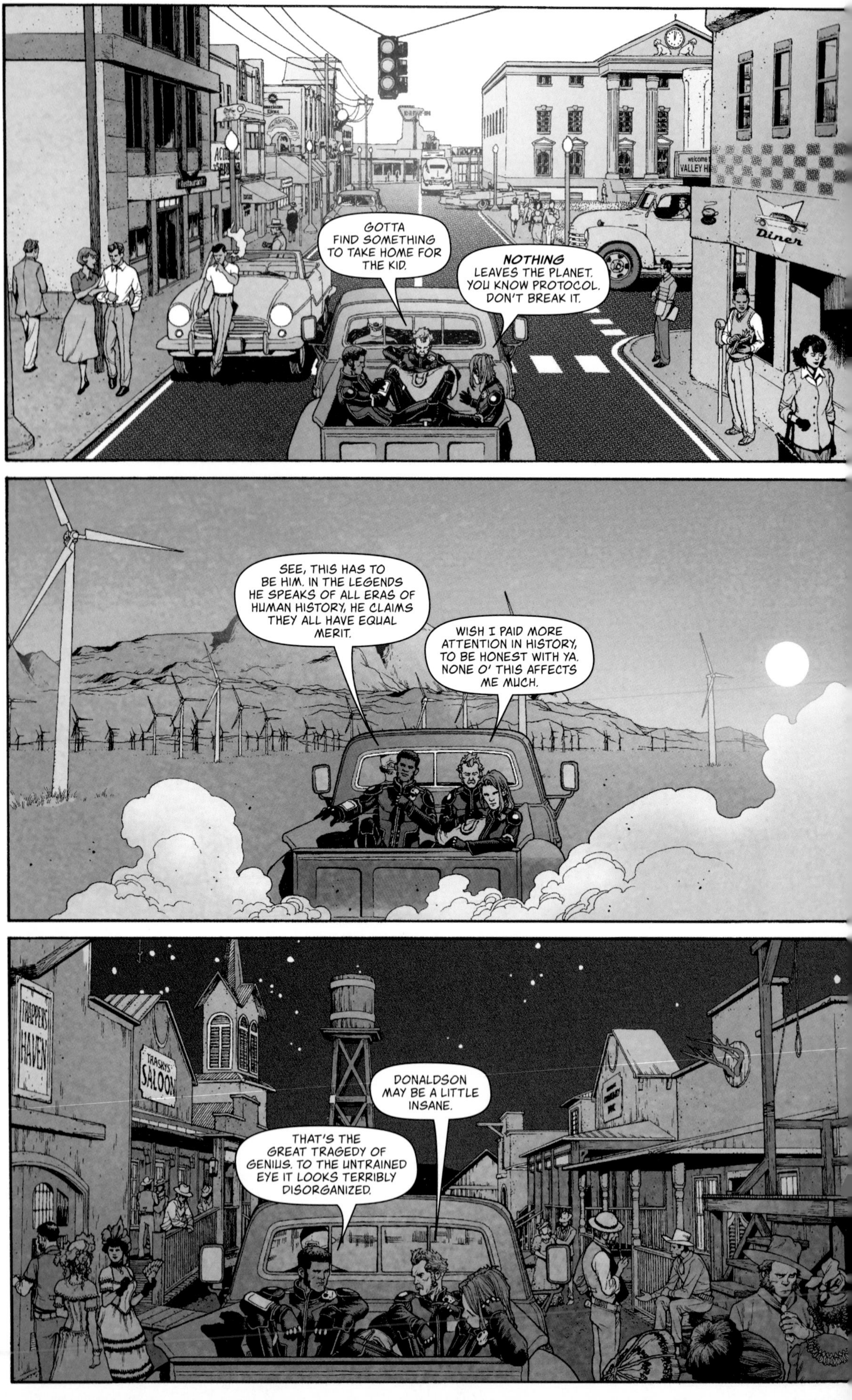
GOTTA FIND SOMETHING TO TAKE HOME FOR THE KID.
NOTHING LEAVES THE PLANET. YOU KNOW PROTOCOL. DON'T BREAK IT.
Diner
SEE, THIS HAS TO BE HIM. IN THE LEGENDS HE SPEAKS OF ALL ERAS OF HUMAN HISTORY, HE CLAIMS THEY ALL HAVE EQUAL MERIT.
WISH I PAID MORE ATTENTION IN HISTORY, TO BE HONEST WITH YA. NONE O' THIS AFFECTS ME MUCH.
TRAPPERS HAVEN
TRASKY'S SALOON
DONALDSON MAY BE A LITTLE INSANE.
THAT'S THE GREAT TRAGEDY OF GENIUS. TO THE UNTRAINED EYE IT LOOKS TERRIBLY DISORGANIZED.

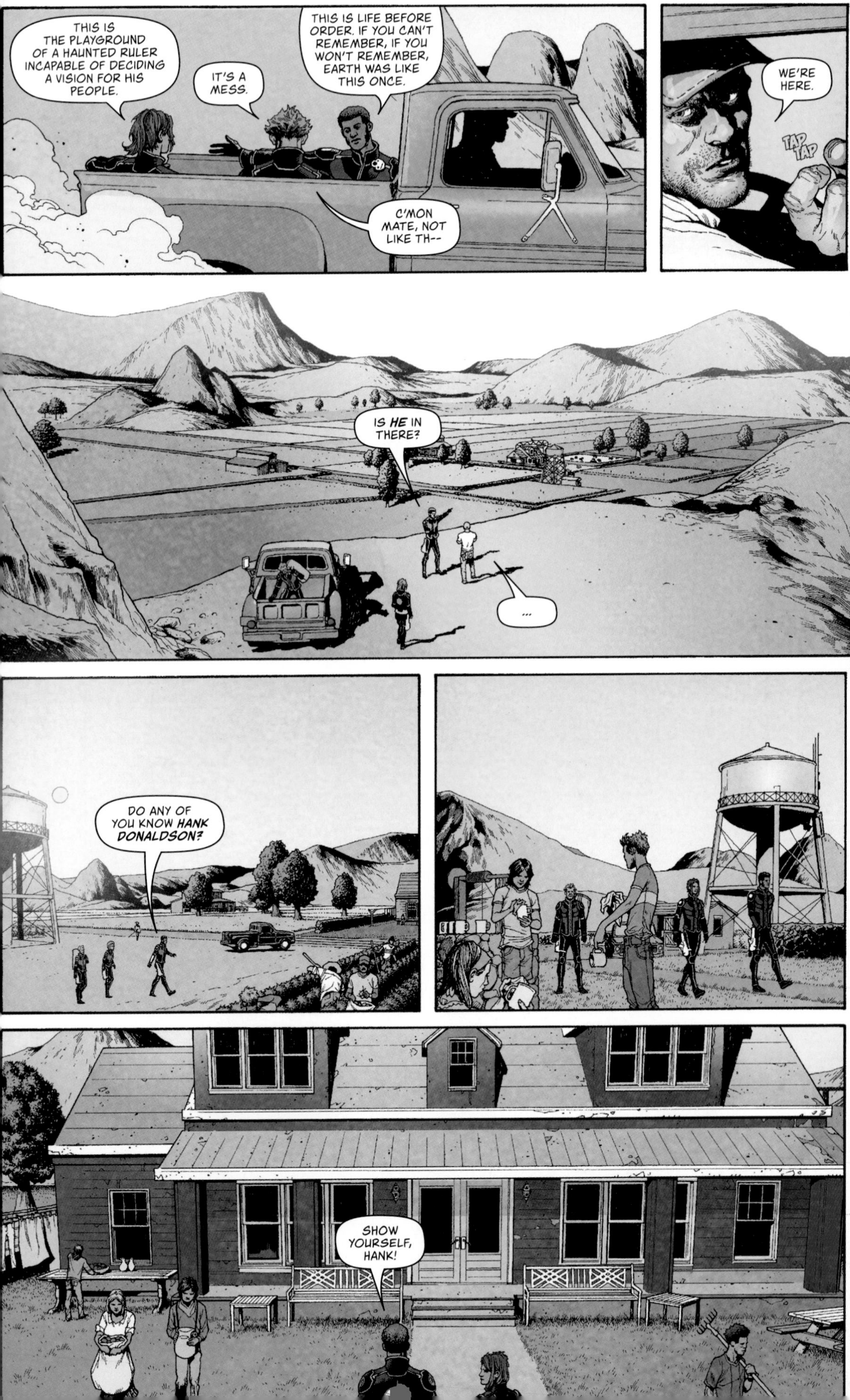
THIS IS THE PLAYGROUND OF A HAUNTED RULER INCAPABLE OF DECIDING A VISION FOR HIS PEOPLE.
IT'S A MESS.
THIS IS LIFE BEFORE ORDER. IF YOU CAN'T REMEMBER, IF YOU WON'T REMEMBER, EARTH WAS LIKE THIS ONCE.
C'MON MATE, NOT LIKE TH--
WE'RE HERE.
TAP TAP
IS HE IN THERE?
...
DO ANY OF YOU KNOW HANK DONALDSON?
SHOW YOURSELF, HANK!

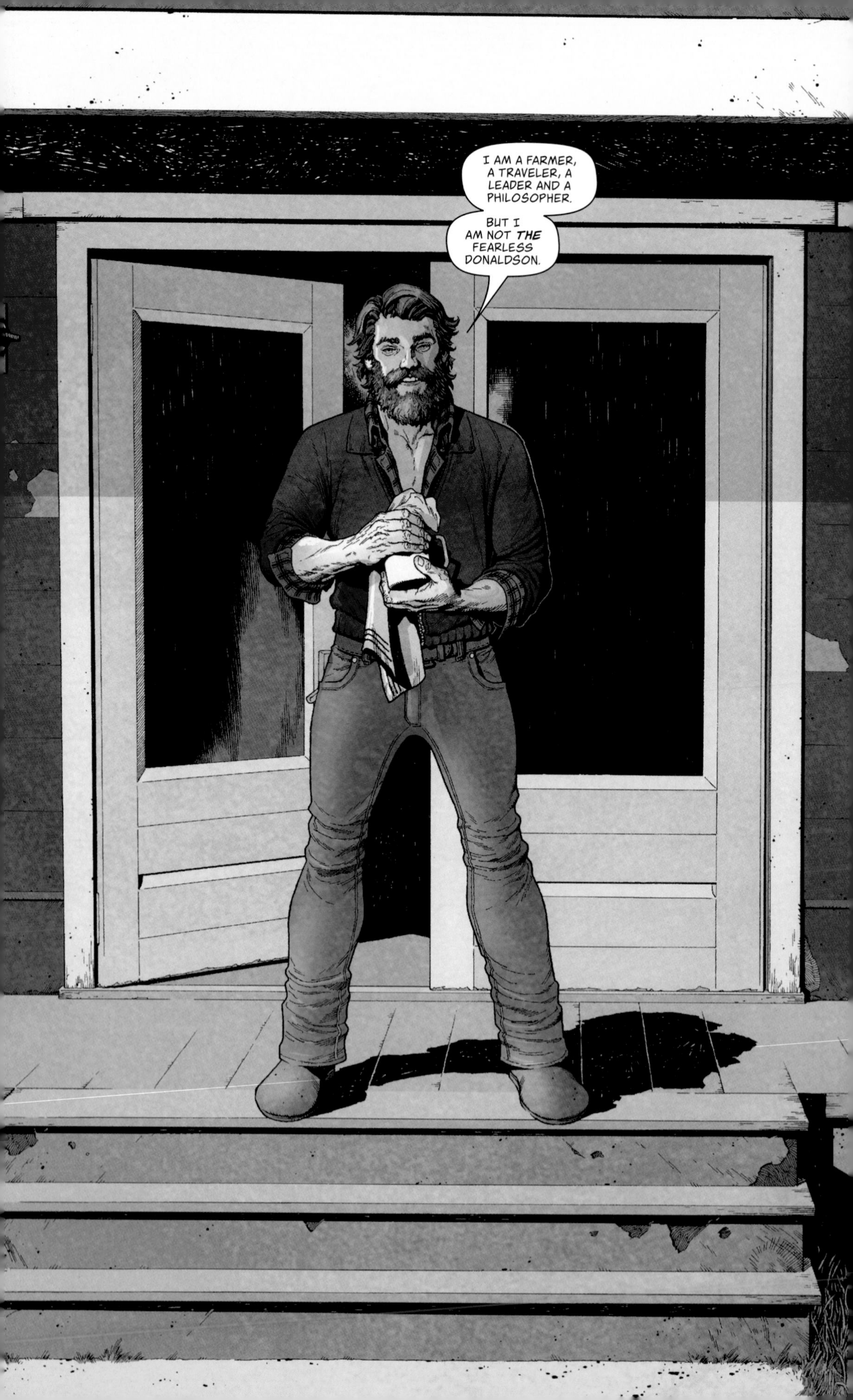
I AM A FARMER, A TRAVELER, A LEADER AND A PHILOSOPHER.
BUT I AM NOT *THE* FEARLESS DONALDSON.

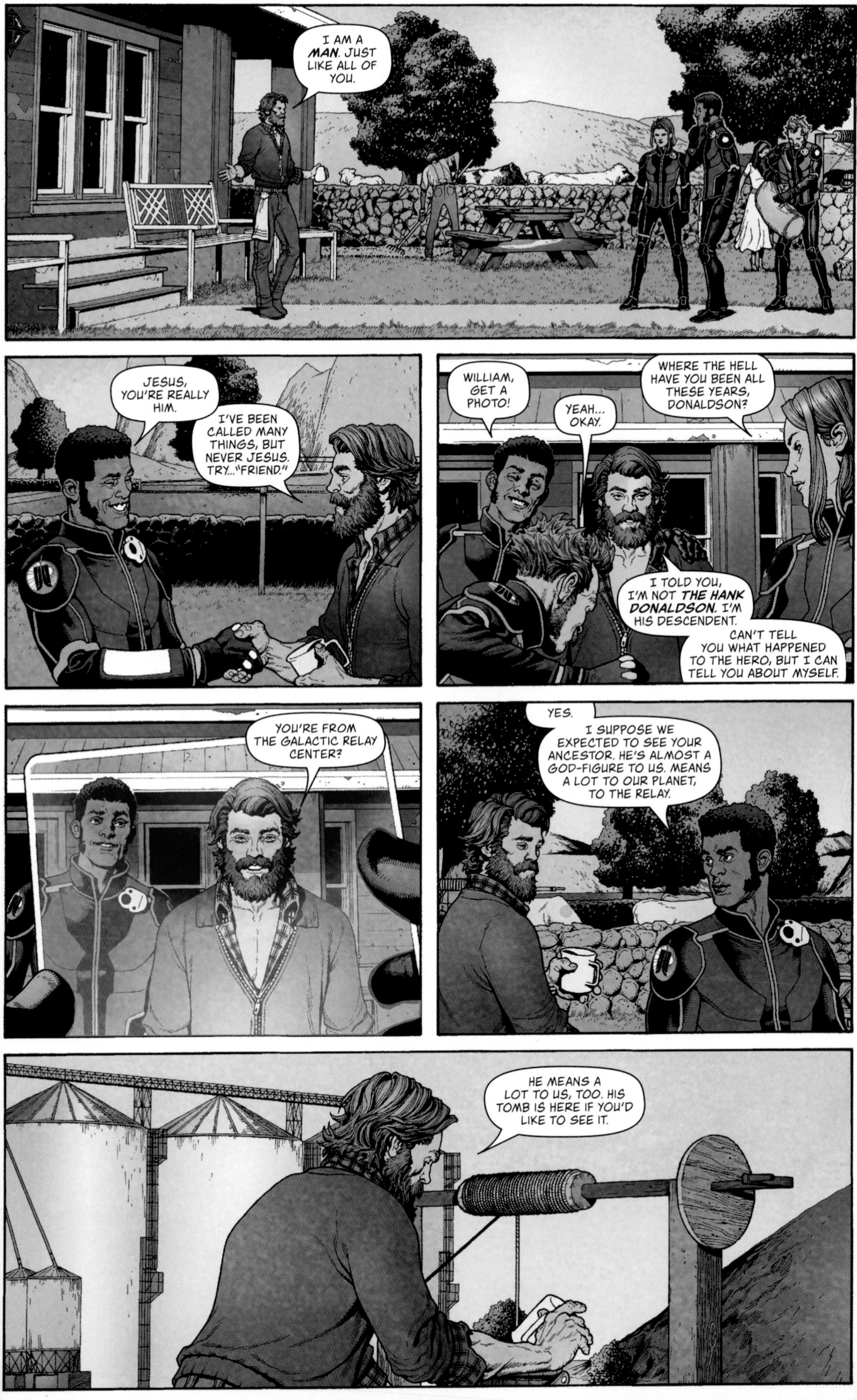
I AM A MAN. JUST LIKE ALL OF YOU.
JESUS, YOU'RE REALLY HIM.
I'VE BEEN CALLED MANY THINGS, BUT NEVER JESUS. TRY..."FRIEND."
WILLIAM, GET A PHOTO!
YEAH... OKAY.
WHERE THE HELL HAVE YOU BEEN ALL THESE YEARS, DONALDSON?
I TOLD YOU, I'M NOT THE HANK DONALDSON. I'M HIS DESCENDENT.
CAN'T TELL YOU WHAT HAPPENED TO THE HERO, BUT I CAN TELL YOU ABOUT MYSELF.
YOU'RE FROM THE GALACTIC RELAY CENTER?
YES.
I SUPPOSE WE EXPECTED TO SEE YOUR ANCESTOR. HE'S ALMOST A GOD-FIGURE TO US. MEANS A LOT TO OUR PLANET, TO THE RELAY.
HE MEANS A LOT TO US, TOO. HIS TOMB IS HERE IF YOU'D LIKE TO SEE IT.

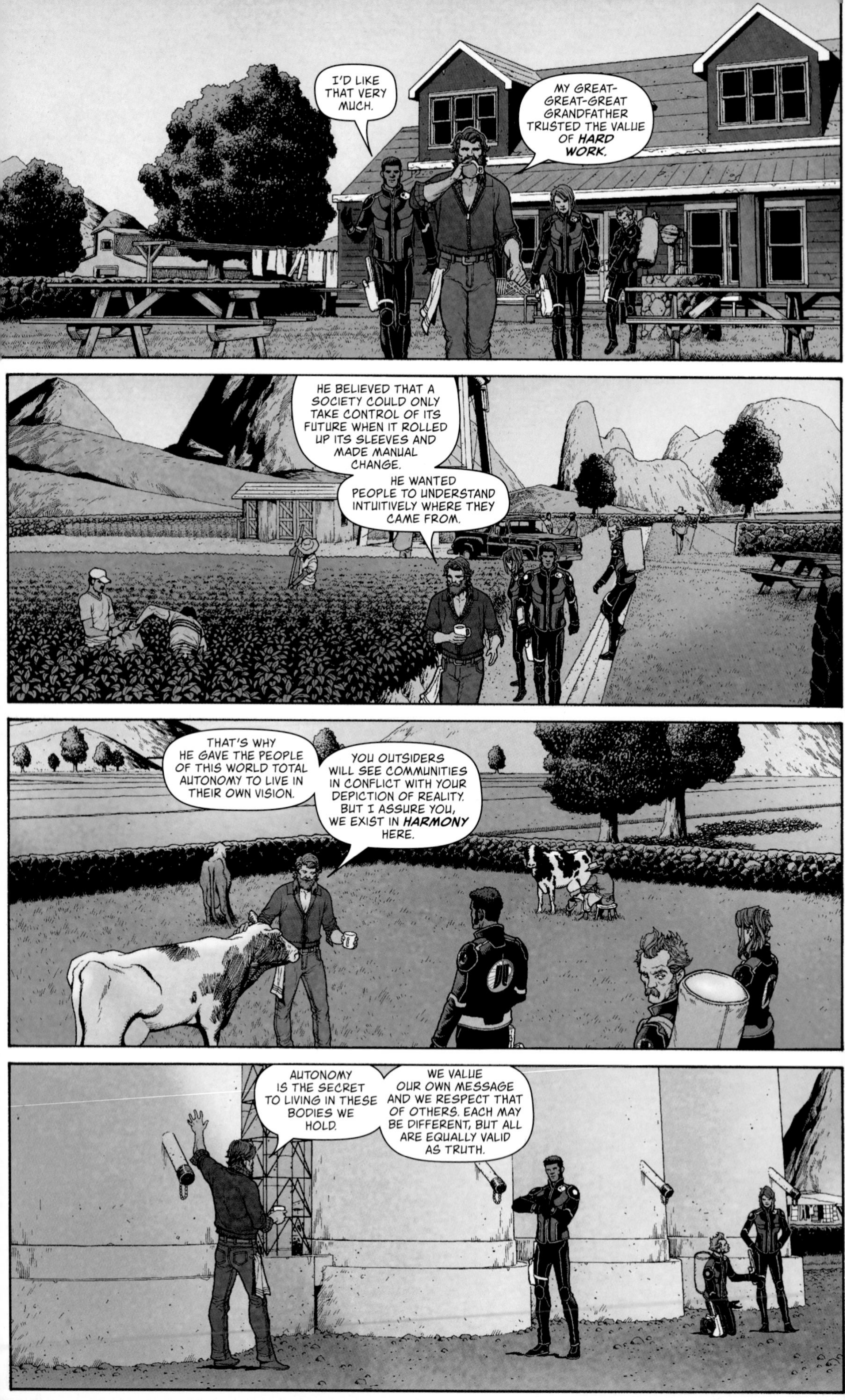
I'D LIKE THAT VERY MUCH.
MY GREAT-GREAT-GREAT GRANDFATHER TRUSTED THE VALUE OF **HARD WORK.**
HE BELIEVED THAT A SOCIETY COULD ONLY TAKE CONTROL OF ITS FUTURE WHEN IT ROLLED UP ITS SLEEVES AND MADE MANUAL CHANGE.
HE WANTED PEOPLE TO UNDERSTAND INTUITIVELY WHERE THEY CAME FROM.
THAT'S WHY HE GAVE THE PEOPLE OF THIS WORLD TOTAL AUTONOMY TO LIVE IN THEIR OWN VISION.
YOU OUTSIDERS WILL SEE COMMUNITIES IN CONFLICT WITH YOUR DEPICTION OF REALITY. BUT I ASSURE YOU, WE EXIST IN **HARMONY** HERE.
AUTONOMY IS THE SECRET TO LIVING IN THESE BODIES WE HOLD.
WE VALUE OUR OWN MESSAGE AND WE RESPECT THAT OF OTHERS. EACH MAY BE DIFFERENT, BUT ALL ARE EQUALLY VALID AS TRUTH.

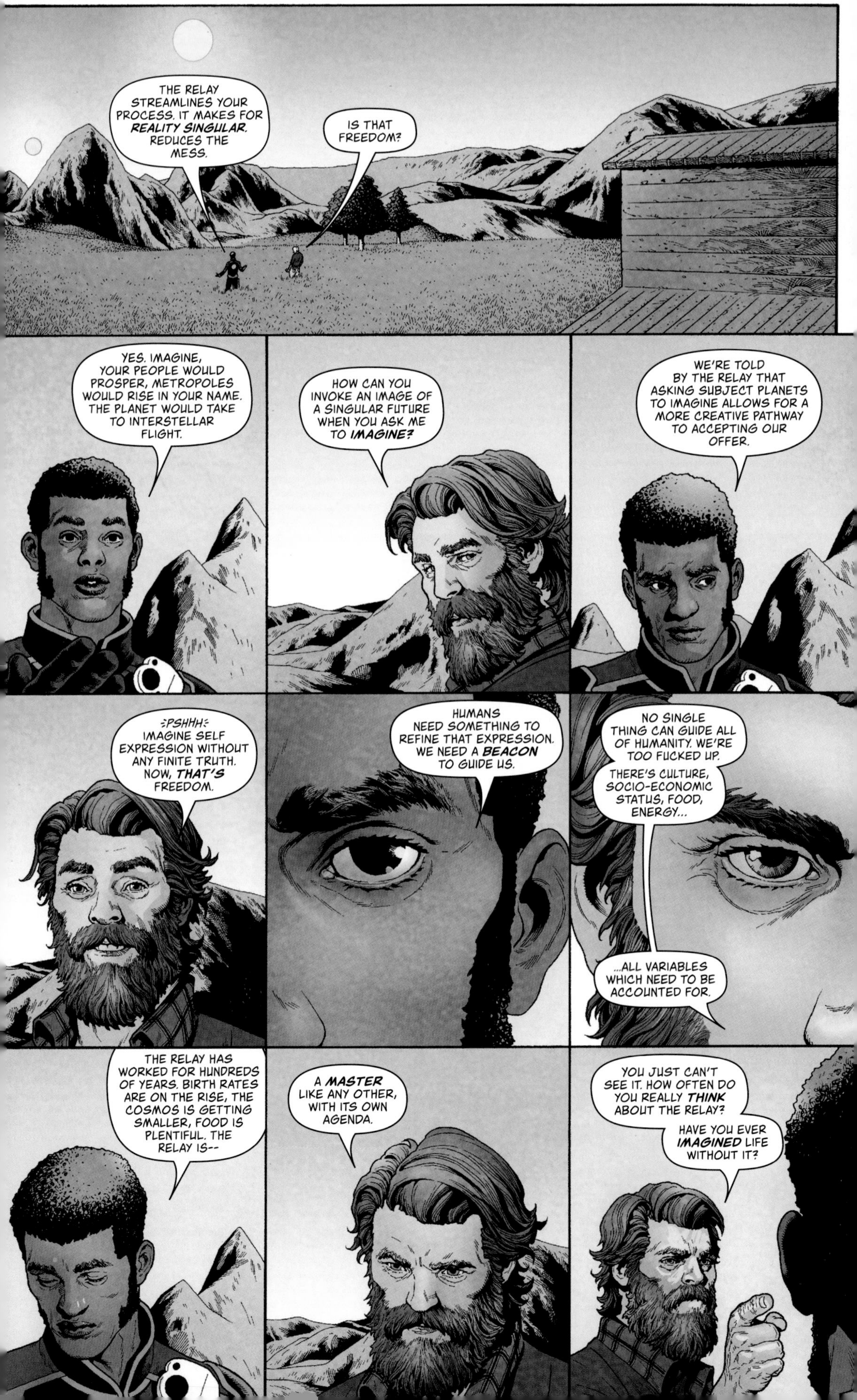
THE RELAY STREAMLINES YOUR PROCESS. IT MAKES FOR REALITY SINGULAR. REDUCES THE MESS.
IS THAT FREEDOM?
YES. IMAGINE, YOUR PEOPLE WOULD PROSPER, METROPOLES WOULD RISE IN YOUR NAME. THE PLANET WOULD TAKE TO INTERSTELLAR FLIGHT.
HOW CAN YOU INVOKE AN IMAGE OF A SINGULAR FUTURE WHEN YOU ASK ME TO IMAGINE?
WE'RE TOLD BY THE RELAY THAT ASKING SUBJECT PLANETS TO IMAGINE ALLOWS FOR A MORE CREATIVE PATHWAY TO ACCEPTING OUR OFFER.
=PSHHH= IMAGINE SELF EXPRESSION WITHOUT ANY FINITE TRUTH. NOW, THAT'S FREEDOM.
HUMANS NEED SOMETHING TO REFINE THAT EXPRESSION. WE NEED A BEACON TO GUIDE US.
NO SINGLE THING CAN GUIDE ALL OF HUMANITY. WE'RE TOO FUCKED UP.
THERE'S CULTURE, SOCIO-ECONOMIC STATUS, FOOD, ENERGY...
...ALL VARIABLES WHICH NEED TO BE ACCOUNTED FOR.
THE RELAY HAS WORKED FOR HUNDREDS OF YEARS. BIRTH RATES ARE ON THE RISE, THE COSMOS IS GETTING SMALLER, FOOD IS PLENTIFUL. THE RELAY IS--
A MASTER LIKE ANY OTHER, WITH ITS OWN AGENDA.
YOU JUST CAN'T SEE IT. HOW OFTEN DO YOU REALLY THINK ABOUT THE RELAY?
HAVE YOU EVER IMAGINED LIFE WITHOUT IT?

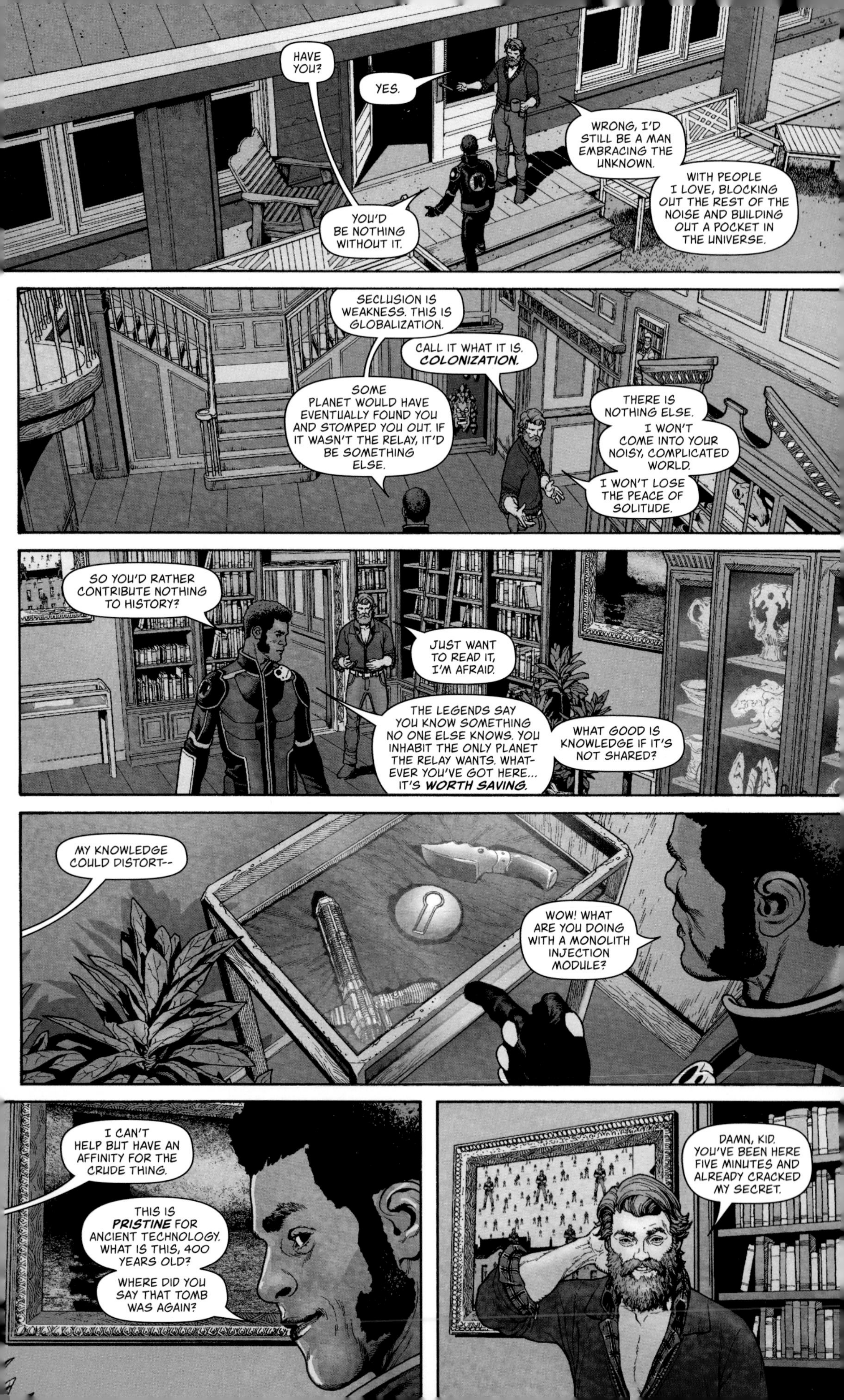
HAVE YOU?
YES.
YOU'D BE NOTHING WITHOUT IT.
WRONG, I'D STILL BE A MAN EMBRACING THE UNKNOWN.
WITH PEOPLE I LOVE, BLOCKING OUT THE REST OF THE NOISE AND BUILDING OUT A POCKET IN THE UNIVERSE.
SECLUSION IS WEAKNESS. THIS IS GLOBALIZATION.
CALL IT WHAT IT IS. COLONIZATION.
SOME PLANET WOULD HAVE EVENTUALLY FOUND YOU AND STOMPED YOU OUT. IF IT WASN'T THE RELAY, IT'D BE SOMETHING ELSE.
THERE IS NOTHING ELSE.
I WON'T COME INTO YOUR NOISY, COMPLICATED WORLD.
I WON'T LOSE THE PEACE OF SOLITUDE.
SO YOU'D RATHER CONTRIBUTE NOTHING TO HISTORY?
JUST WANT TO READ IT, I'M AFRAID.
THE LEGENDS SAY YOU KNOW SOMETHING NO ONE ELSE KNOWS. YOU INHABIT THE ONLY PLANET THE RELAY WANTS. WHAT-EVER YOU'VE GOT HERE... IT'S WORTH SAVING.
WHAT GOOD IS KNOWLEDGE IF IT'S NOT SHARED?
MY KNOWLEDGE COULD DISTORT--
WOW! WHAT ARE YOU DOING WITH A MONOLITH INJECTION MODULE?
I CAN'T HELP BUT HAVE AN AFFINITY FOR THE CRUDE THING.
THIS IS PRISTINE FOR ANCIENT TECHNOLOGY. WHAT IS THIS, 400 YEARS OLD?
WHERE DID YOU SAY THAT TOMB WAS AGAIN?
DAMN, KID. YOU'VE BEEN HERE FIVE MINUTES AND ALREADY CRACKED MY SECRET.

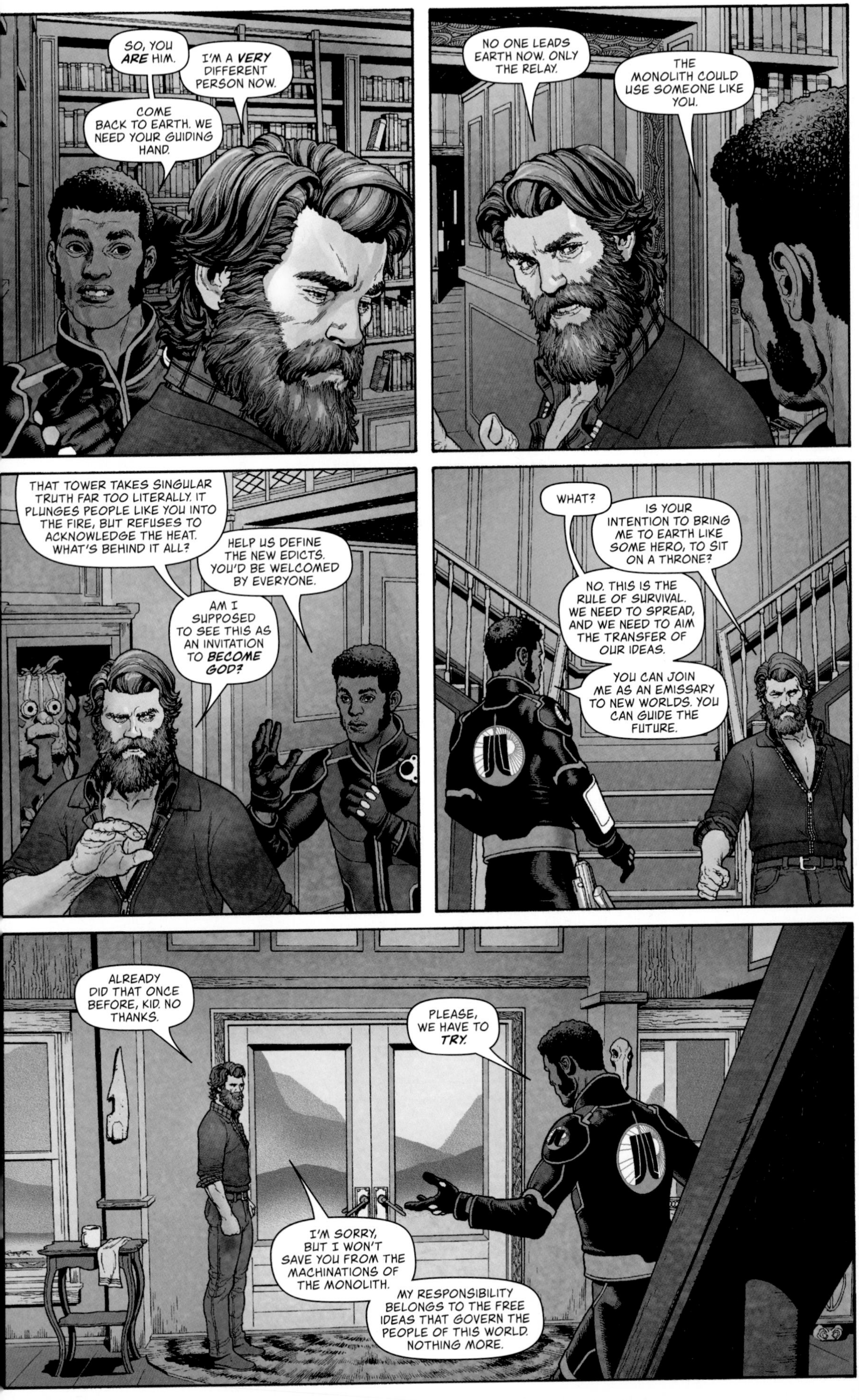

SO, YOU ARE HIM.
COME BACK TO EARTH. WE NEED YOUR GUIDING HAND.
I'M A VERY DIFFERENT PERSON NOW.
NO ONE LEADS EARTH NOW. ONLY THE RELAY.
THE MONOLITH COULD USE SOMEONE LIKE YOU.
THAT TOWER TAKES SINGULAR TRUTH FAR TOO LITERALLY. IT PLUNGES PEOPLE LIKE YOU INTO THE FIRE, BUT REFUSES TO ACKNOWLEDGE THE HEAT. WHAT'S BEHIND IT ALL?
HELP US DEFINE THE NEW EDICTS. YOU'D BE WELCOMED BY EVERYONE.
AM I SUPPOSED TO SEE THIS AS AN INVITATION TO BECOME GOD?
WHAT?
IS YOUR INTENTION TO BRING ME TO EARTH LIKE SOME HERO, TO SIT ON A THRONE?
NO. THIS IS THE RULE OF SURVIVAL. WE NEED TO SPREAD, AND WE NEED TO AIM THE TRANSFER OF OUR IDEAS.
YOU CAN JOIN ME AS AN EMISSARY TO NEW WORLDS. YOU CAN GUIDE THE FUTURE.
ALREADY DID THAT ONCE BEFORE, KID. NO THANKS.
PLEASE, WE HAVE TO TRY.
I'M SORRY, BUT I WON'T SAVE YOU FROM THE MACHINATIONS OF THE MONOLITH.
MY RESPONSIBILITY BELONGS TO THE FREE IDEAS THAT GOVERN THE PEOPLE OF THIS WORLD. NOTHING MORE.

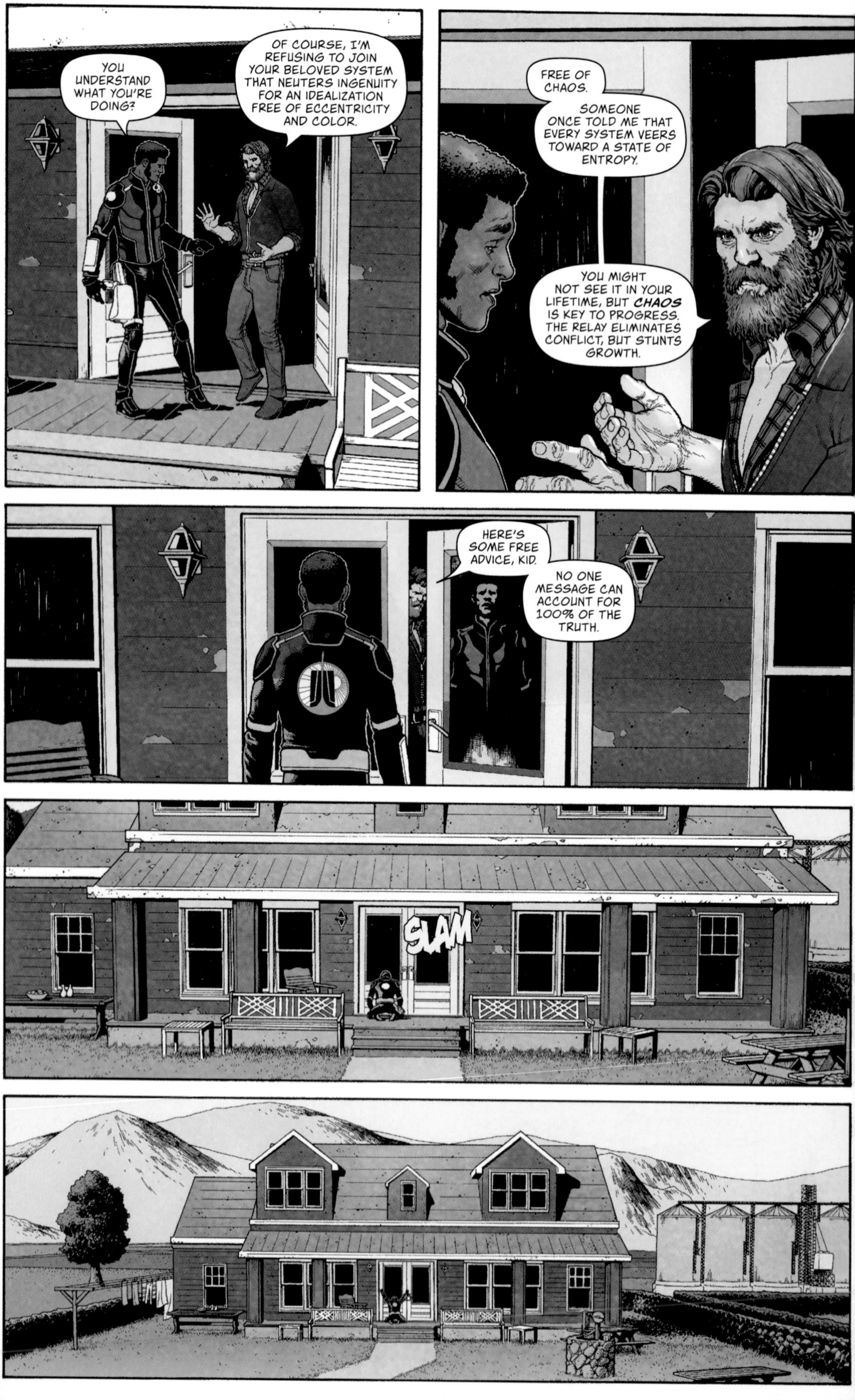
YOU UNDERSTAND WHAT YOU'RE DOING?
OF COURSE, I'M REFUSING TO JOIN YOUR BELOVED SYSTEM THAT NEUTERS INGENUITY FOR AN IDEALIZATION FREE OF ECCENTRICITY AND COLOR.
FREE OF CHAOS.
SOMEONE ONCE TOLD ME THAT EVERY SYSTEM VEERS TOWARD A STATE OF ENTROPY.
YOU MIGHT NOT SEE IT IN YOUR LIFETIME, BUT CHAOS IS KEY TO PROGRESS. THE RELAY ELIMINATES CONFLICT, BUT STUNTS GROWTH.
HERE'S SOME FREE ADVICE, KID.
NO ONE MESSAGE CAN ACCOUNT FOR 100% OF THE TRUTH.
SLAM

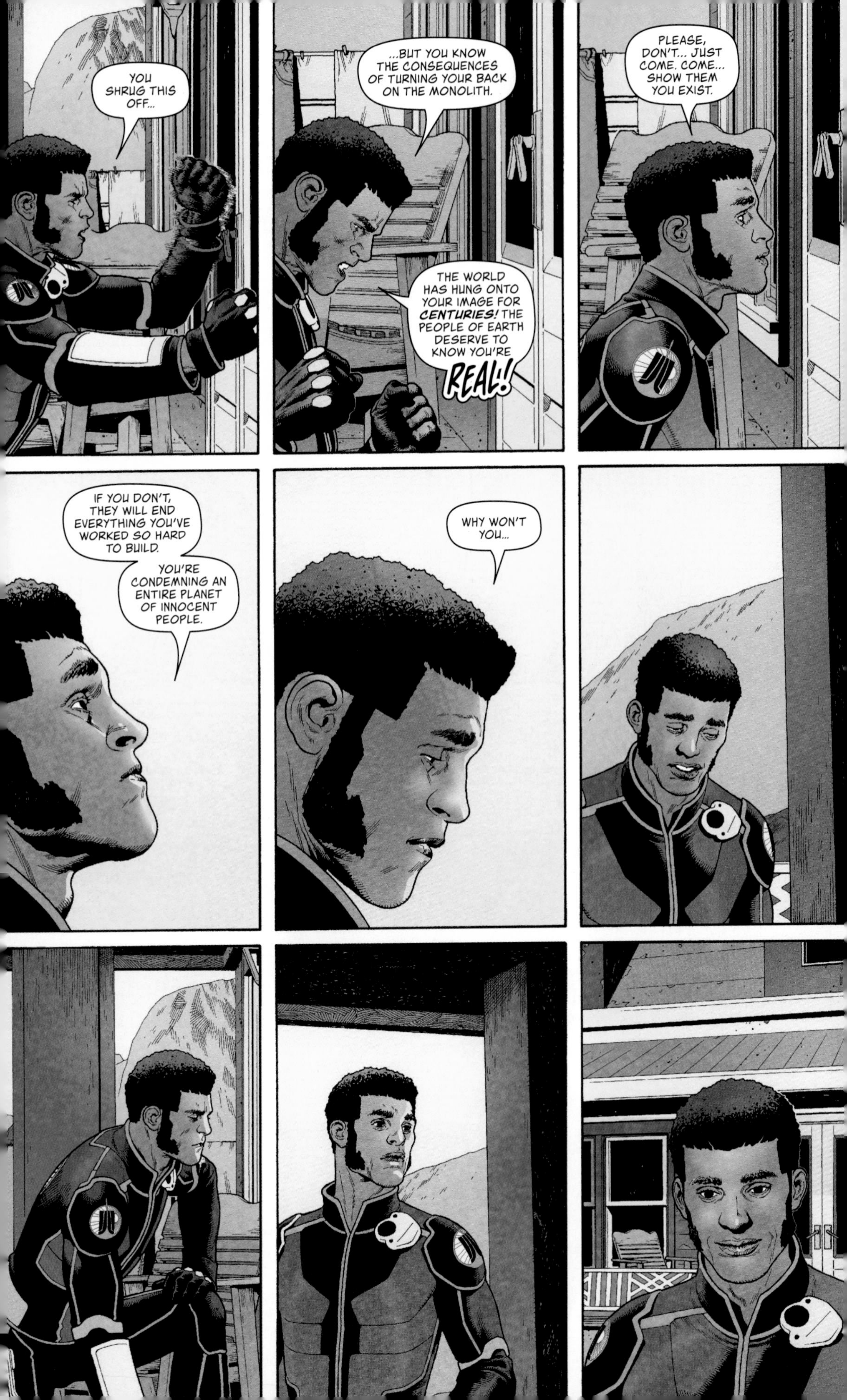
YOU SHRUG THIS OFF...
...BUT YOU KNOW THE CONSEQUENCES OF TURNING YOUR BACK ON THE MONOLITH.
THE WORLD HAS HUNG ONTO YOUR IMAGE FOR CENTURIES! THE PEOPLE OF EARTH DESERVE TO KNOW YOU'RE REAL!!
PLEASE, DON'T... JUST COME. COME... SHOW THEM YOU EXIST.
IF YOU DON'T, THEY WILL END EVERYTHING YOU'VE WORKED SO HARD TO BUILD.
YOU'RE CONDEMNING AN ENTIRE PLANET OF INNOCENT PEOPLE.
WHY WON'T YOU...

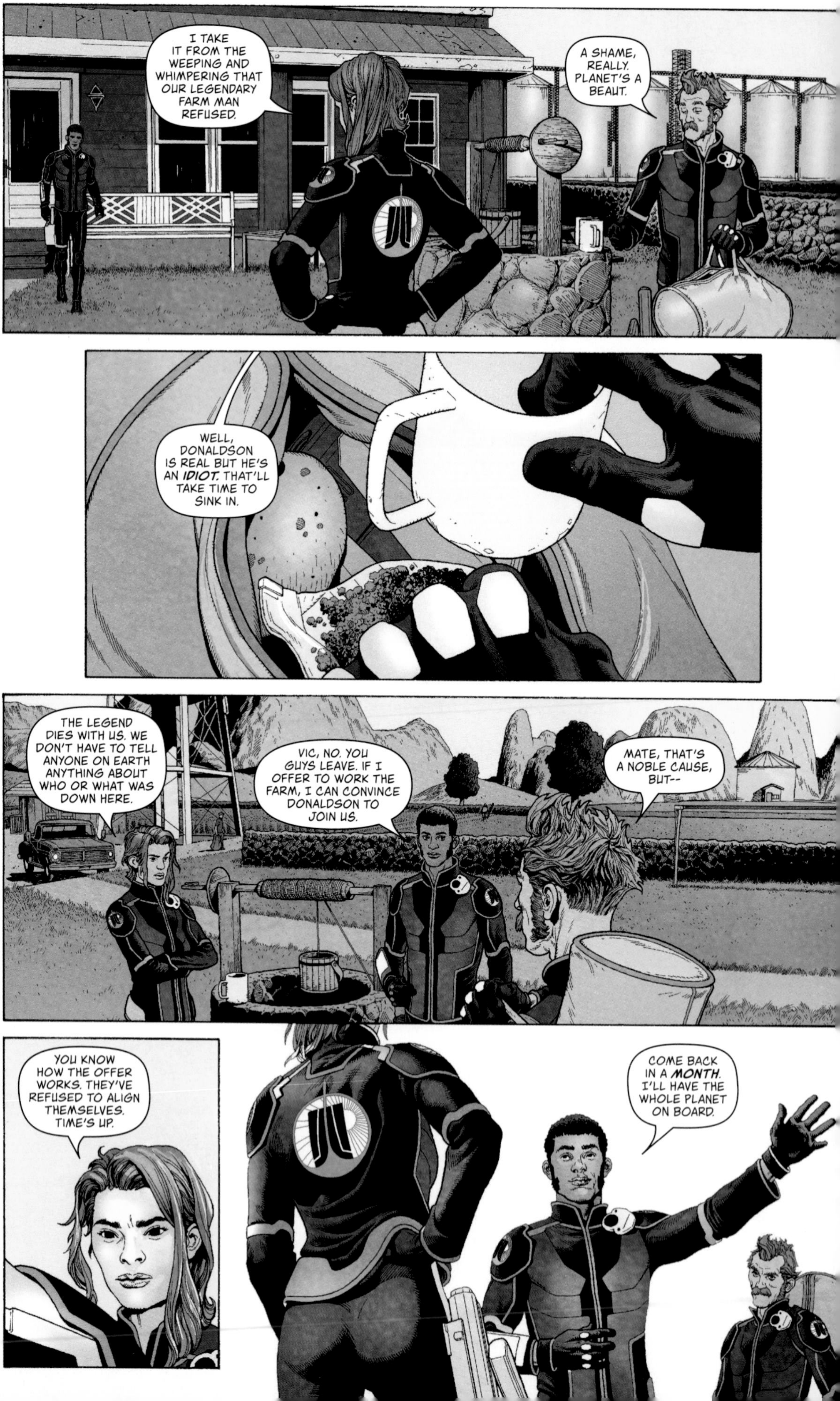
I TAKE IT FROM THE WEEPING AND WHIMPERING THAT OUR LEGENDARY FARM MAN REFUSED.
A SHAME, REALLY. PLANET'S A BEAUT.
WELL, DONALDSON IS REAL BUT HE'S AN *IDIOT.* THAT'LL TAKE TIME TO SINK IN.
THE LEGEND DIES WITH US. WE DON'T HAVE TO TELL ANYONE ON EARTH ANYTHING ABOUT WHO OR WHAT WAS DOWN HERE.
VIC, NO. YOU GUYS LEAVE. IF I OFFER TO WORK THE FARM, I CAN CONVINCE DONALDSON TO JOIN US.
MATE, THAT'S A NOBLE CAUSE, BUT--
YOU KNOW HOW THE OFFER WORKS. THEY'VE REFUSED TO ALIGN THEMSELVES. TIME'S UP.
COME BACK IN A ***MONTH***. I'LL HAVE THE WHOLE PLANET ON BOARD.

ARE YOU INSANE?

PLEASE. HE'S THE *ORIGINAL* DONALDSON. WE CAN'T DO THIS.

"YOU'RE DELUSIONAL. WE CAN'T HAVE A VARIABLE PLANET THIS CLOSE TO TWO OTHER RELAY PLANETS. HE'S NOT WORTH IT."

"WE CAN'T DENY HIS REALITY JUST BECAUSE IT'S UNCERTAIN. MAYBE HIS IDEAS COULD SPREAD."

"SHIT. WHY THE FUCK DID YOU *SAY THAT?* I'M PLACING YOU UNDER PROTECTIVE CUSTODY UNTIL WE'RE DONE HERE."

"YOU CAN'T ERASE THE ONLY THING WE WERE EVER ASKED TO FIND. I WON'T LET YOU."

"DON'T LET YOUR MORALS GET IN THE WAY OF WHAT NEEDS TO BE DONE."

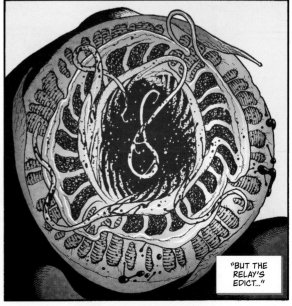

"BUT THE RELAY'S EDICT..."

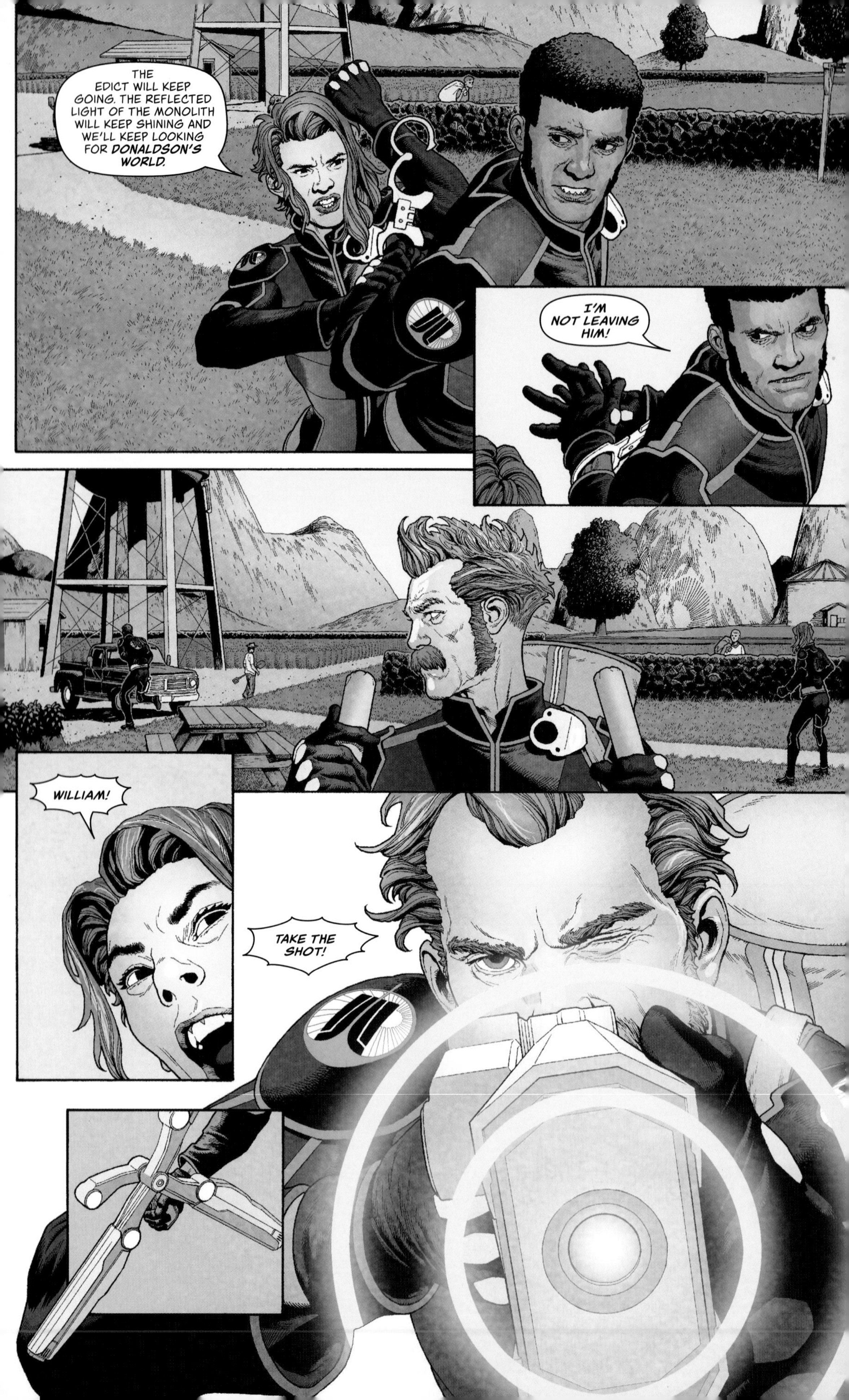
THE EDICT WILL KEEP GOING. THE REFLECTED LIGHT OF THE MONOLITH WILL KEEP SHINING AND WE'LL KEEP LOOKING FOR DONALDSON'S WORLD.
I'M NOT LEAVING HIM!
WILLIAM!
TAKE THE SHOT!

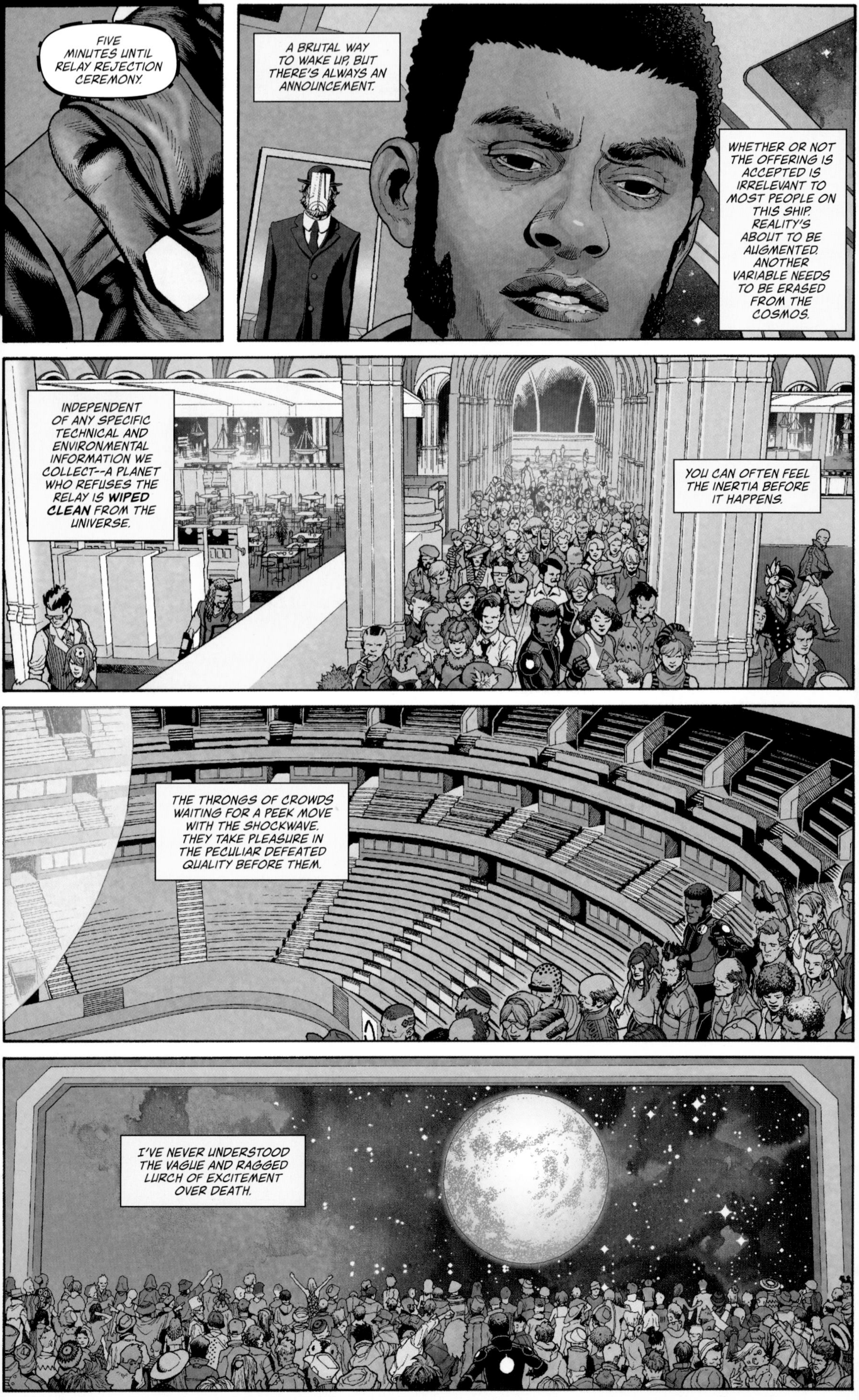
FIVE MINUTES UNTIL RELAY REJECTION CEREMONY.
A BRUTAL WAY TO WAKE UP, BUT THERE'S ALWAYS AN ANNOUNCEMENT.
WHETHER OR NOT THE OFFERING IS ACCEPTED IS IRRELEVANT TO MOST PEOPLE ON THIS SHIP. REALITY'S ABOUT TO BE AUGMENTED. ANOTHER VARIABLE NEEDS TO BE ERASED FROM THE COSMOS.
INDEPENDENT OF ANY SPECIFIC TECHNICAL AND ENVIRONMENTAL INFORMATION WE COLLECT--A PLANET WHO REFUSES THE RELAY IS WIPED CLEAN FROM THE UNIVERSE.
YOU CAN OFTEN FEEL THE INERTIA BEFORE IT HAPPENS.
THE THRONGS OF CROWDS WAITING FOR A PEEK MOVE WITH THE SHOCKWAVE. THEY TAKE PLEASURE IN THE PECULIAR DEFEATED QUALITY BEFORE THEM.
I'VE NEVER UNDERSTOOD THE VAGUE AND RAGGED LURCH OF EXCITEMENT OVER DEATH.

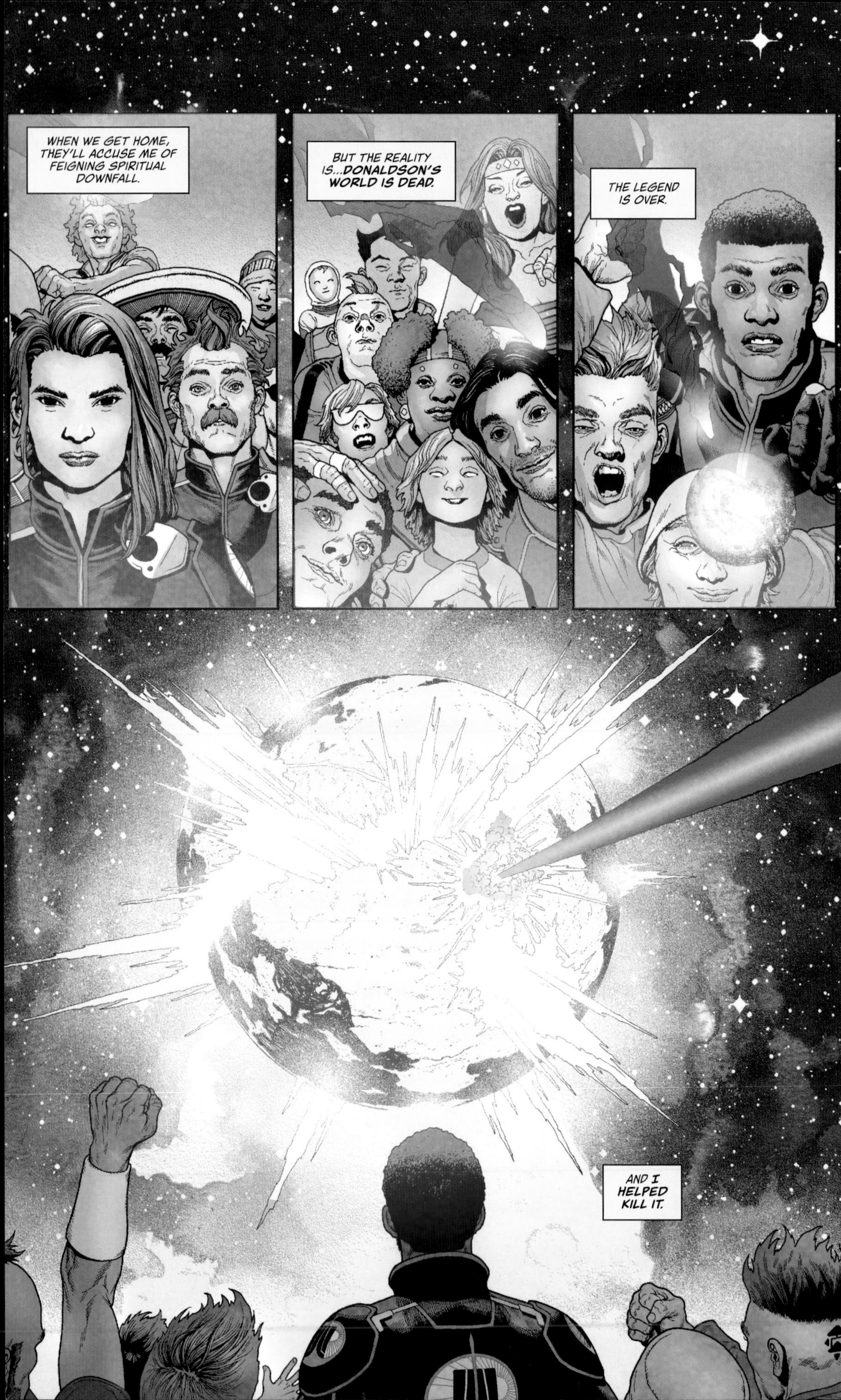

WHEN WE GET HOME, THEY'LL ACCUSE ME OF FEIGNING SPIRITUAL DOWNFALL.
BUT THE REALITY IS...DONALDSON'S WORLD IS DEAD.
THE LEGEND IS OVER.
AND I HELPED KILL IT.

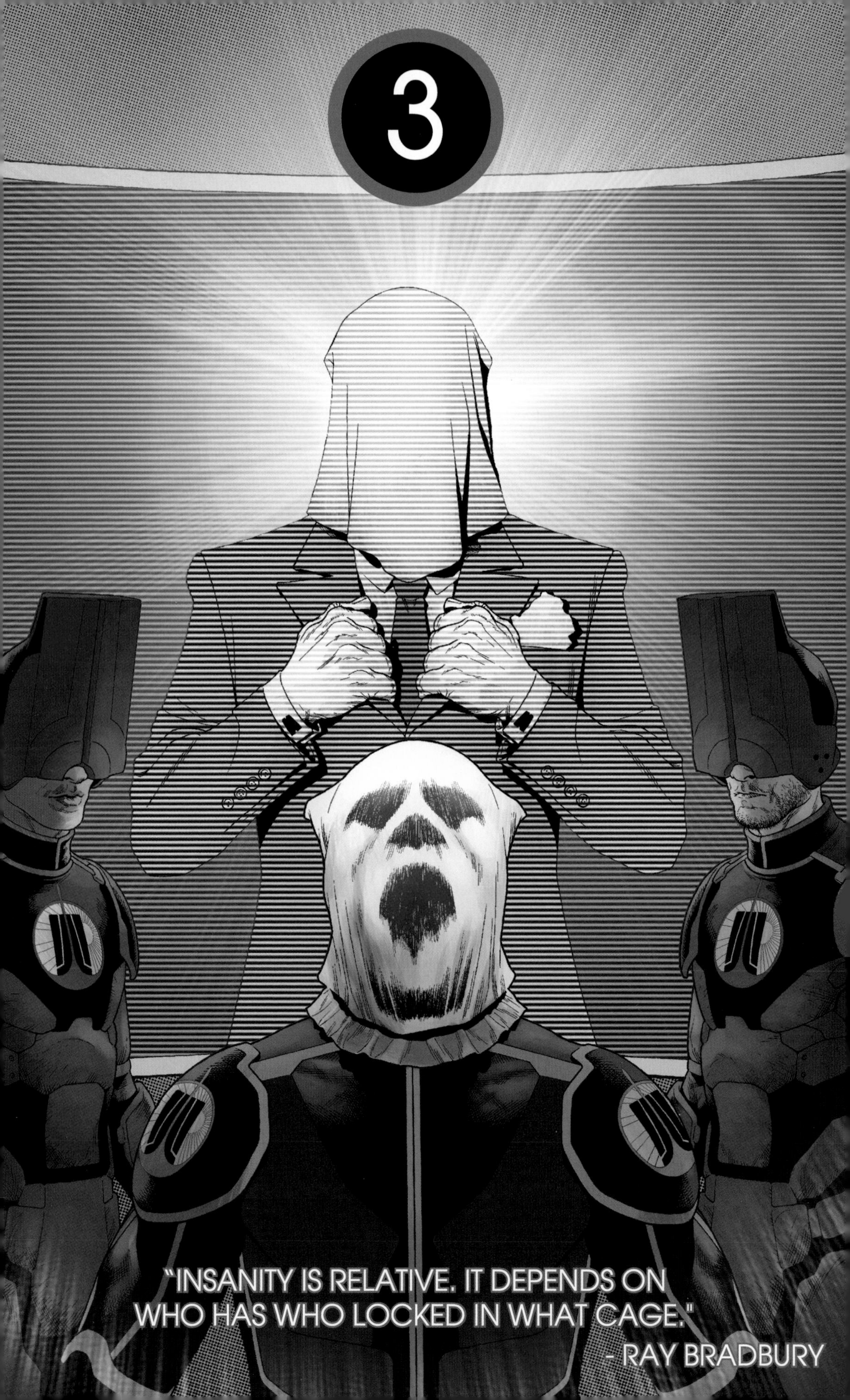
3
"INSANITY IS RELATIVE. IT DEPENDS ON
WHO HAS WHO LOCKED IN WHAT CAGE."
- RAY BRADBURY

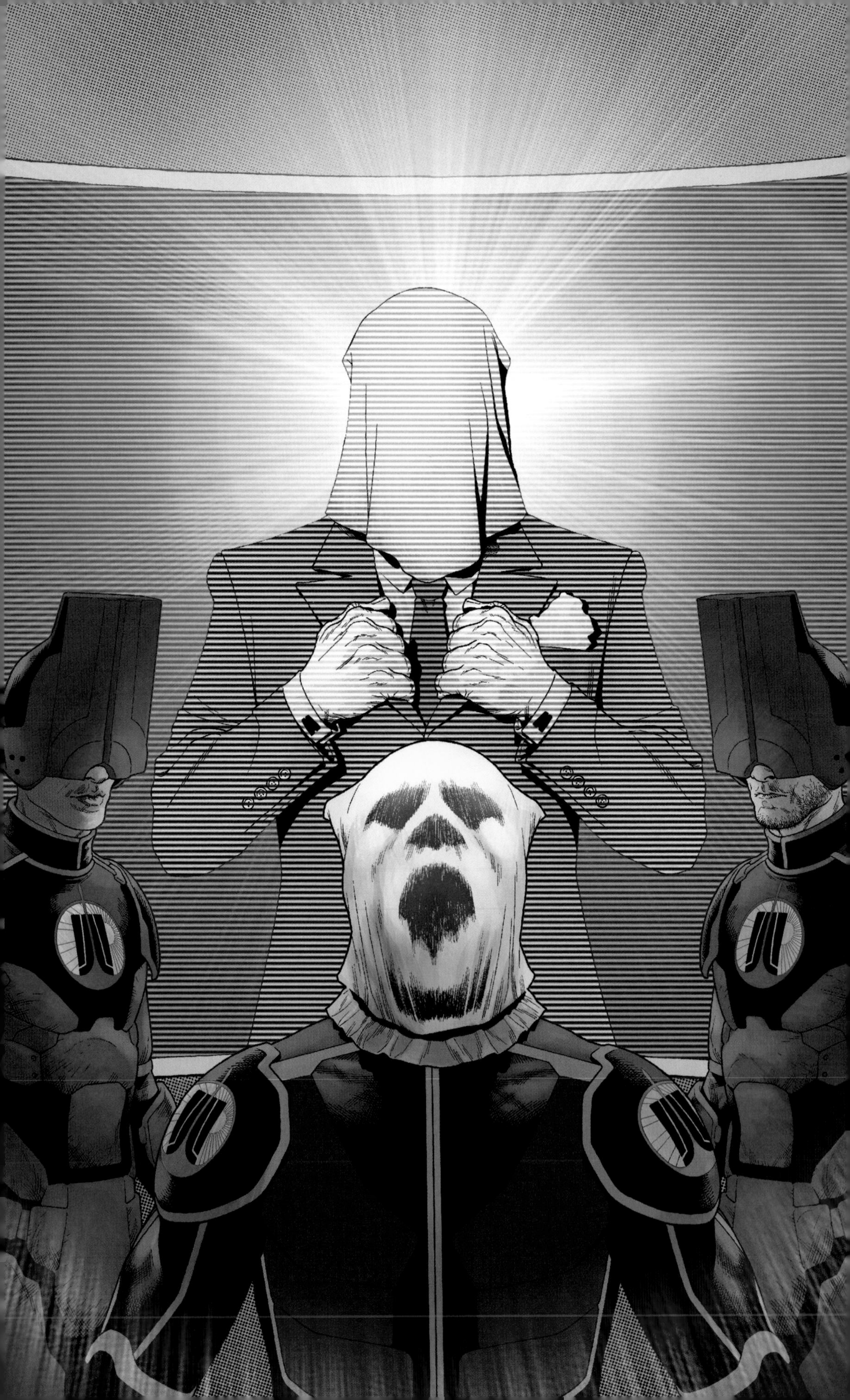

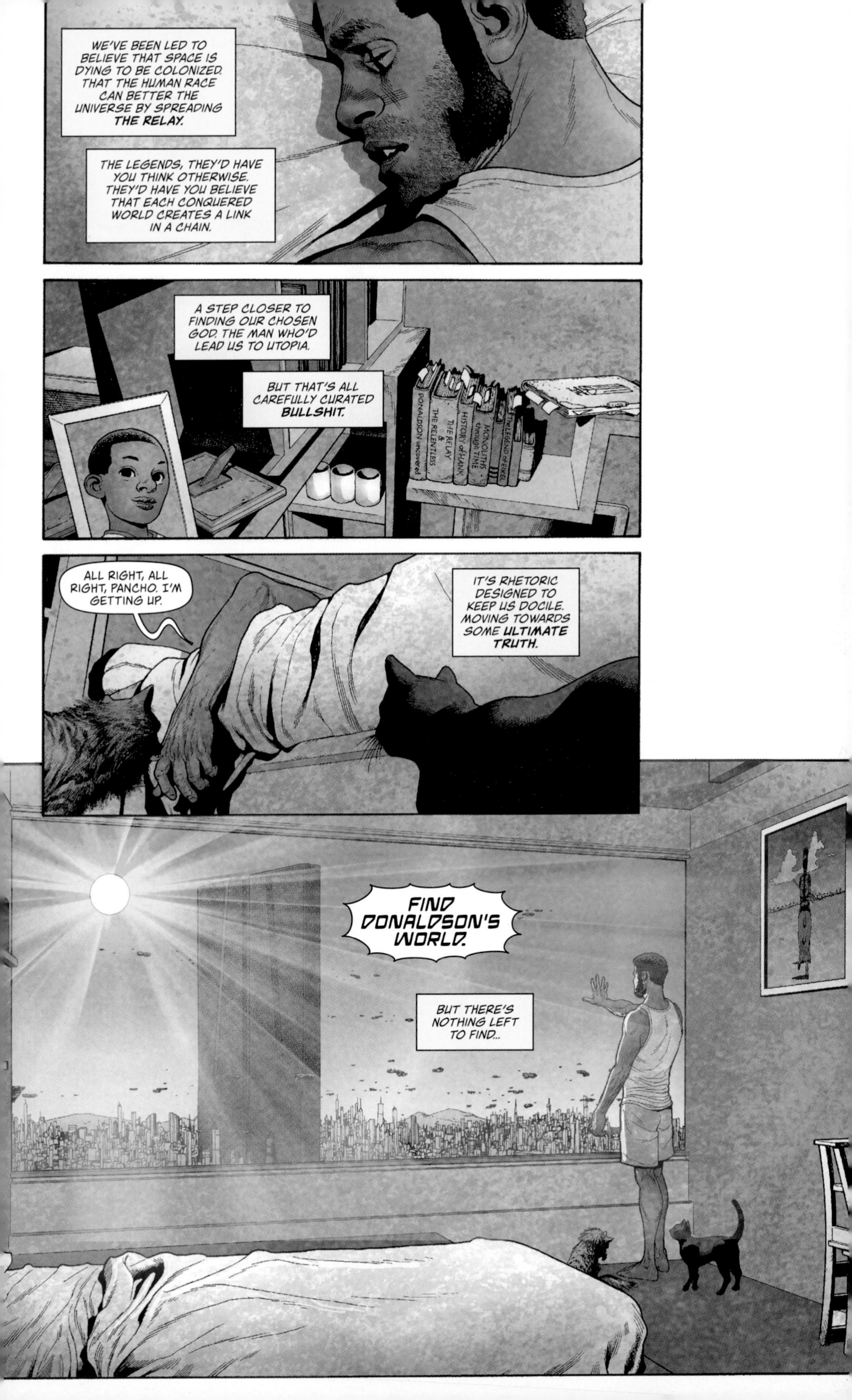
WE'VE BEEN LED TO BELIEVE THAT SPACE IS DYING TO BE COLONIZED. THAT THE HUMAN RACE CAN BETTER THE UNIVERSE BY SPREADING THE RELAY.
THE LEGENDS, THEY'D HAVE YOU THINK OTHERWISE. THEY'D HAVE YOU BELIEVE THAT EACH CONQUERED WORLD CREATES A LINK IN A CHAIN.
A STEP CLOSER TO FINDING OUR CHOSEN GOD. THE MAN WHO'D LEAD US TO UTOPIA.
BUT THAT'S ALL CAREFULLY CURATED BULLSHIT.
DONALDSON uncovered
THE RELAY & THE RELENTLESS
HISTORY of HANK
MONOLITHS through TIME
The LEGEND of EIXEL
ALL RIGHT, ALL RIGHT, PANCHO. I'M GETTING UP.
IT'S RHETORIC DESIGNED TO KEEP US DOCILE. MOVING TOWARDS SOME ULTIMATE TRUTH.
FIND DONALDSON'S WORLD.
BUT THERE'S NOTHING LEFT TO FIND...

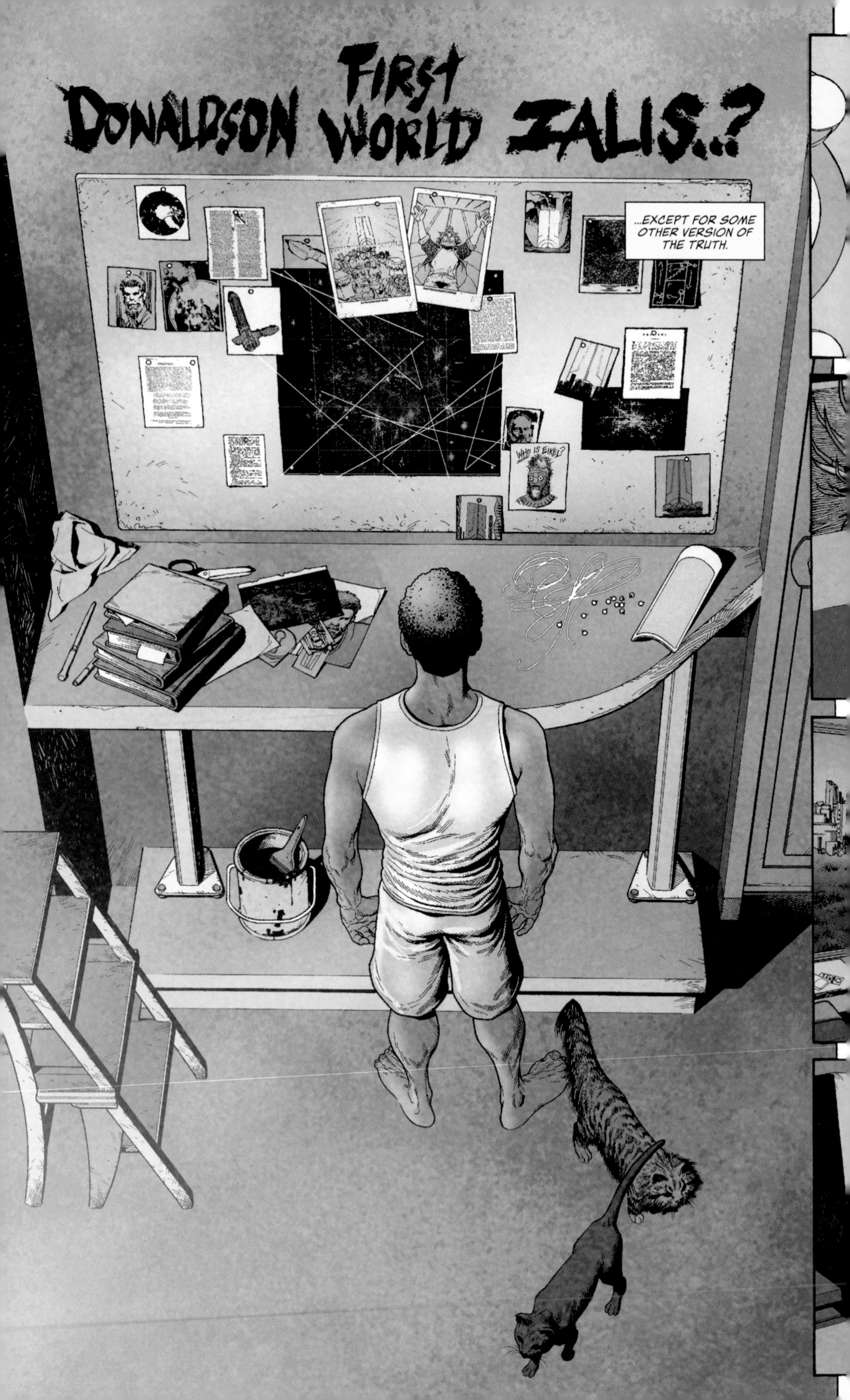
DONALDSON FIRST WORLD ZALIS..?
...EXCEPT FOR SOME OTHER VERSION OF THE TRUTH.
WHO IS EIKEL?

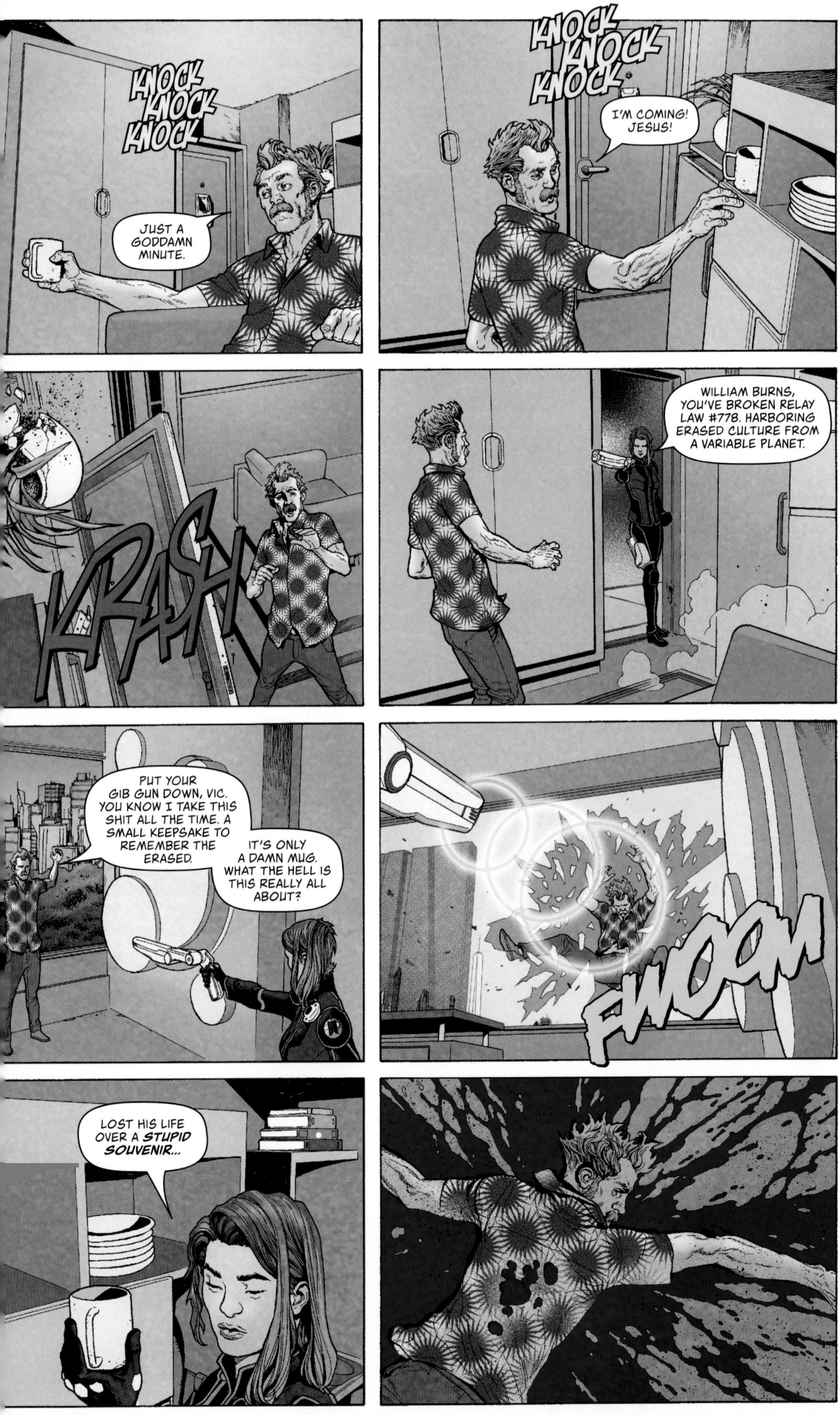
KNOCK KNOCK KNOCK
JUST A GODDAMN MINUTE.
KNOCK KNOCK KNOCK
I'M COMING! JESUS!
KRASH
WILLIAM BURNS, YOU'VE BROKEN RELAY LAW #778. HARBORING ERASED CULTURE FROM A VARIABLE PLANET.
PUT YOUR GIB GUN DOWN, VIC. YOU KNOW I TAKE THIS SHIT ALL THE TIME. A SMALL KEEPSAKE TO REMEMBER THE ERASED.
IT'S ONLY A DAMN MUG. WHAT THE HELL IS THIS REALLY ALL ABOUT?
FWOOM
LOST HIS LIFE OVER A **STUPID SOUVENIR...**

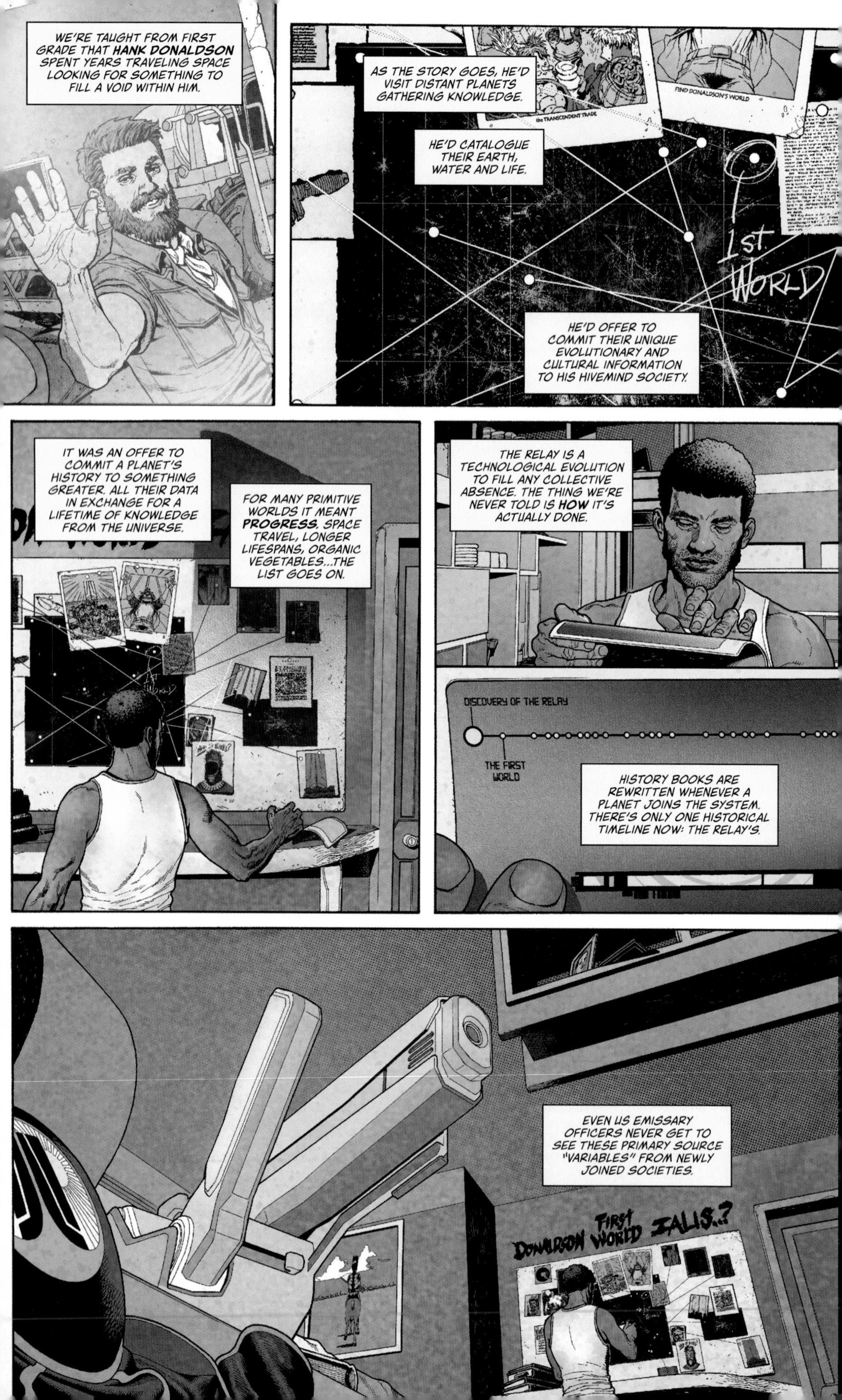

WE'RE TAUGHT FROM FIRST GRADE THAT **HANK DONALDSON** SPENT YEARS TRAVELING SPACE LOOKING FOR SOMETHING TO FILL A VOID WITHIN HIM.
AS THE STORY GOES, HE'D VISIT DISTANT PLANETS GATHERING KNOWLEDGE.
the TRANSCENDENT TRADE
FIND DONALDSON'S WORLD
HE'D CATALOGUE THEIR EARTH, WATER AND LIFE.
1st WORLD
HE'D OFFER TO COMMIT THEIR UNIQUE EVOLUTIONARY AND CULTURAL INFORMATION TO HIS HIVEMIND SOCIETY.
IT WAS AN OFFER TO COMMIT A PLANET'S HISTORY TO SOMETHING GREATER. ALL THEIR DATA IN EXCHANGE FOR A LIFETIME OF KNOWLEDGE FROM THE UNIVERSE.
FOR MANY PRIMITIVE WORLDS IT MEANT **PROGRESS.** SPACE TRAVEL, LONGER LIFESPANS, ORGANIC VEGETABLES...THE LIST GOES ON.
THE RELAY IS A TECHNOLOGICAL EVOLUTION TO FILL ANY COLLECTIVE ABSENCE. THE THING WE'RE NEVER TOLD IS **HOW** IT'S ACTUALLY DONE.
DISCOVERY OF THE RELAY
THE FIRST WORLD
HISTORY BOOKS ARE REWRITTEN WHENEVER A PLANET JOINS THE SYSTEM. THERE'S ONLY ONE HISTORICAL TIMELINE NOW: THE RELAY'S.
EVEN US EMISSARY OFFICERS NEVER GET TO SEE THESE PRIMARY SOURCE "VARIABLES" FROM NEWLY JOINED SOCIETIES.
DONALDSON FIRST WORLD IALIS..?

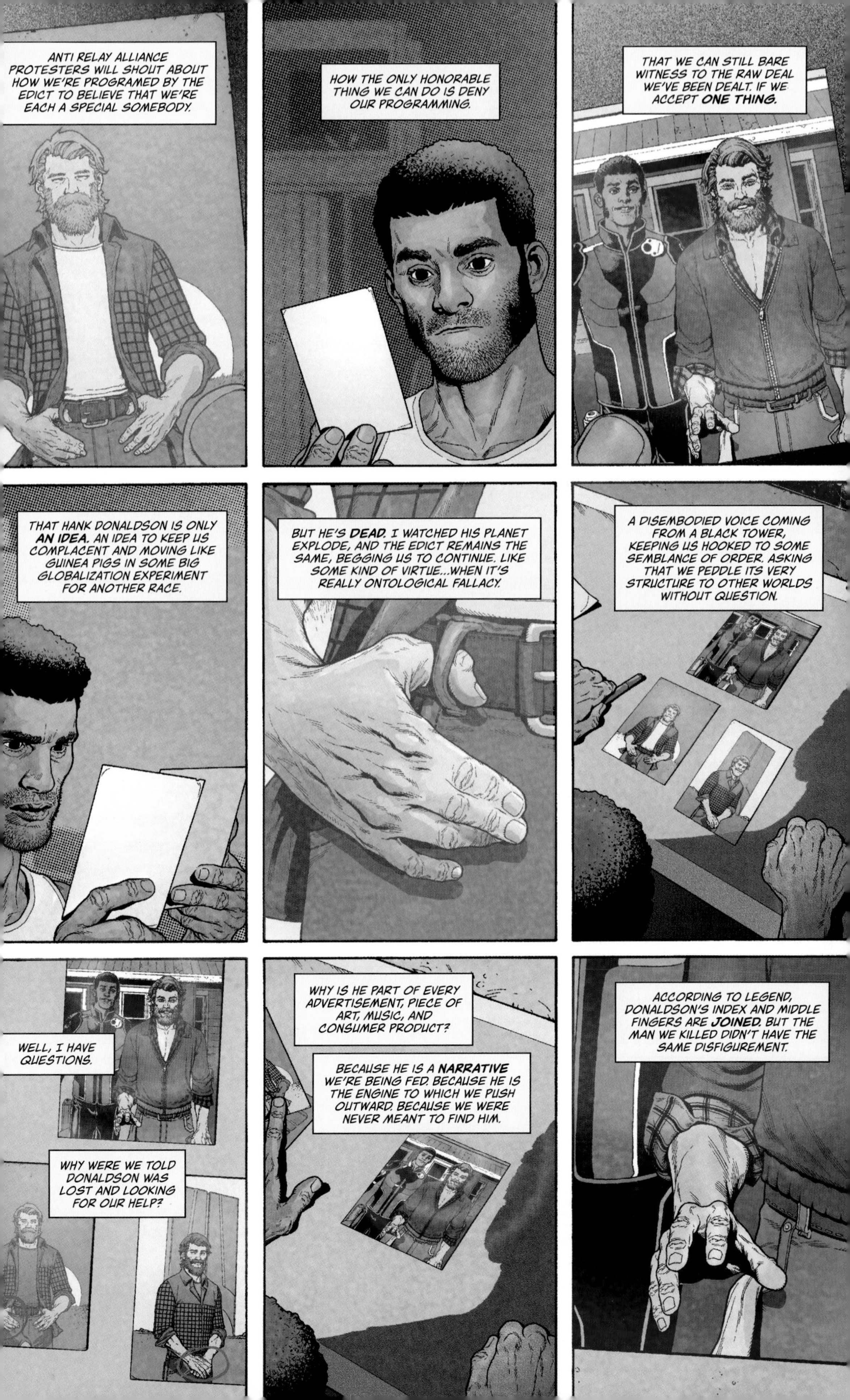
ANTI RELAY ALLIANCE PROTESTERS WILL SHOUT ABOUT HOW WE'RE PROGRAMED BY THE EDICT TO BELIEVE THAT WE'RE EACH A SPECIAL SOMEBODY.
HOW THE ONLY HONORABLE THING WE CAN DO IS DENY OUR PROGRAMMING.
THAT WE CAN STILL BARE WITNESS TO THE RAW DEAL WE'VE BEEN DEALT. IF WE ACCEPT **ONE THING.**
THAT HANK DONALDSON IS ONLY **AN IDEA.** AN IDEA TO KEEP US COMPLACENT AND MOVING LIKE GUINEA PIGS IN SOME BIG GLOBALIZATION EXPERIMENT FOR ANOTHER RACE.
BUT HE'S **DEAD.** I WATCHED HIS PLANET EXPLODE, AND THE EDICT REMAINS THE SAME, BEGGING US TO CONTINUE. LIKE SOME KIND OF VIRTUE...WHEN IT'S REALLY ONTOLOGICAL FALLACY.
A DISEMBODIED VOICE COMING FROM A BLACK TOWER, KEEPING US HOOKED TO SOME SEMBLANCE OF ORDER. ASKING THAT WE PEDDLE ITS VERY STRUCTURE TO OTHER WORLDS WITHOUT QUESTION.
WELL, I HAVE QUESTIONS.
WHY WERE WE TOLD DONALDSON WAS LOST AND LOOKING FOR OUR HELP?
WHY IS HE PART OF EVERY ADVERTISEMENT, PIECE OF ART, MUSIC, AND CONSUMER PRODUCT?
BECAUSE HE IS A **NARRATIVE** WE'RE BEING FED. BECAUSE HE IS THE ENGINE TO WHICH WE PUSH OUTWARD. BECAUSE WE WERE NEVER MEANT TO FIND HIM.
ACCORDING TO LEGEND, DONALDSON'S INDEX AND MIDDLE FINGERS ARE **JOINED.** BUT THE MAN WE KILLED DIDN'T HAVE THE SAME DISFIGUREMENT.

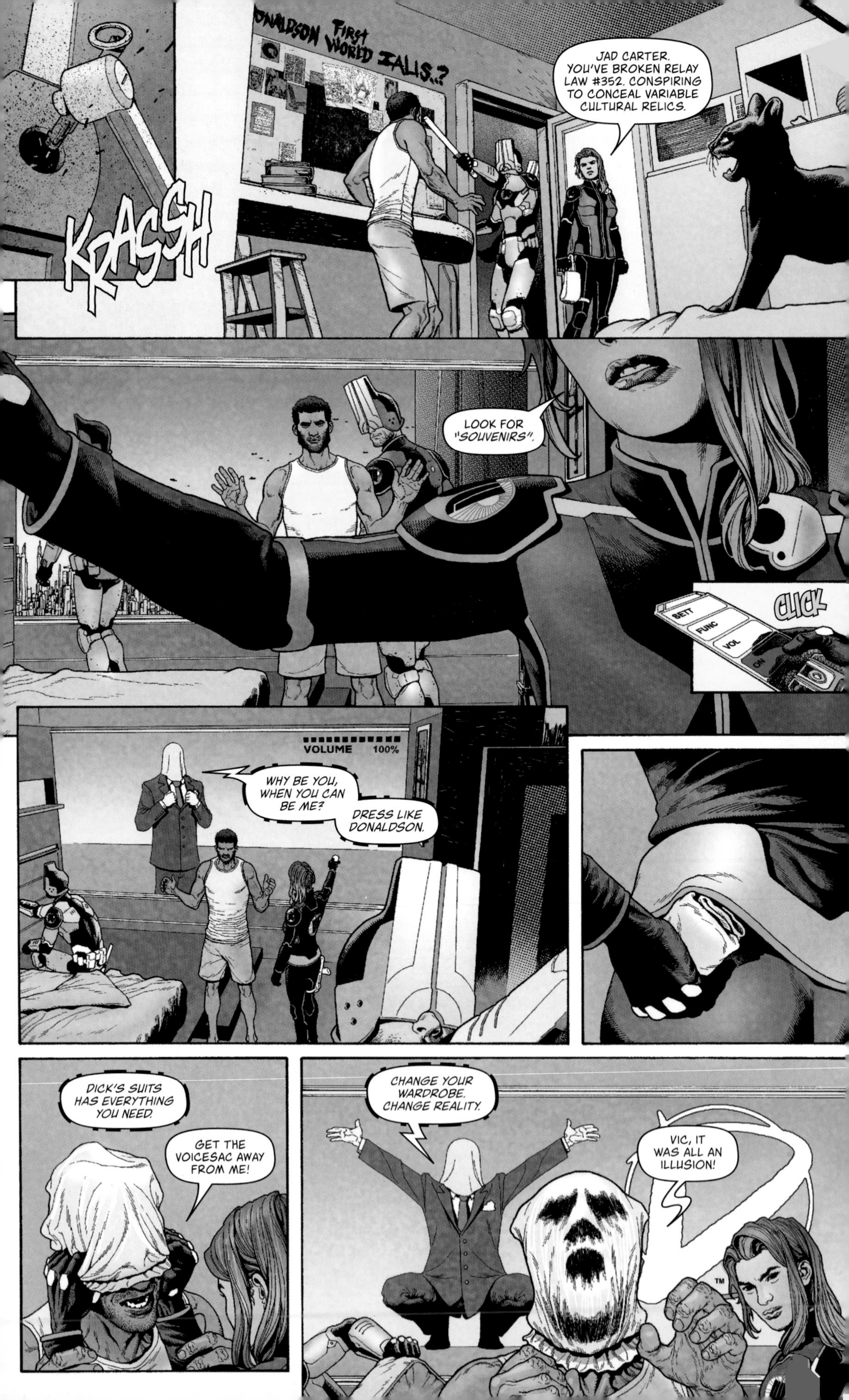
DONALDSON First WORLD ZALIS..?
KRASSH
JAD CARTER. YOU'VE BROKEN RELAY LAW #352. CONSPIRING TO CONCEAL VARIABLE CULTURAL RELICS.
LOOK FOR "SOUVENIRS".
CLICK
SETT
FUNC
VOL
ON
VOLUME 100%
WHY BE YOU, WHEN YOU CAN BE ME?
DRESS LIKE DONALDSON.
DICK'S SUITS HAS EVERYTHING YOU NEED.
GET THE VOICESAC AWAY FROM ME!
CHANGE YOUR WARDROBE. CHANGE REALITY.
VIC, IT WAS ALL AN ILLUSION!
™

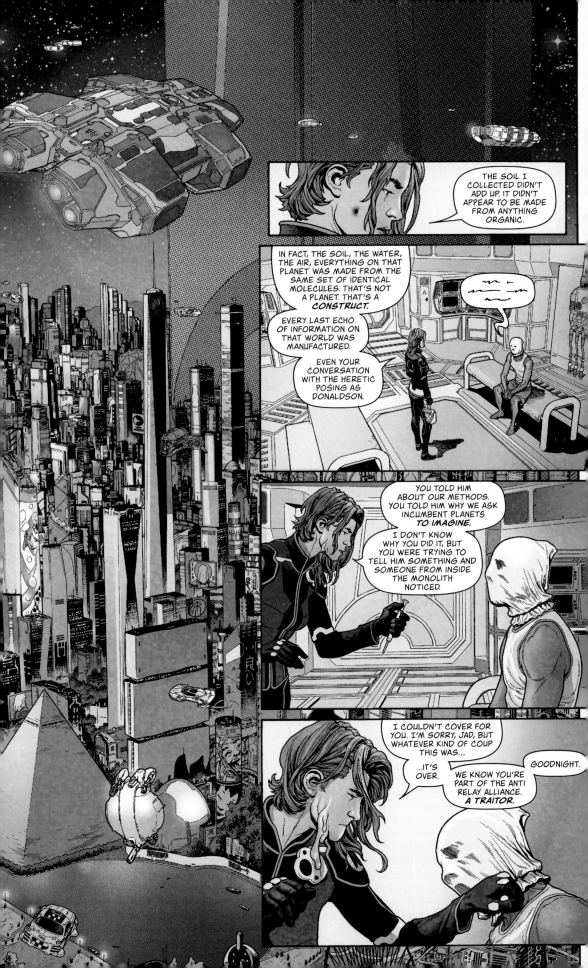

THE SOIL I COLLECTED DIDN'T ADD UP. IT DIDN'T APPEAR TO BE MADE FROM ANYTHING ORGANIC.

IN FACT, THE SOIL, THE WATER, THE AIR, EVERYTHING ON THAT PLANET WAS MADE FROM THE SAME SET OF IDENTICAL MOLECULES. THAT'S NOT A PLANET. THAT'S A *CONSTRUCT.*

EVERY LAST ECHO OF INFORMATION ON THAT WORLD WAS MANUFACTURED.

EVEN YOUR CONVERSATION WITH THE HERETIC POSING AS DONALDSON.

YOU TOLD HIM ABOUT OUR METHODS. YOU TOLD HIM WHY WE ASK INCUMBENT PLANETS *TO IMAGINE.*

I DON'T KNOW WHY YOU DID IT, BUT YOU WERE TRYING TO TELL HIM SOMETHING AND SOMEONE FROM INSIDE THE MONOLITH NOTICED.

I COULDN'T COVER FOR YOU. I'M SORRY, JAD, BUT WHATEVER KIND OF COUP THIS WAS...

...IT'S OVER.

WE KNOW YOU'RE PART OF THE ANTI RELAY ALLIANCE. *A TRAITOR.*

GOODNIGHT.

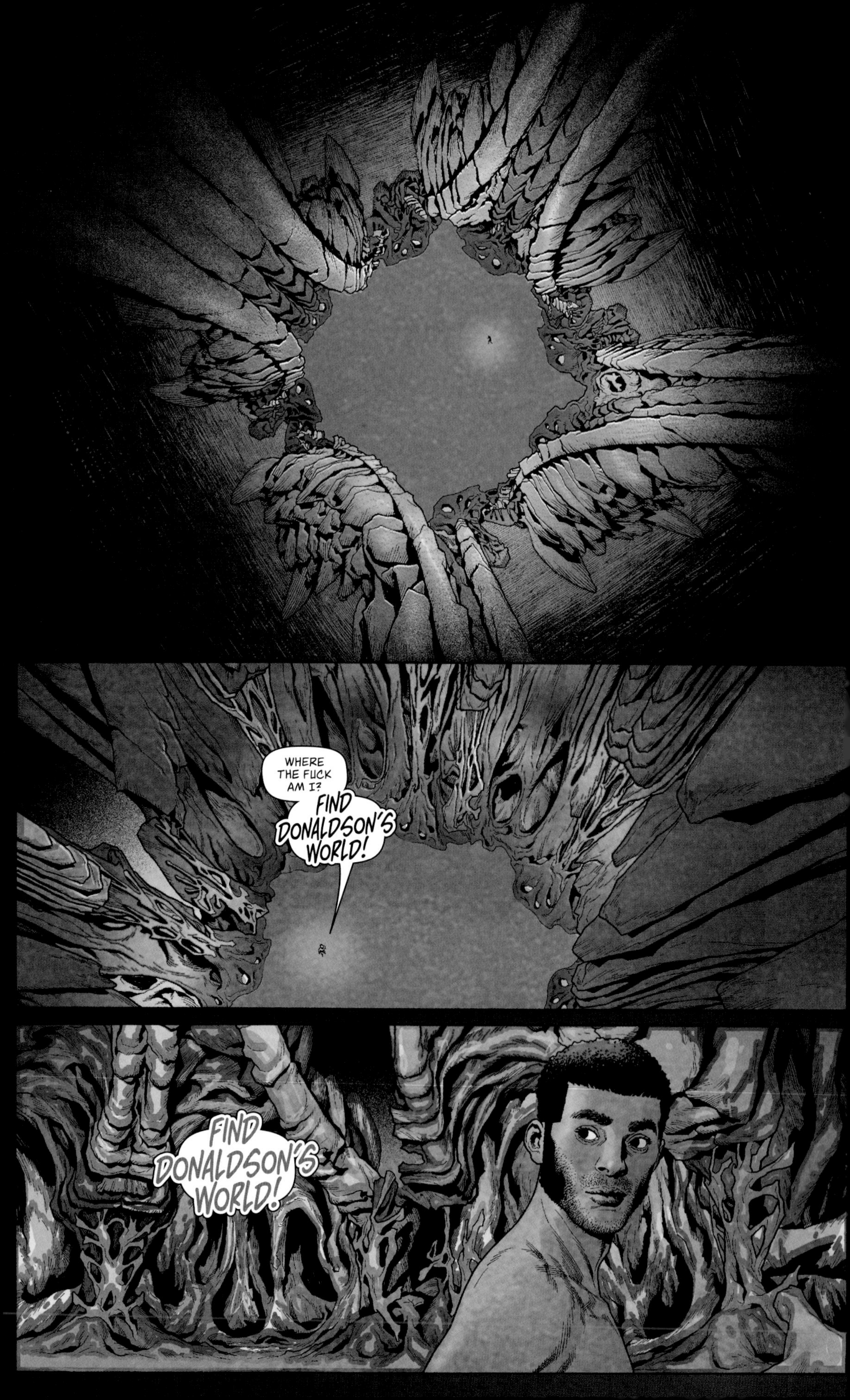
WHERE THE FUCK AM I?
FIND DONALDSON'S WORLD!
FIND DONALDSON'S WORLD!

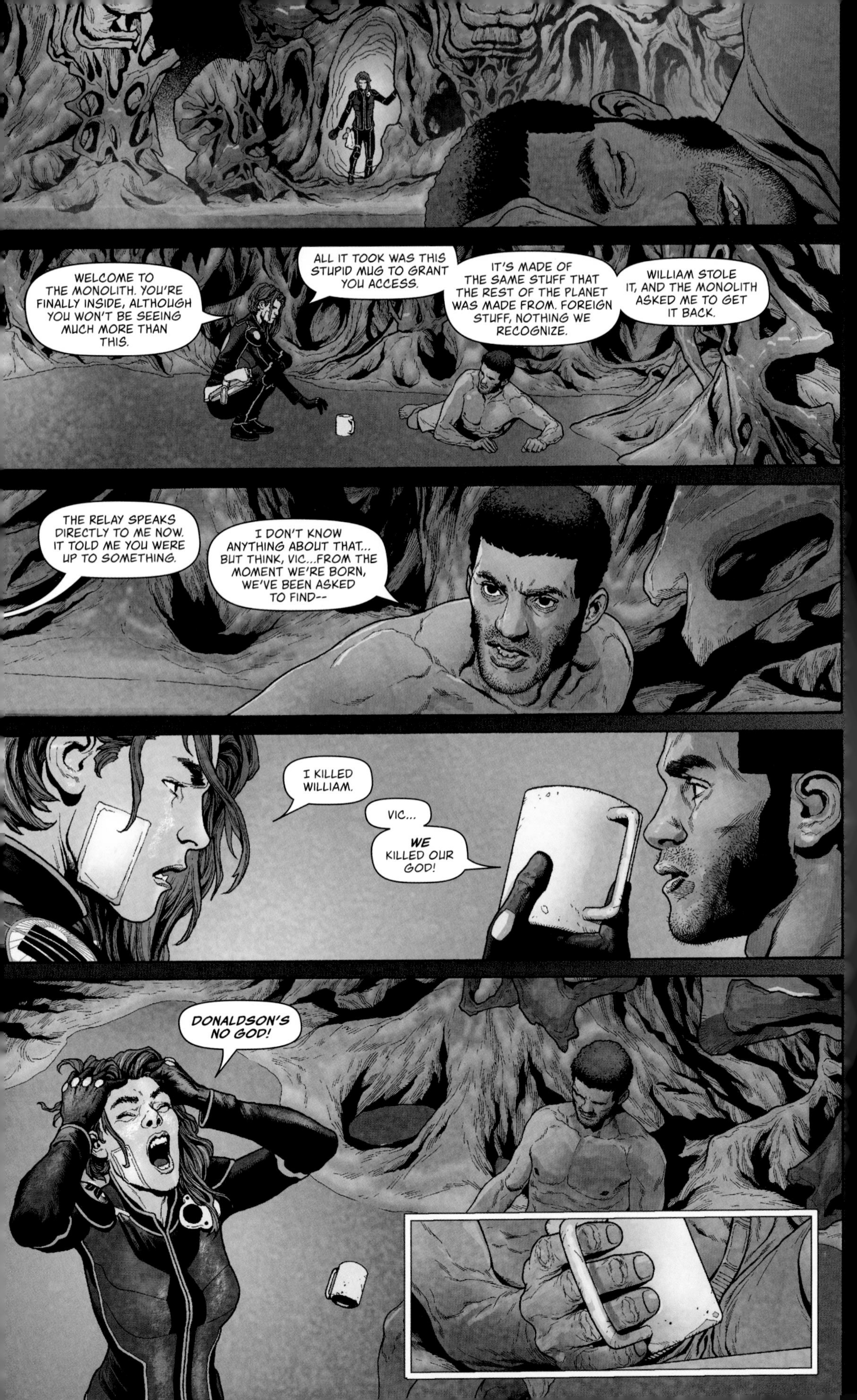
WELCOME TO THE MONOLITH. YOU'RE FINALLY INSIDE, ALTHOUGH YOU WON'T BE SEEING MUCH MORE THAN THIS.
ALL IT TOOK WAS THIS STUPID MUG TO GRANT YOU ACCESS.
IT'S MADE OF THE SAME STUFF THAT THE REST OF THE PLANET WAS MADE FROM. FOREIGN STUFF, NOTHING WE RECOGNIZE.
WILLIAM STOLE IT, AND THE MONOLITH ASKED ME TO GET IT BACK.
THE RELAY SPEAKS DIRECTLY TO ME NOW. IT TOLD ME YOU WERE UP TO SOMETHING.
I DON'T KNOW ANYTHING ABOUT THAT... BUT THINK, VIC...FROM THE MOMENT WE'RE BORN, WE'VE BEEN ASKED TO FIND--
I KILLED WILLIAM.
VIC...
WE KILLED OUR GOD!
DONALDSON'S NO GOD!

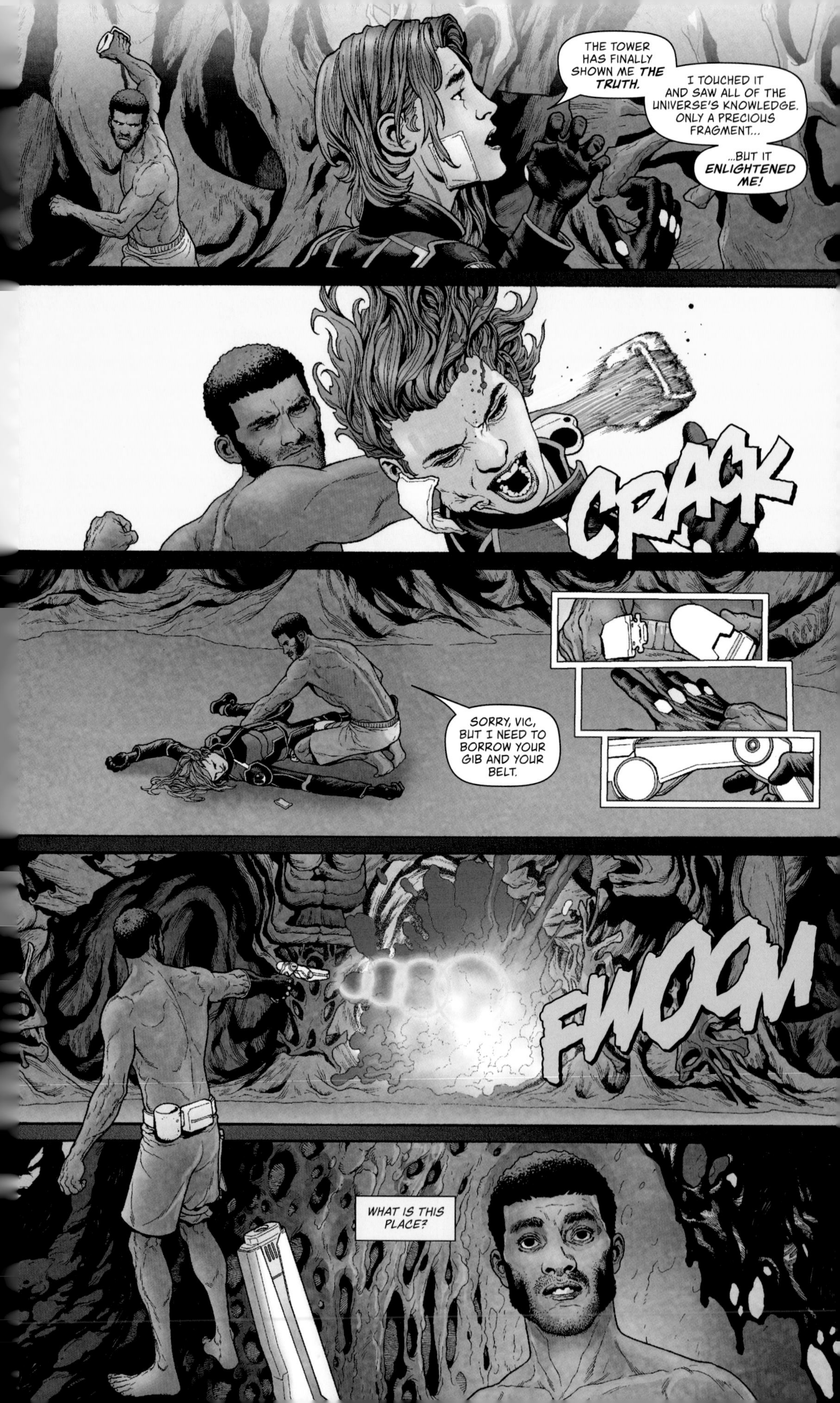

THE TOWER HAS FINALLY SHOWN ME THE TRUTH.
I TOUCHED IT AND SAW ALL OF THE UNIVERSE'S KNOWLEDGE. ONLY A PRECIOUS FRAGMENT...
...BUT IT ENLIGHTENED ME!
CRACK
SORRY, VIC, BUT I NEED TO BORROW YOUR GIB AND YOUR BELT.
FWOOM
WHAT IS THIS PLACE?

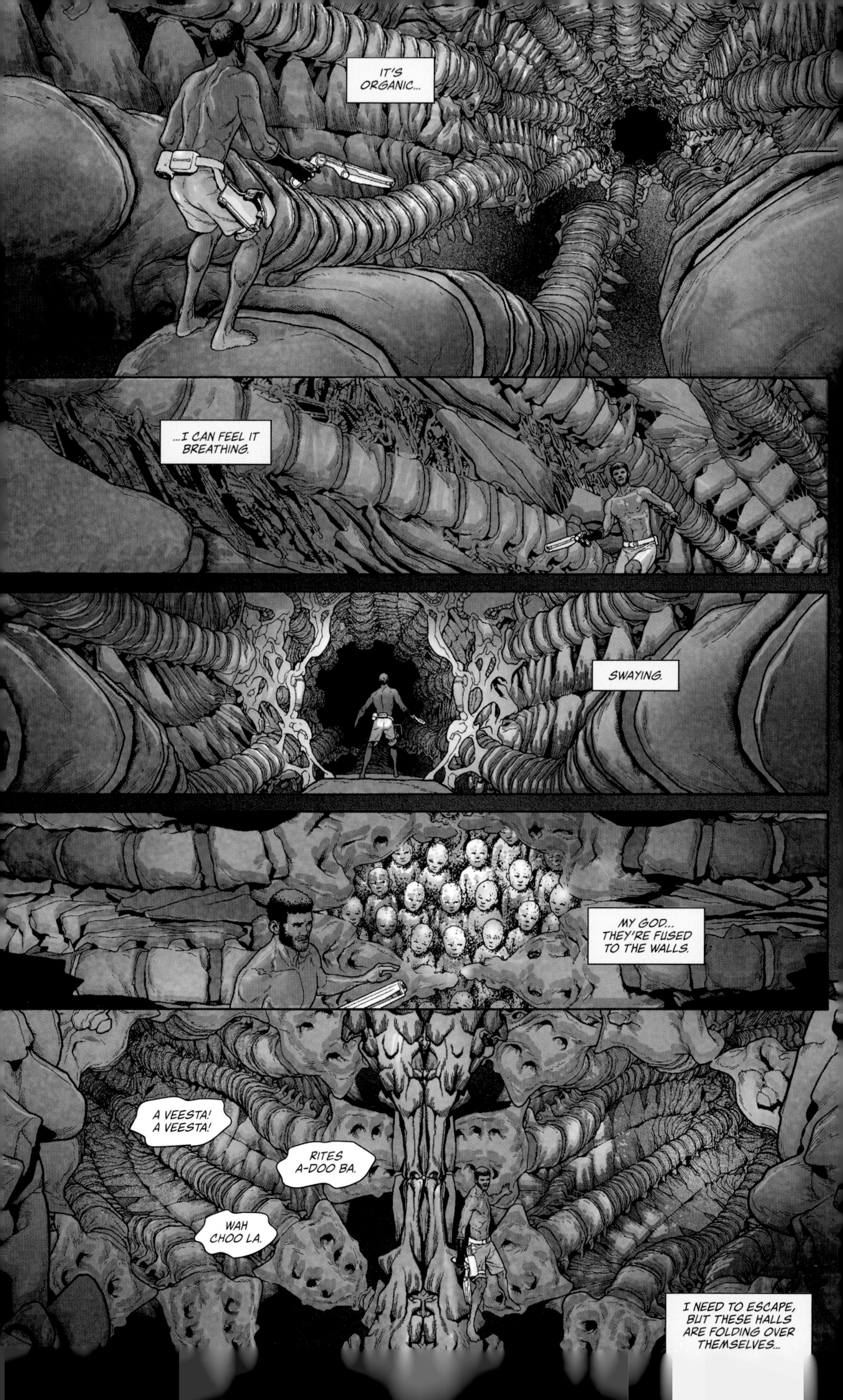

IT'S ORGANIC...
...I CAN FEEL IT BREATHING.
SWAYING.
MY GOD... THEY'RE FUSED TO THE WALLS.
A VEESTA! A VEESTA!
RITES A-DOO BA.
WAH CHOO LA.
I NEED TO ESCAPE, BUT THESE HALLS ARE FOLDING OVER THEMSELVES...

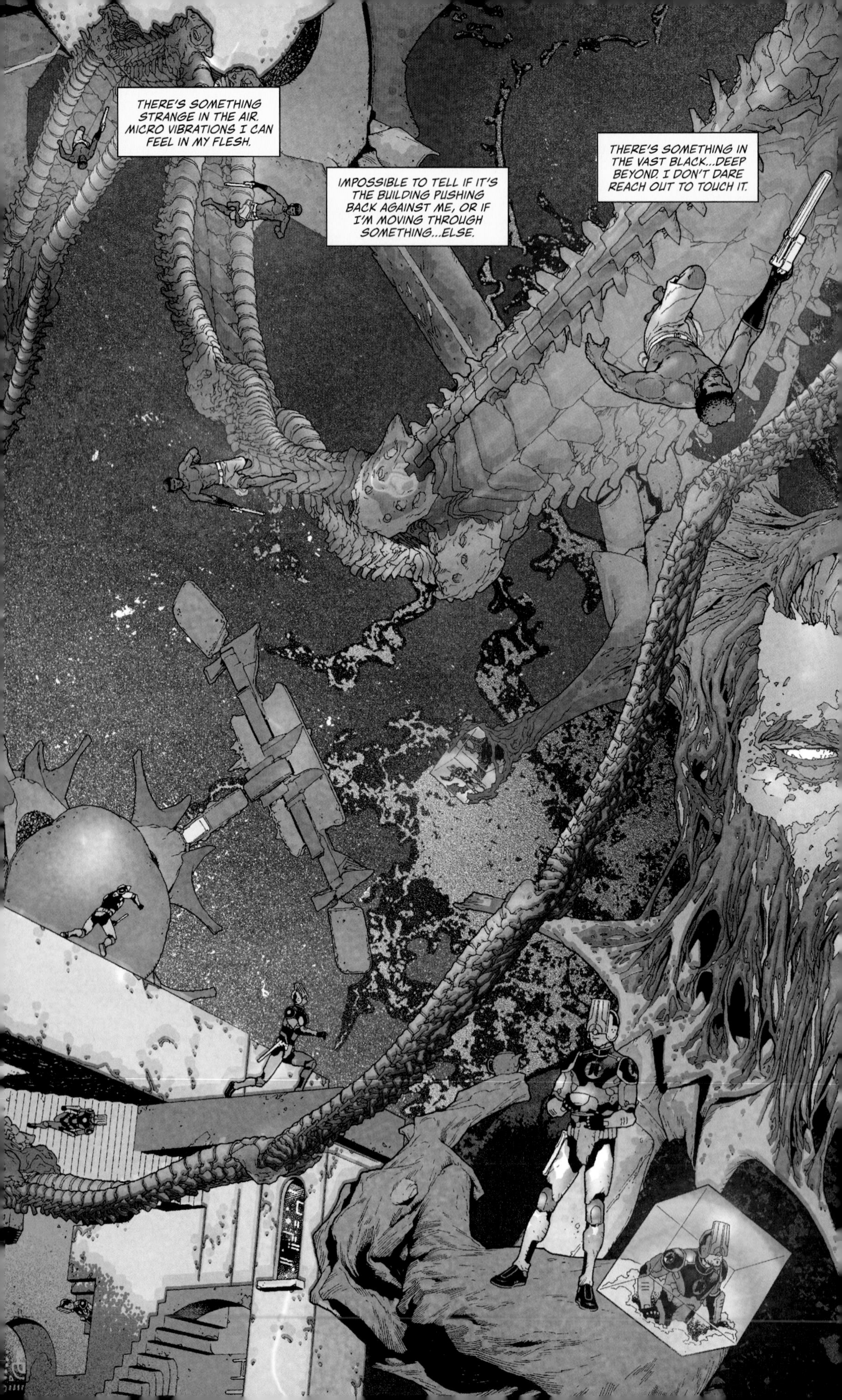
THERE'S SOMETHING STRANGE IN THE AIR. MICRO VIBRATIONS I CAN FEEL IN MY FLESH.
IMPOSSIBLE TO TELL IF IT'S THE BUILDING PUSHING BACK AGAINST ME, OR IF I'M MOVING THROUGH SOMETHING...ELSE.
THERE'S SOMETHING IN THE VAST BLACK...DEEP BEYOND. I DON'T DARE REACH OUT TO TOUCH IT.

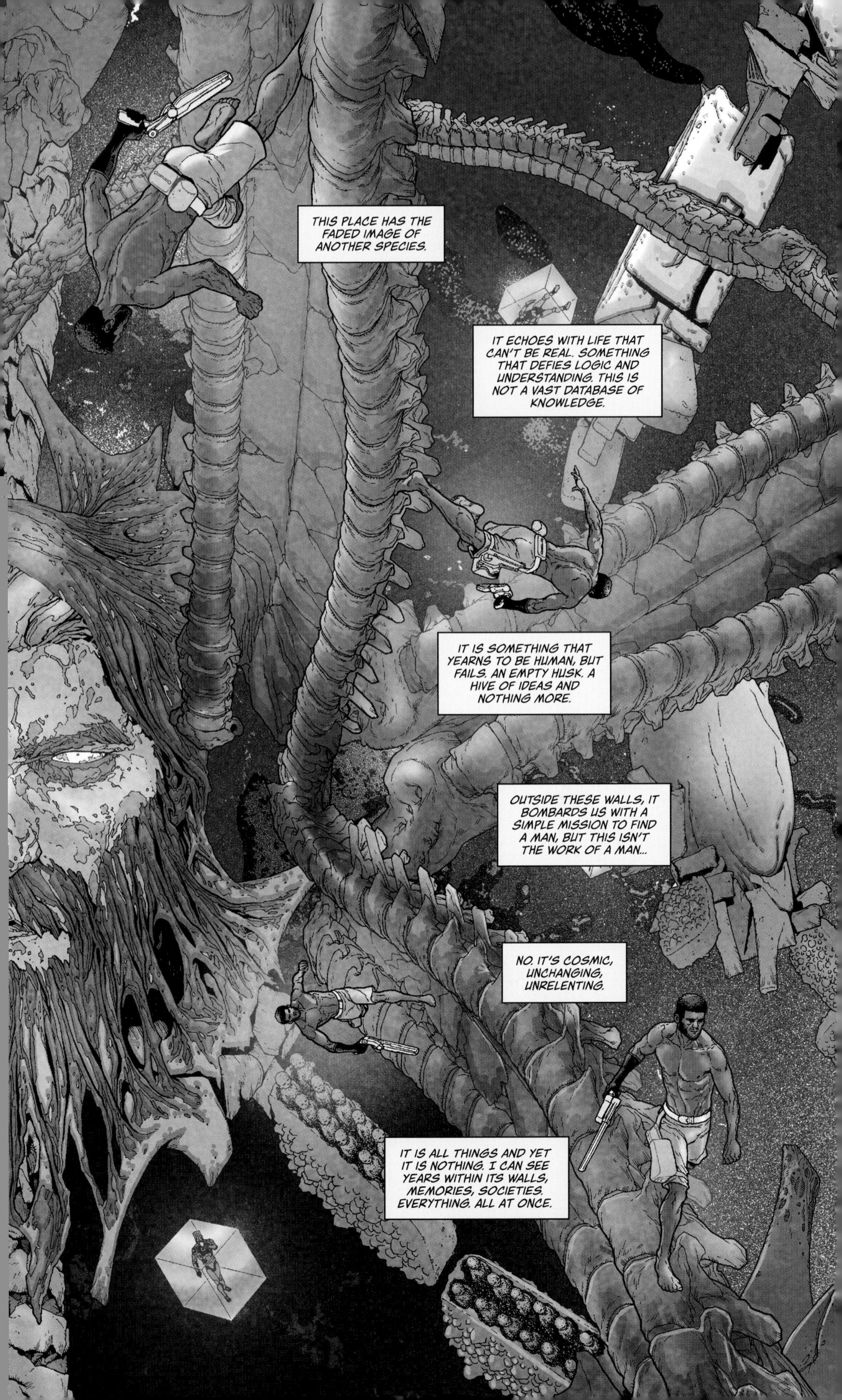
THIS PLACE HAS THE FADED IMAGE OF ANOTHER SPECIES.
IT ECHOES WITH LIFE THAT CAN'T BE REAL. SOMETHING THAT DEFIES LOGIC AND UNDERSTANDING. THIS IS NOT A VAST DATABASE OF KNOWLEDGE.
IT IS SOMETHING THAT YEARNS TO BE HUMAN, BUT FAILS. AN EMPTY HUSK. A HIVE OF IDEAS AND NOTHING MORE.
OUTSIDE THESE WALLS, IT BOMBARDS US WITH A SIMPLE MISSION TO FIND A MAN, BUT THIS ISN'T THE WORK OF A MAN...
NO. IT'S COSMIC, UNCHANGING, UNRELENTING.
IT IS ALL THINGS AND YET IT IS NOTHING. I CAN SEE YEARS WITHIN ITS WALLS, MEMORIES, SOCIETIES. EVERYTHING. ALL AT ONCE.

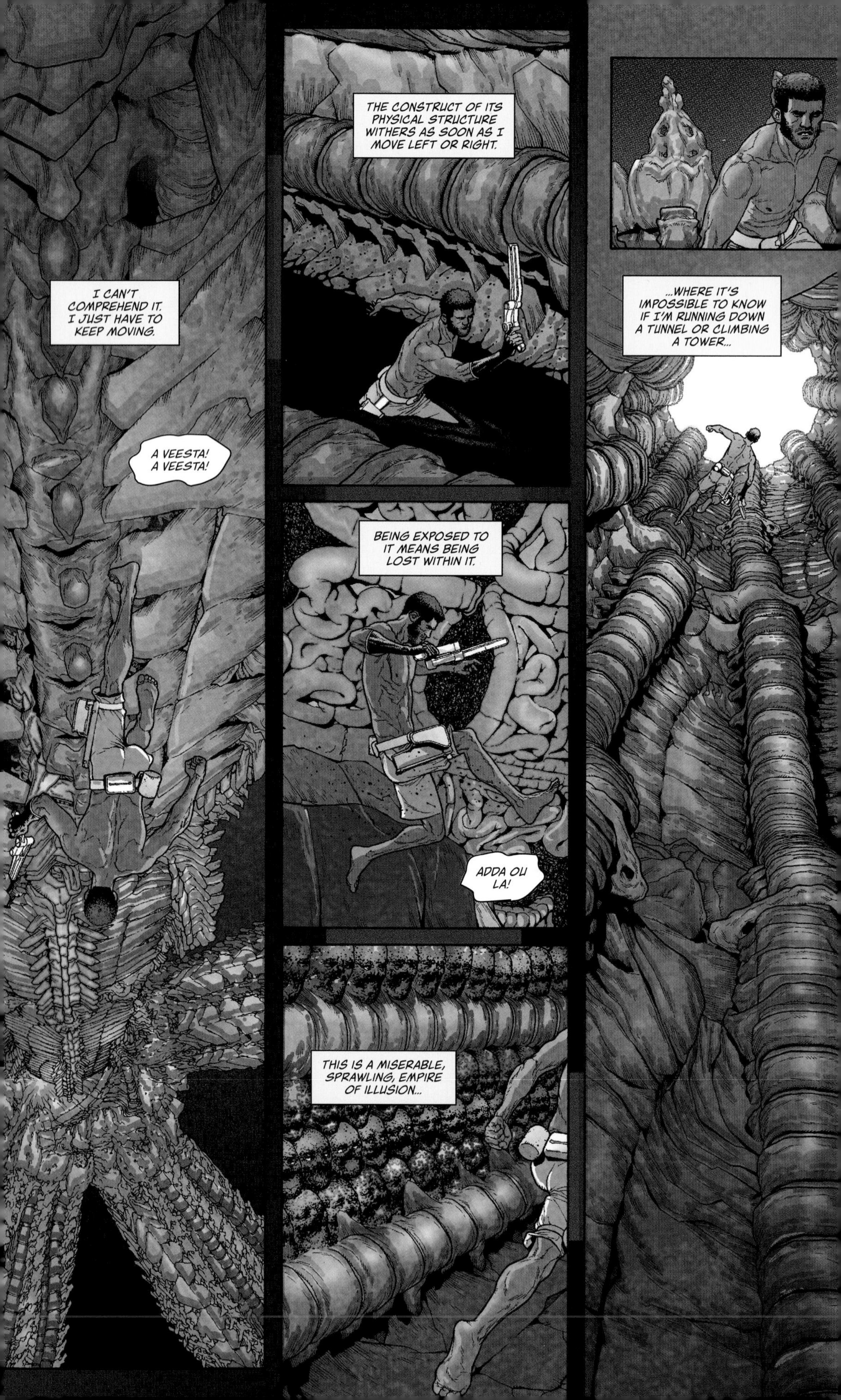
I CAN'T COMPREHEND IT. I JUST HAVE TO KEEP MOVING.
A VEESTA! A VEESTA!
THE CONSTRUCT OF ITS PHYSICAL STRUCTURE WITHERS AS SOON AS I MOVE LEFT OR RIGHT.
BEING EXPOSED TO IT MEANS BEING LOST WITHIN IT.
ADDA OU LA!
THIS IS A MISERABLE, SPRAWLING, EMPIRE OF ILLUSION...
...WHERE IT'S IMPOSSIBLE TO KNOW IF I'M RUNNING DOWN A TUNNEL OR CLIMBING A TOWER...

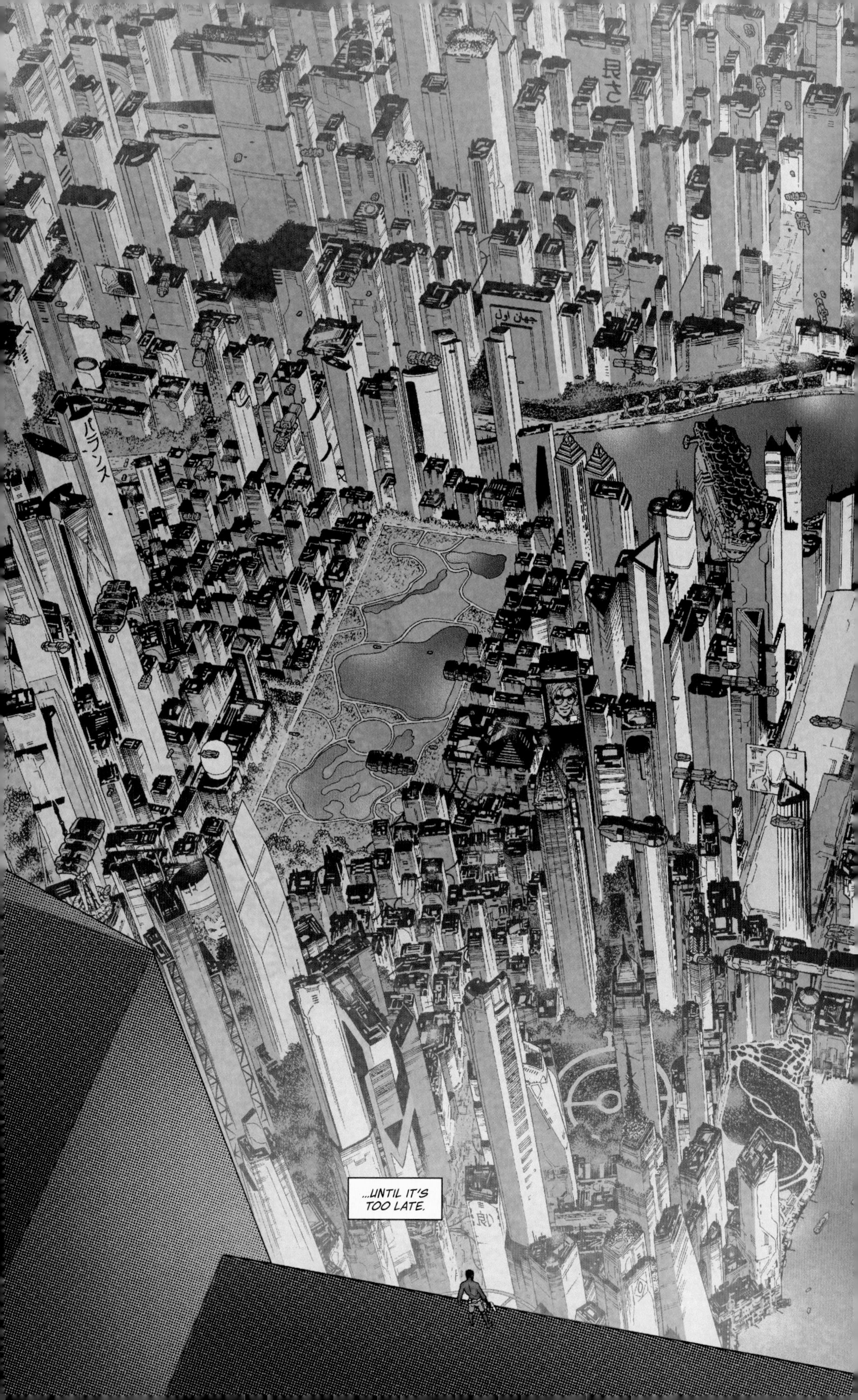
...UNTIL IT'S TOO LATE.

MY GIB GUN WORKS ON SOUND...

...SOUND BOUNCES OFF ALL THINGS.

I HOPE...

FWOOM

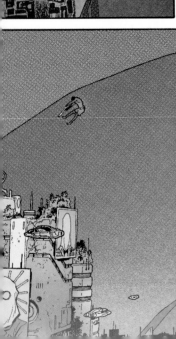

FWOOM

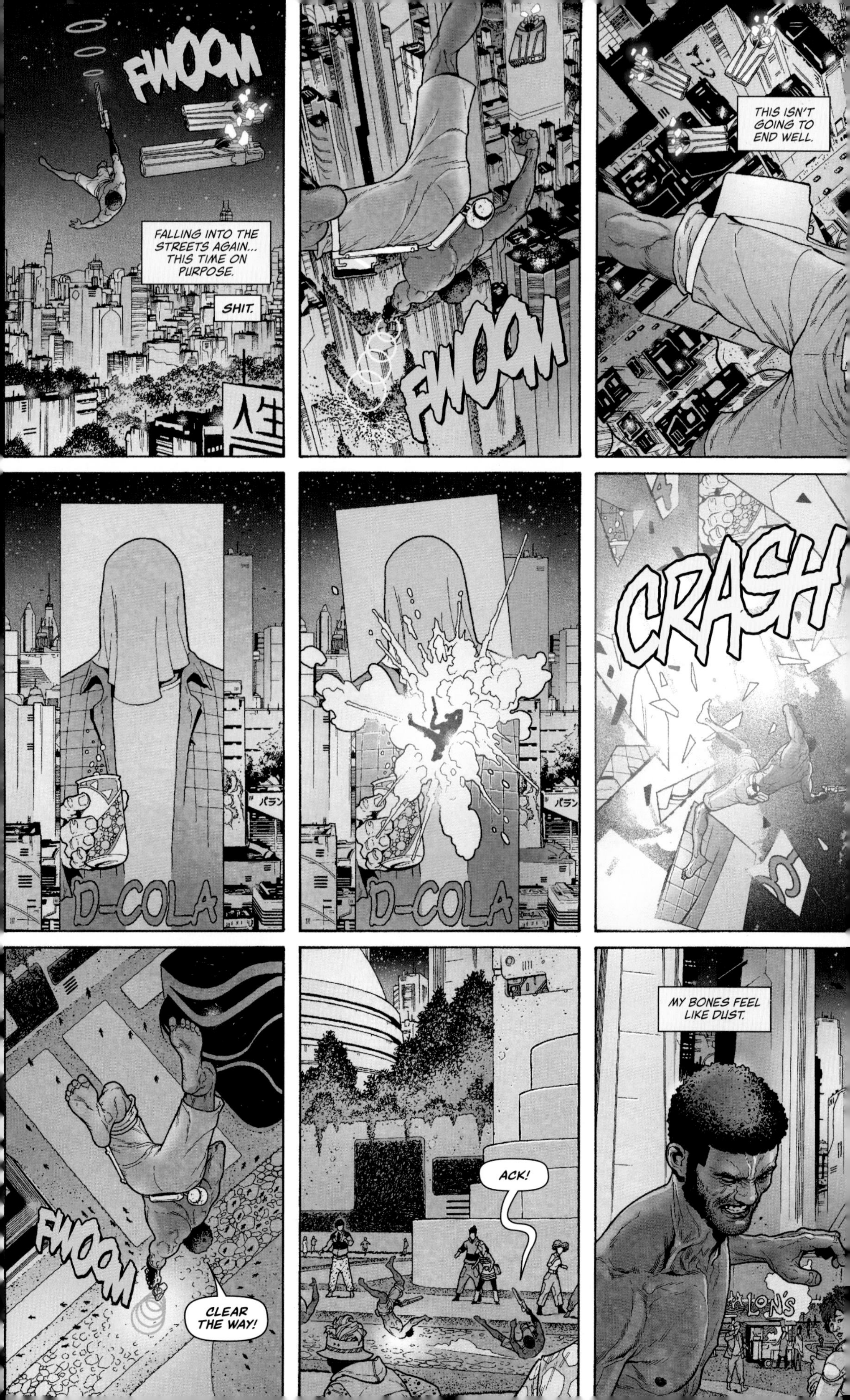
FWOOM
FALLING INTO THE STREETS AGAIN... THIS TIME ON PURPOSE.
SHIT.
人生
FWOOM
THIS ISN'T GOING TO END WELL.
D-COLA
バラン
D-COLA
バラン
CRASH
FWOOM
CLEAR THE WAY!
ACK!
MY BONES FEEL LIKE DUST.

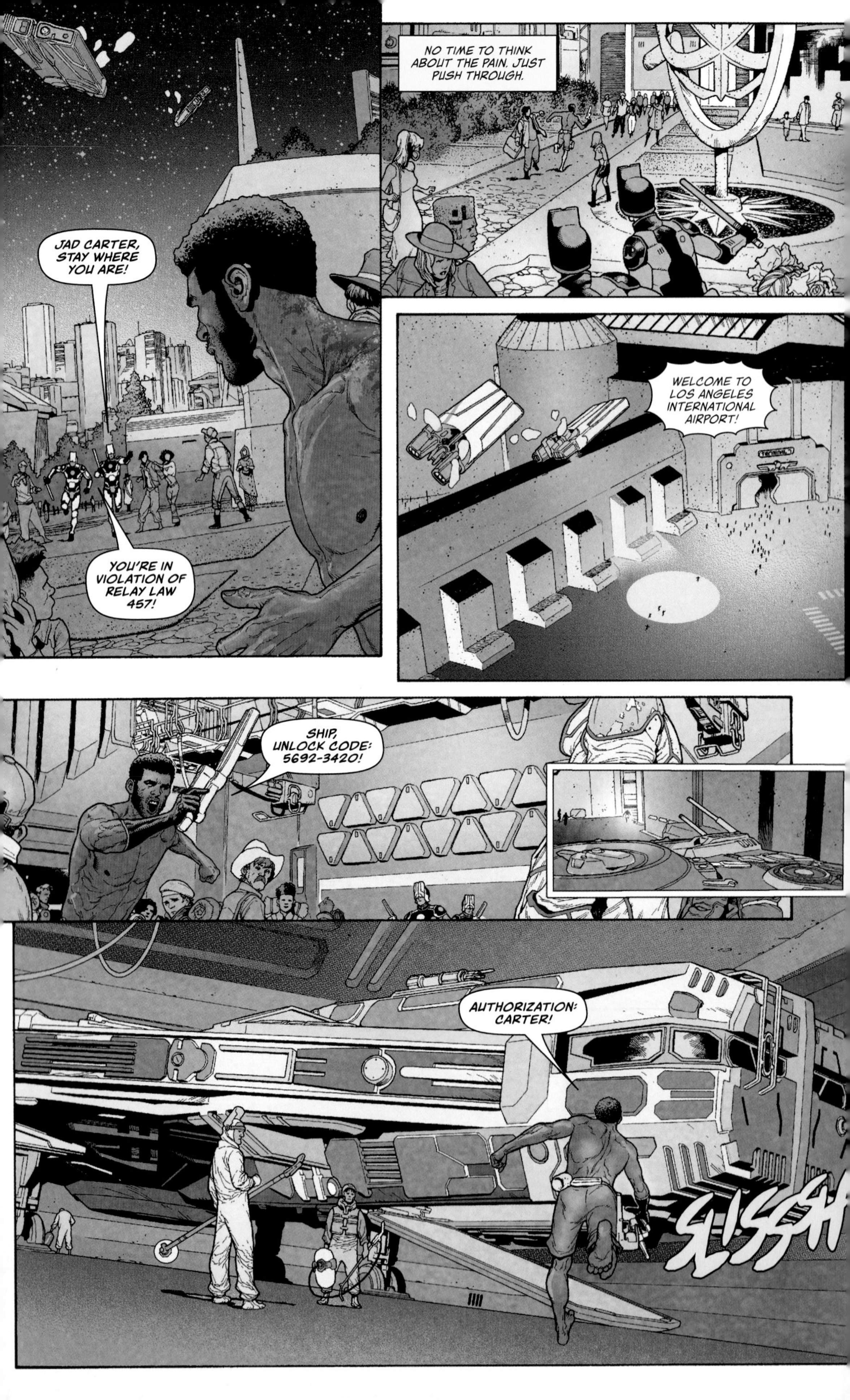
JAD CARTER, STAY WHERE YOU ARE!
YOU'RE IN VIOLATION OF RELAY LAW 457!
NO TIME TO THINK ABOUT THE PAIN. JUST PUSH THROUGH.
WELCOME TO LOS ANGELES INTERNATIONAL AIRPORT!
TERMINAL 7
SHIP, UNLOCK CODE: 5692-3420!
AUTHORIZATION: CARTER!
SLISSH

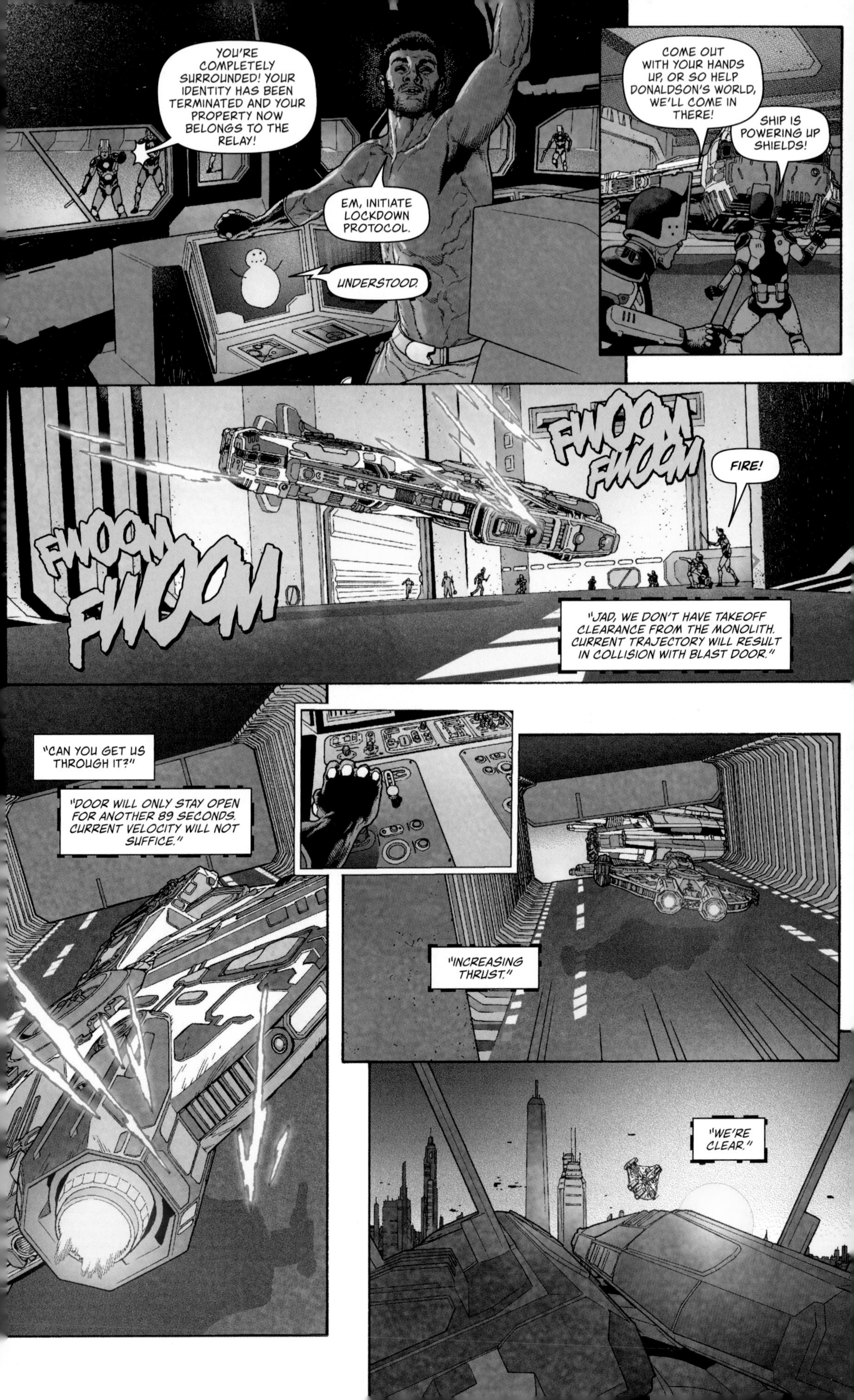
YOU'RE COMPLETELY SURROUNDED! YOUR IDENTITY HAS BEEN TERMINATED AND YOUR PROPERTY NOW BELONGS TO THE RELAY!
EM, INITIATE LOCKDOWN PROTOCOL.
UNDERSTOOD.
COME OUT WITH YOUR HANDS UP, OR SO HELP DONALDSON'S WORLD, WE'LL COME IN THERE!
SHIP IS POWERING UP SHIELDS!
FWOOM FWOOM
FIRE!
FWOOM FWOOM
"JAD, WE DON'T HAVE TAKEOFF CLEARANCE FROM THE MONOLITH. CURRENT TRAJECTORY WILL RESULT IN COLLISION WITH BLAST DOOR."
"CAN YOU GET US THROUGH IT?"
"DOOR WILL ONLY STAY OPEN FOR ANOTHER 89 SECONDS. CURRENT VELOCITY WILL NOT SUFFICE."
"INCREASING THRUST."
"WE'RE CLEAR."

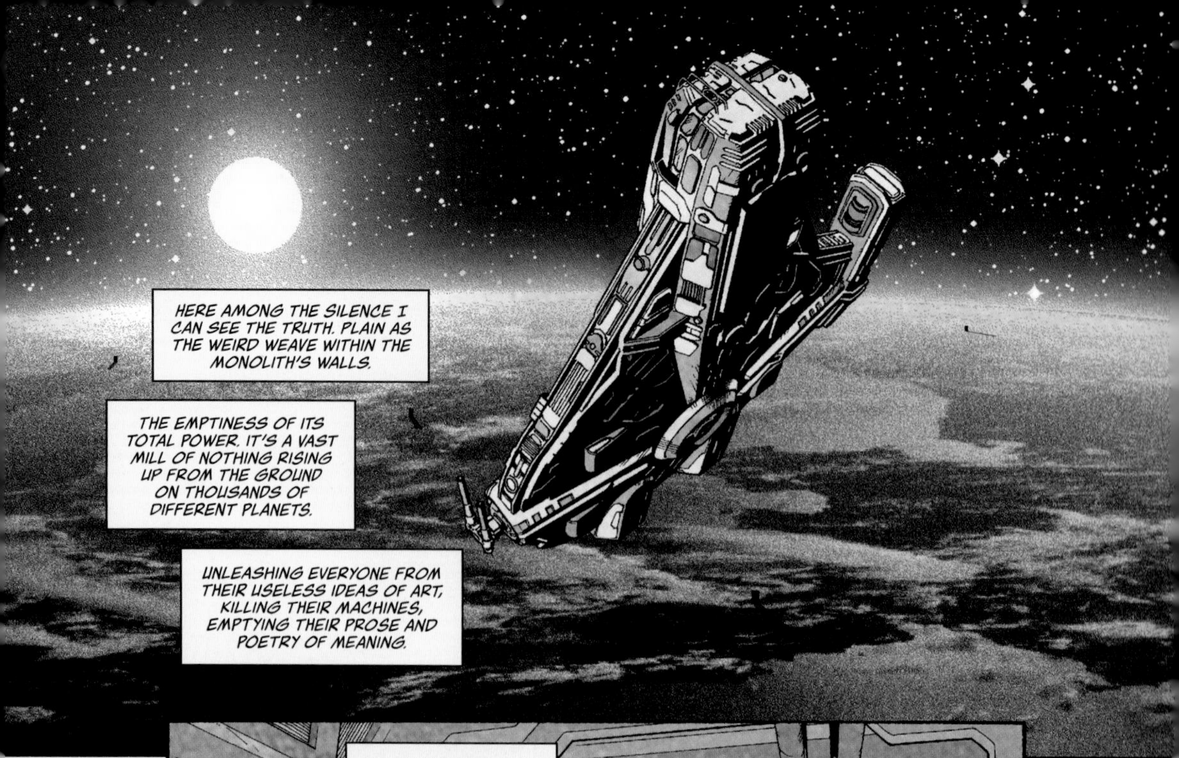
HERE AMONG THE SILENCE I CAN SEE THE TRUTH. PLAIN AS THE WEIRD WEAVE WITHIN THE MONOLITH'S WALLS.
THE EMPTINESS OF ITS TOTAL POWER. IT'S A VAST MILL OF NOTHING RISING UP FROM THE GROUND ON THOUSANDS OF DIFFERENT PLANETS.
UNLEASHING EVERYONE FROM THEIR USELESS IDEAS OF ART, KILLING THEIR MACHINES, EMPTYING THEIR PROSE AND POETRY OF MEANING.

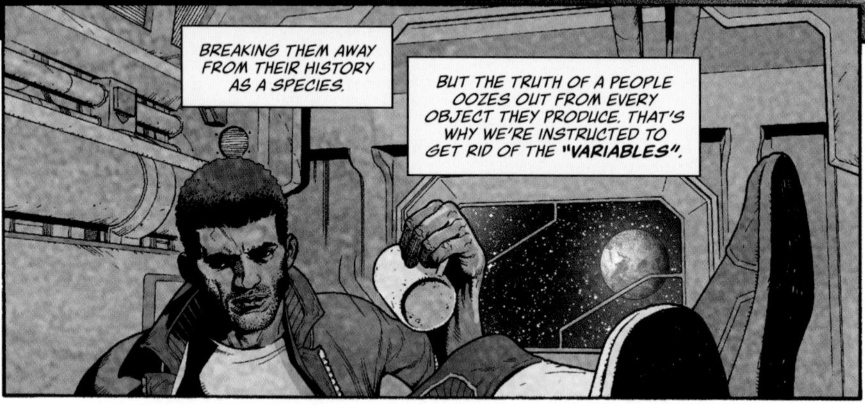
BREAKING THEM AWAY FROM THEIR HISTORY AS A SPECIES.
BUT THE TRUTH OF A PEOPLE OOZES OUT FROM EVERY OBJECT THEY PRODUCE. THAT'S WHY WE'RE INSTRUCTED TO GET RID OF THE **"VARIABLES"**.

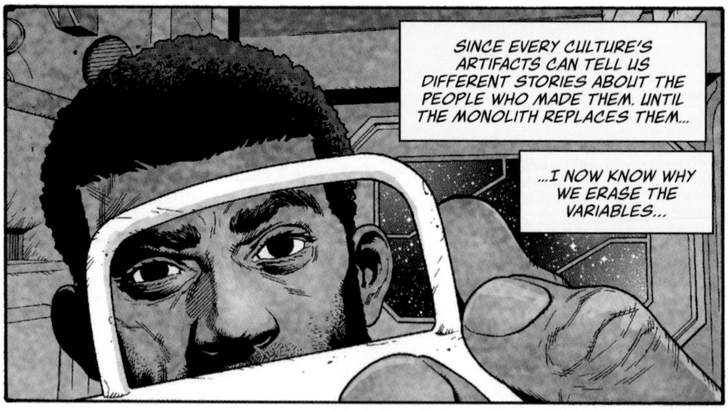
SINCE EVERY CULTURE'S ARTIFACTS CAN TELL US DIFFERENT STORIES ABOUT THE PEOPLE WHO MADE THEM. UNTIL THE MONOLITH REPLACES THEM...
...I NOW KNOW WHY WE ERASE THE VARIABLES...

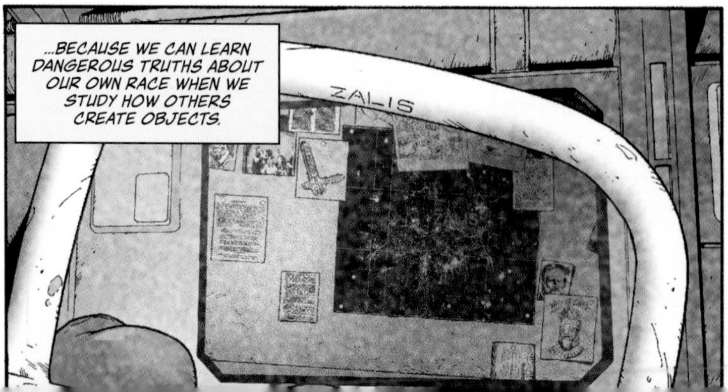
...BECAUSE WE CAN LEARN DANGEROUS TRUTHS ABOUT OUR OWN RACE WHEN WE STUDY HOW OTHERS CREATE OBJECTS.
ZALIS

4

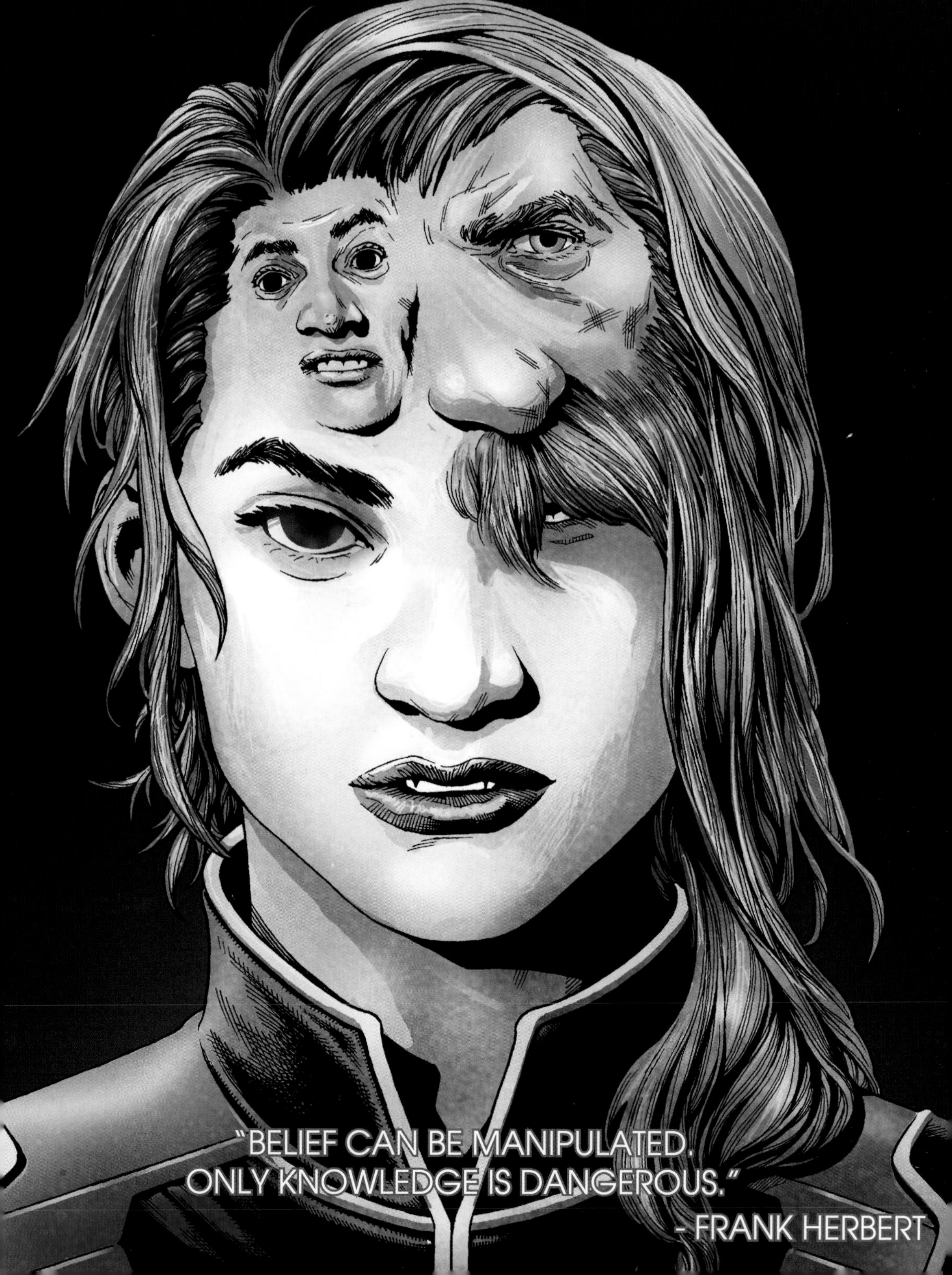

"BELIEF CAN BE MANIPULATED.
ONLY KNOWLEDGE IS DANGEROUS."
- FRANK HERBERT

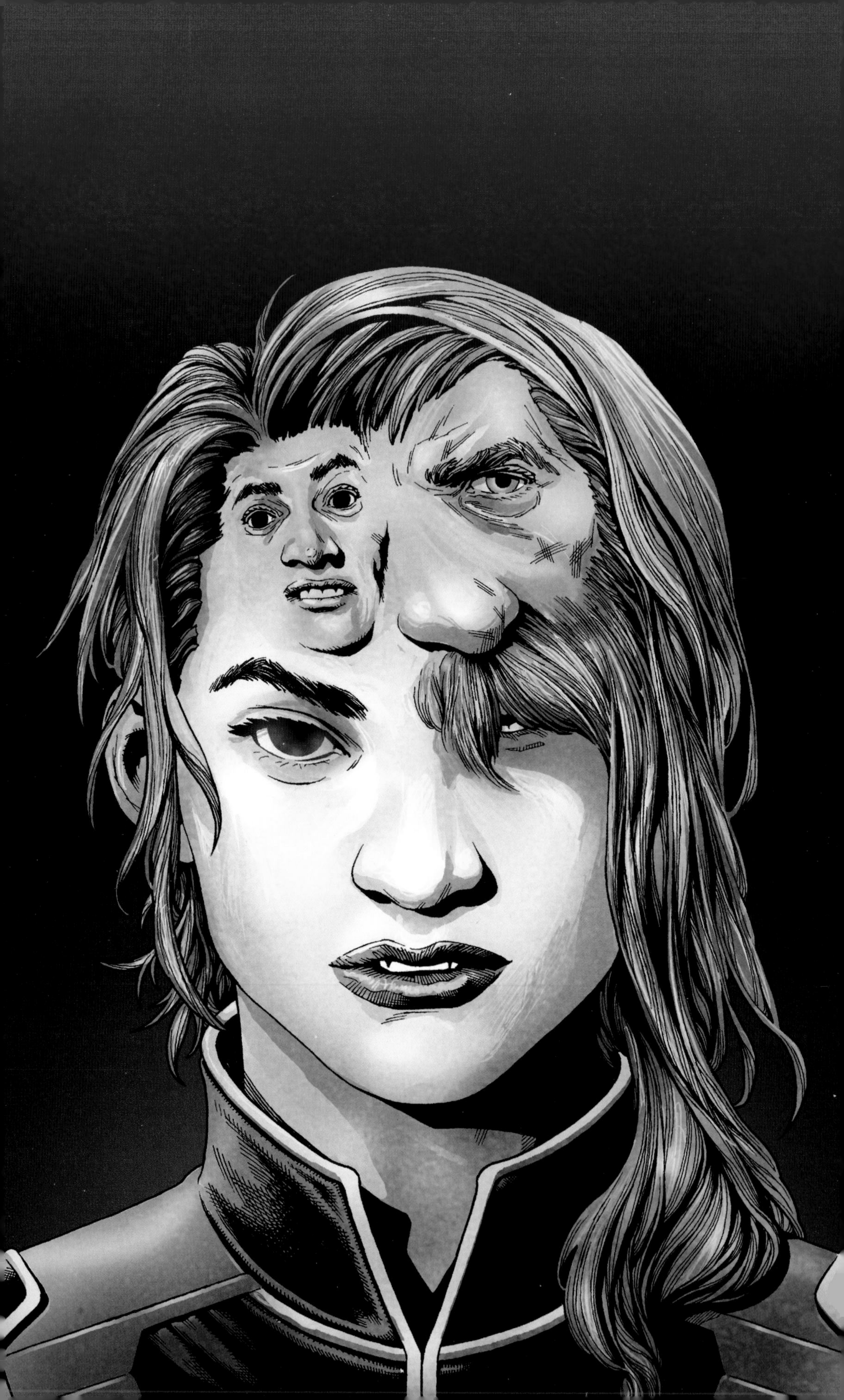

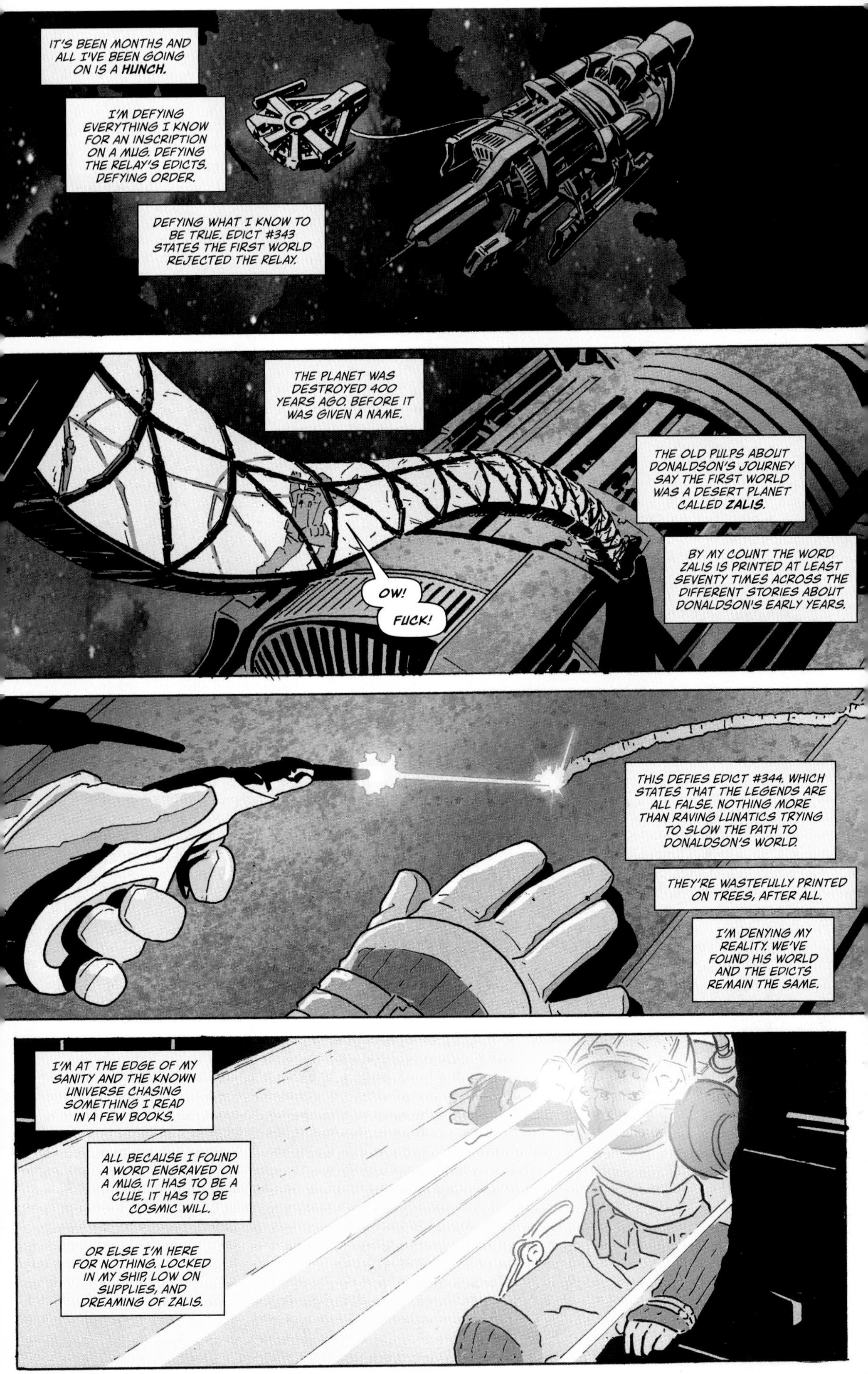
IT'S BEEN MONTHS AND ALL I'VE BEEN GOING ON IS A **HUNCH.**
I'M DEFYING EVERYTHING I KNOW FOR AN INSCRIPTION ON A MUG. DEFYING THE RELAY'S EDICTS. DEFYING ORDER.
DEFYING WHAT I KNOW TO BE TRUE. EDICT #343 STATES THE FIRST WORLD REJECTED THE RELAY.
THE PLANET WAS DESTROYED 400 YEARS AGO. BEFORE IT WAS GIVEN A NAME.
THE OLD PULPS ABOUT DONALDSON'S JOURNEY SAY THE FIRST WORLD WAS A DESERT PLANET CALLED **ZALIS.**
OW!
FUCK!
BY MY COUNT THE WORD ZALIS IS PRINTED AT LEAST SEVENTY TIMES ACROSS THE DIFFERENT STORIES ABOUT DONALDSON'S EARLY YEARS.
THIS DEFIES EDICT #344. WHICH STATES THAT THE LEGENDS ARE ALL FALSE. NOTHING MORE THAN RAVING LUNATICS TRYING TO SLOW THE PATH TO DONALDSON'S WORLD.
THEY'RE WASTEFULLY PRINTED ON TREES, AFTER ALL.
I'M DENYING MY REALITY. WE'VE FOUND HIS WORLD AND THE EDICTS REMAIN THE SAME.
I'M AT THE EDGE OF MY SANITY AND THE KNOWN UNIVERSE CHASING SOMETHING I READ IN A FEW BOOKS.
ALL BECAUSE I FOUND A WORD ENGRAVED ON A MUG. IT HAS TO BE A CLUE. IT HAS TO BE COSMIC WILL.
OR ELSE I'M HERE FOR NOTHING. LOCKED IN MY SHIP, LOW ON SUPPLIES, AND DREAMING OF ZALIS.

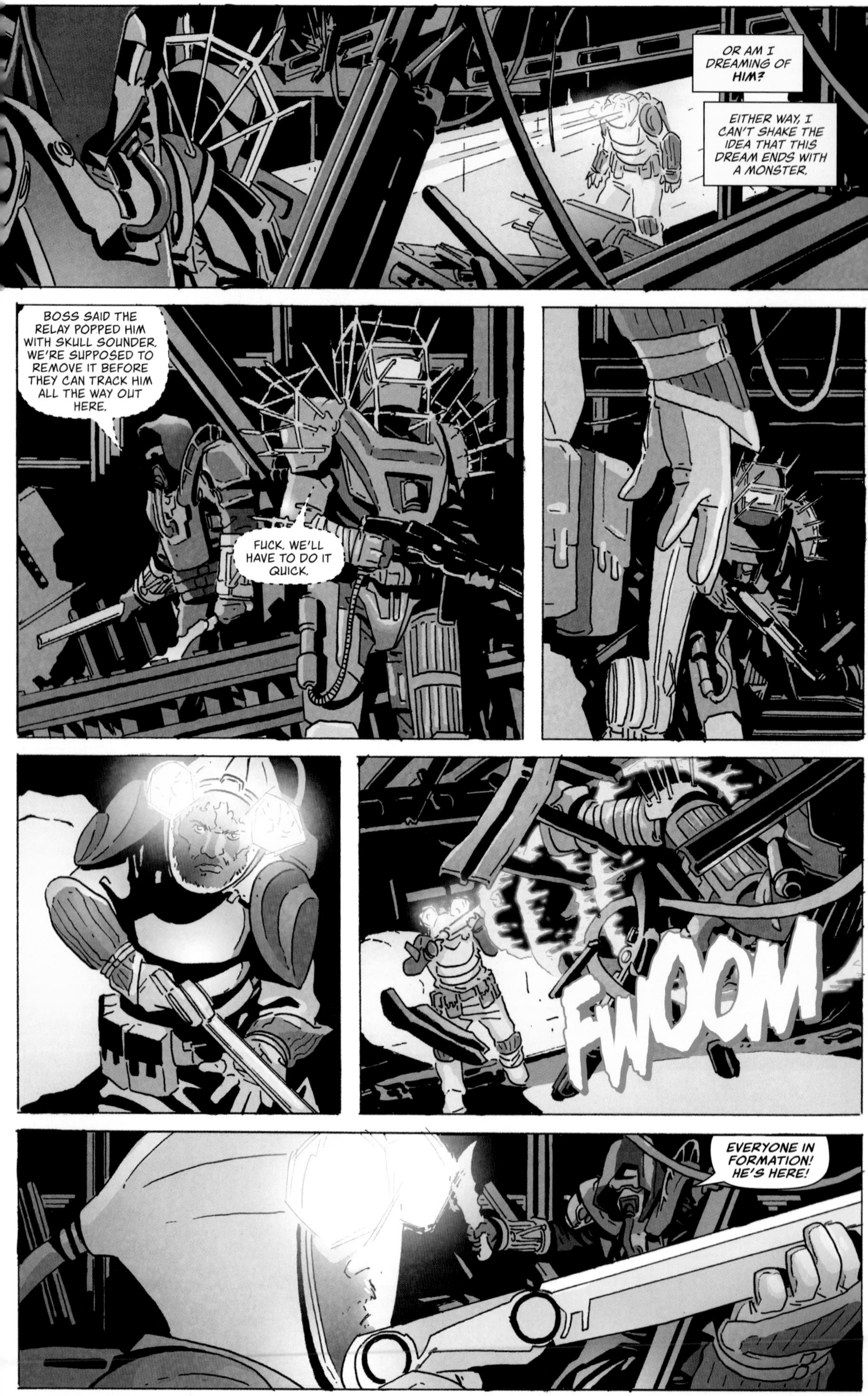
OR AM I DREAMING OF HIM?
EITHER WAY, I CAN'T SHAKE THE IDEA THAT THIS DREAM ENDS WITH A MONSTER.
BOSS SAID THE RELAY POPPED HIM WITH SKULL SOUNDER. WE'RE SUPPOSED TO REMOVE IT BEFORE THEY CAN TRACK HIM ALL THE WAY OUT HERE.
FUCK. WE'LL HAVE TO DO IT QUICK.
FWOOM
EVERYONE IN FORMATION! HE'S HERE!

BARAKKA
BARAKKA

TING
TING
TING

FWOOM

ARGH!

AHHHH!

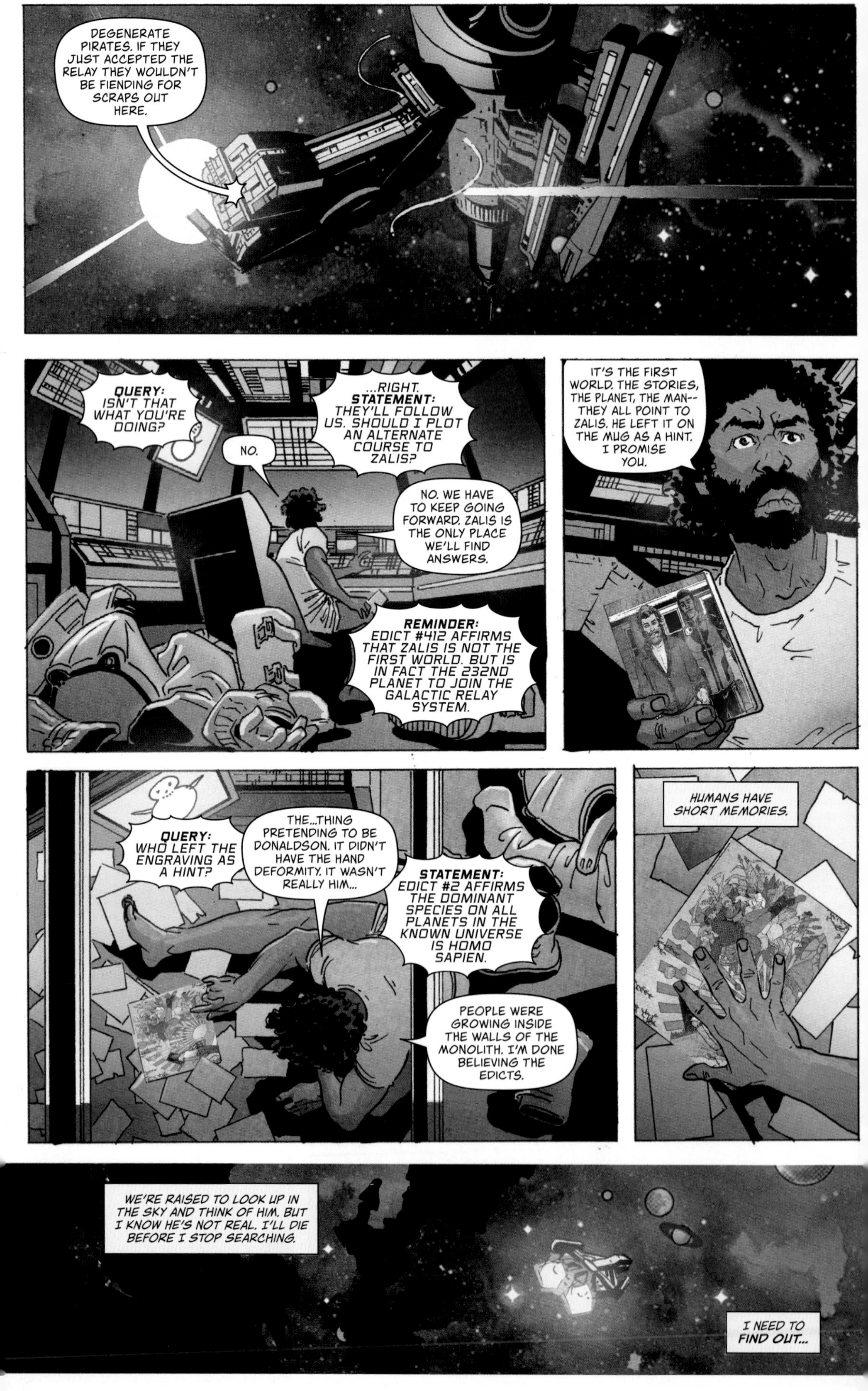
DEGENERATE PIRATES. IF THEY JUST ACCEPTED THE RELAY THEY WOULDN'T BE FIENDING FOR SCRAPS OUT HERE.
QUERY: ISN'T THAT WHAT YOU'RE DOING?
NO.
...RIGHT. STATEMENT: THEY'LL FOLLOW US. SHOULD I PLOT AN ALTERNATE COURSE TO ZALIS?
NO. WE HAVE TO KEEP GOING FORWARD. ZALIS IS THE ONLY PLACE WE'LL FIND ANSWERS.
REMINDER: EDICT #412 AFFIRMS THAT ZALIS IS NOT THE FIRST WORLD. BUT IS IN FACT THE 232ND PLANET TO JOIN THE GALACTIC RELAY SYSTEM.
IT'S THE FIRST WORLD. THE STORIES, THE PLANET, THE MAN-- THEY ALL POINT TO ZALIS. HE LEFT IT ON THE MUG AS A HINT. I PROMISE YOU.
QUERY: WHO LEFT THE ENGRAVING AS A HINT?
THE...THING PRETENDING TO BE DONALDSON. IT DIDN'T HAVE THE HAND DEFORMITY. IT WASN'T REALLY HIM...
STATEMENT: EDICT #2 AFFIRMS THE DOMINANT SPECIES ON ALL PLANETS IN THE KNOWN UNIVERSE IS HOMO SAPIEN.
PEOPLE WERE GROWING INSIDE THE WALLS OF THE MONOLITH. I'M DONE BELIEVING THE EDICTS.
HUMANS HAVE SHORT MEMORIES.
WE'RE RAISED TO LOOK UP IN THE SKY AND THINK OF HIM. BUT I KNOW HE'S NOT REAL. I'LL DIE BEFORE I STOP SEARCHING.
I NEED TO FIND OUT...

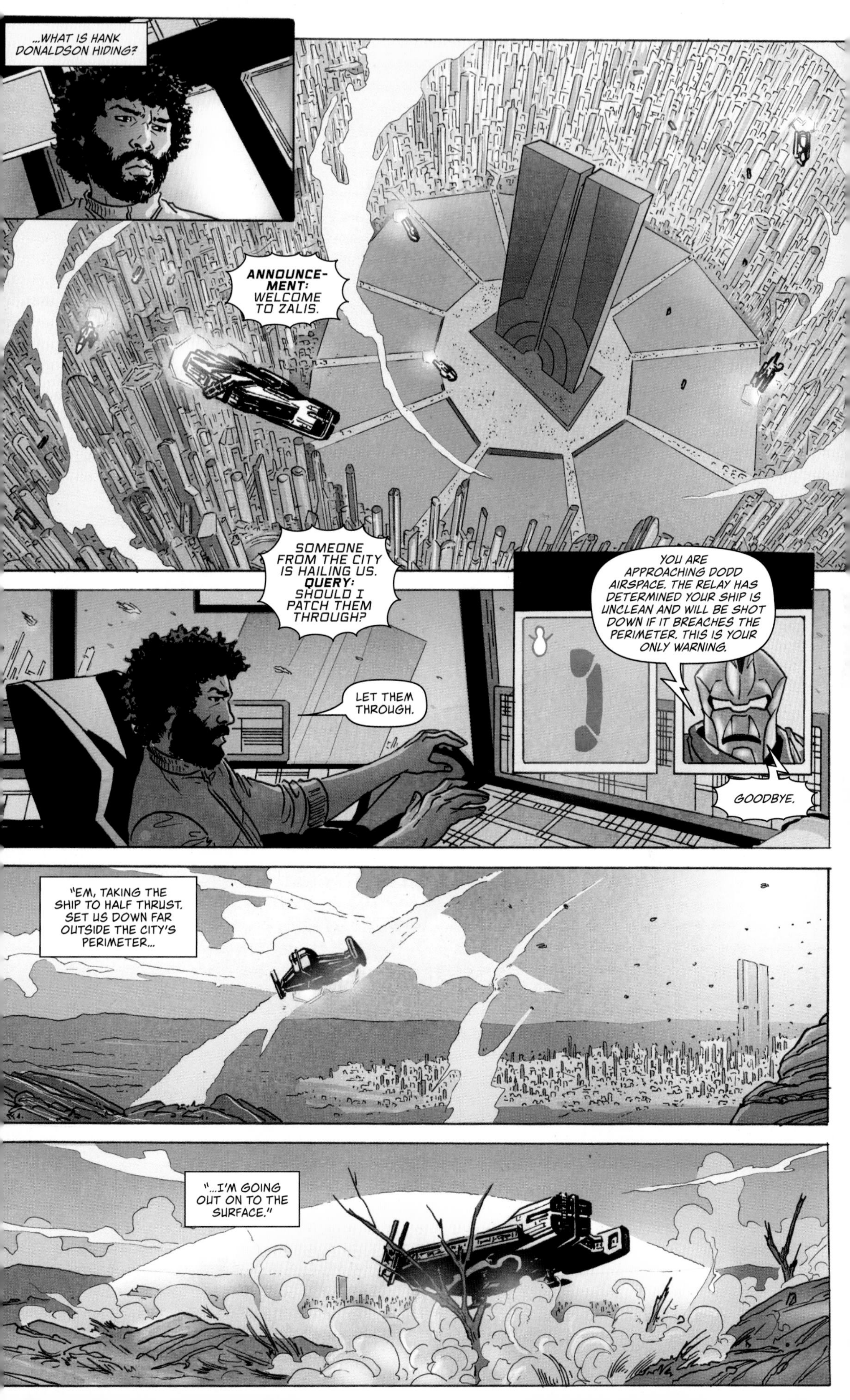
...WHAT IS HANK DONALDSON HIDING?
ANNOUNCEMENT: WELCOME TO ZALIS.
SOMEONE FROM THE CITY IS HAILING US. QUERY: SHOULD I PATCH THEM THROUGH?
LET THEM THROUGH.
YOU ARE APPROACHING DODD AIRSPACE. THE RELAY HAS DETERMINED YOUR SHIP IS UNCLEAN AND WILL BE SHOT DOWN IF IT BREACHES THE PERIMETER. THIS IS YOUR ONLY WARNING.
GOODBYE.
"EM, TAKING THE SHIP TO HALF THRUST. SET US DOWN FAR OUTSIDE THE CITY'S PERIMETER...
"...I'M GOING OUT ON TO THE SURFACE."

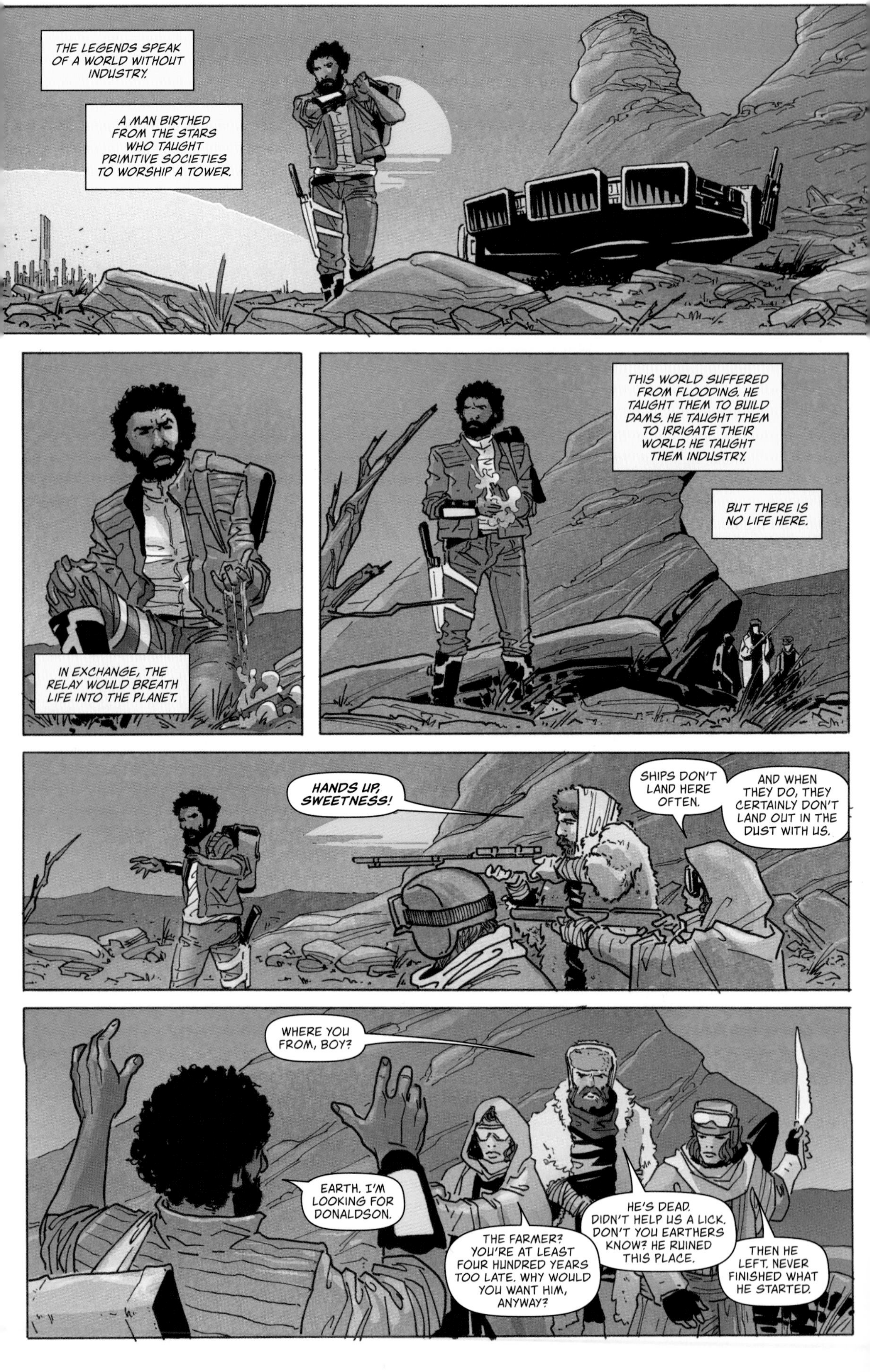
THE LEGENDS SPEAK OF A WORLD WITHOUT INDUSTRY.
A MAN BIRTHED FROM THE STARS WHO TAUGHT PRIMITIVE SOCIETIES TO WORSHIP A TOWER.
IN EXCHANGE, THE RELAY WOULD BREATH LIFE INTO THE PLANET.
THIS WORLD SUFFERED FROM FLOODING. HE TAUGHT THEM TO BUILD DAMS. HE TAUGHT THEM TO IRRIGATE THEIR WORLD. HE TAUGHT THEM INDUSTRY.
BUT THERE IS NO LIFE HERE.
HANDS UP, SWEETNESS!
SHIPS DON'T LAND HERE OFTEN.
AND WHEN THEY DO, THEY CERTAINLY DON'T LAND OUT IN THE DUST WITH US.
WHERE YOU FROM, BOY?
EARTH. I'M LOOKING FOR DONALDSON.
THE FARMER? YOU'RE AT LEAST FOUR HUNDRED YEARS TOO LATE. WHY WOULD YOU WANT HIM, ANYWAY?
HE'S DEAD. DIDN'T HELP US A LICK. DON'T YOU EARTHERS KNOW? HE RUINED THIS PLACE.
THEN HE LEFT. NEVER FINISHED WHAT HE STARTED.

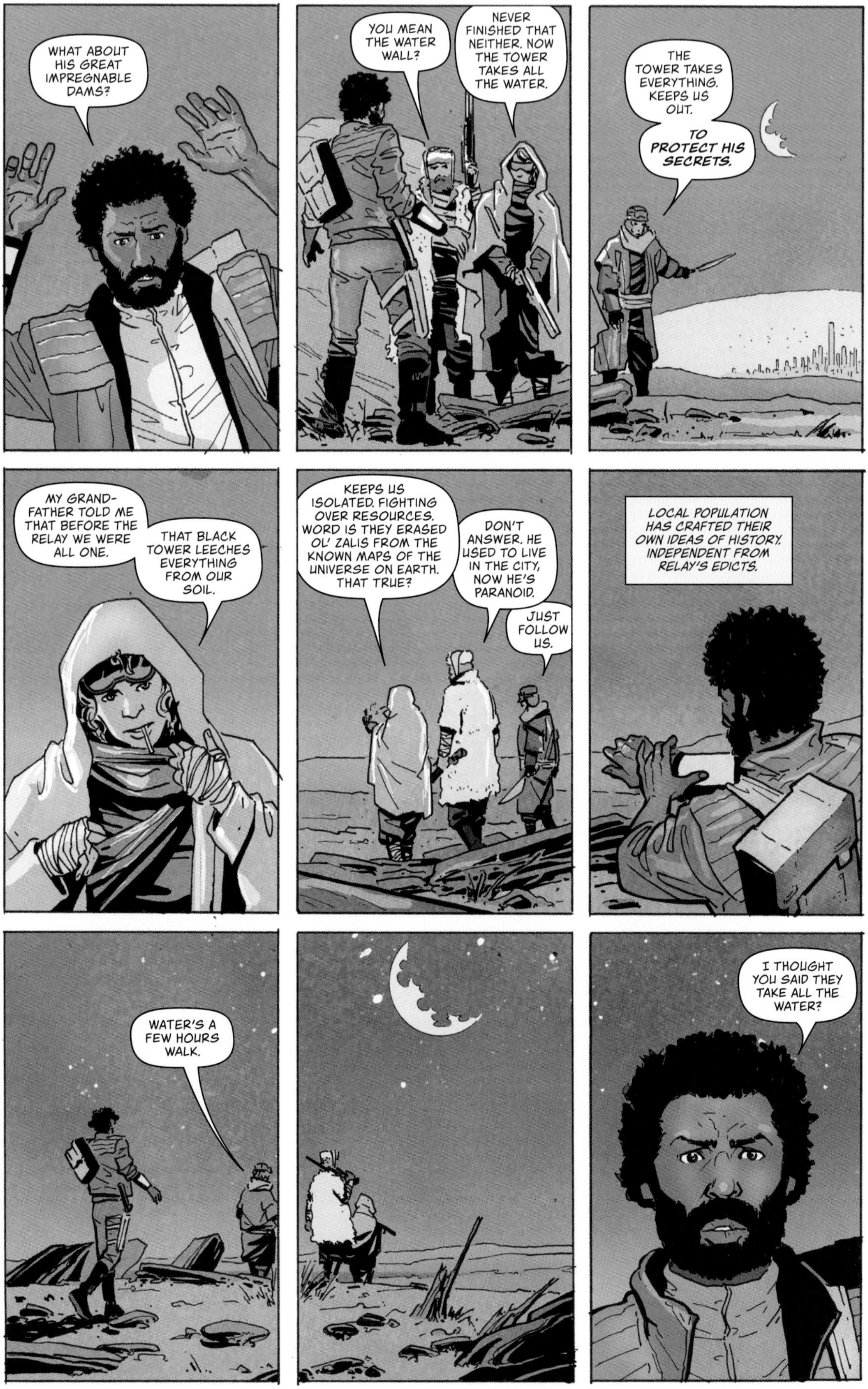
WHAT ABOUT HIS GREAT IMPREGNABLE DAMS?
YOU MEAN THE WATER WALL?
NEVER FINISHED THAT NEITHER. NOW THE TOWER TAKES ALL THE WATER.
THE TOWER TAKES EVERYTHING. KEEPS US OUT.
TO PROTECT HIS SECRETS.
MY GRAND-FATHER TOLD ME THAT BEFORE THE RELAY WE WERE ALL ONE.
THAT BLACK TOWER LEECHES EVERYTHING FROM OUR SOIL.
KEEPS US ISOLATED. FIGHTING OVER RESOURCES. WORD IS THEY ERASED OL' ZALIS FROM THE KNOWN MAPS OF THE UNIVERSE ON EARTH. THAT TRUE?
DON'T ANSWER. HE USED TO LIVE IN THE CITY, NOW HE'S PARANOID.
JUST FOLLOW US.
LOCAL POPULATION HAS CRAFTED THEIR OWN IDEAS OF HISTORY. INDEPENDENT FROM RELAY'S EDICTS.
WATER'S A FEW HOURS WALK.
I THOUGHT YOU SAID THEY TAKE ALL THE WATER?

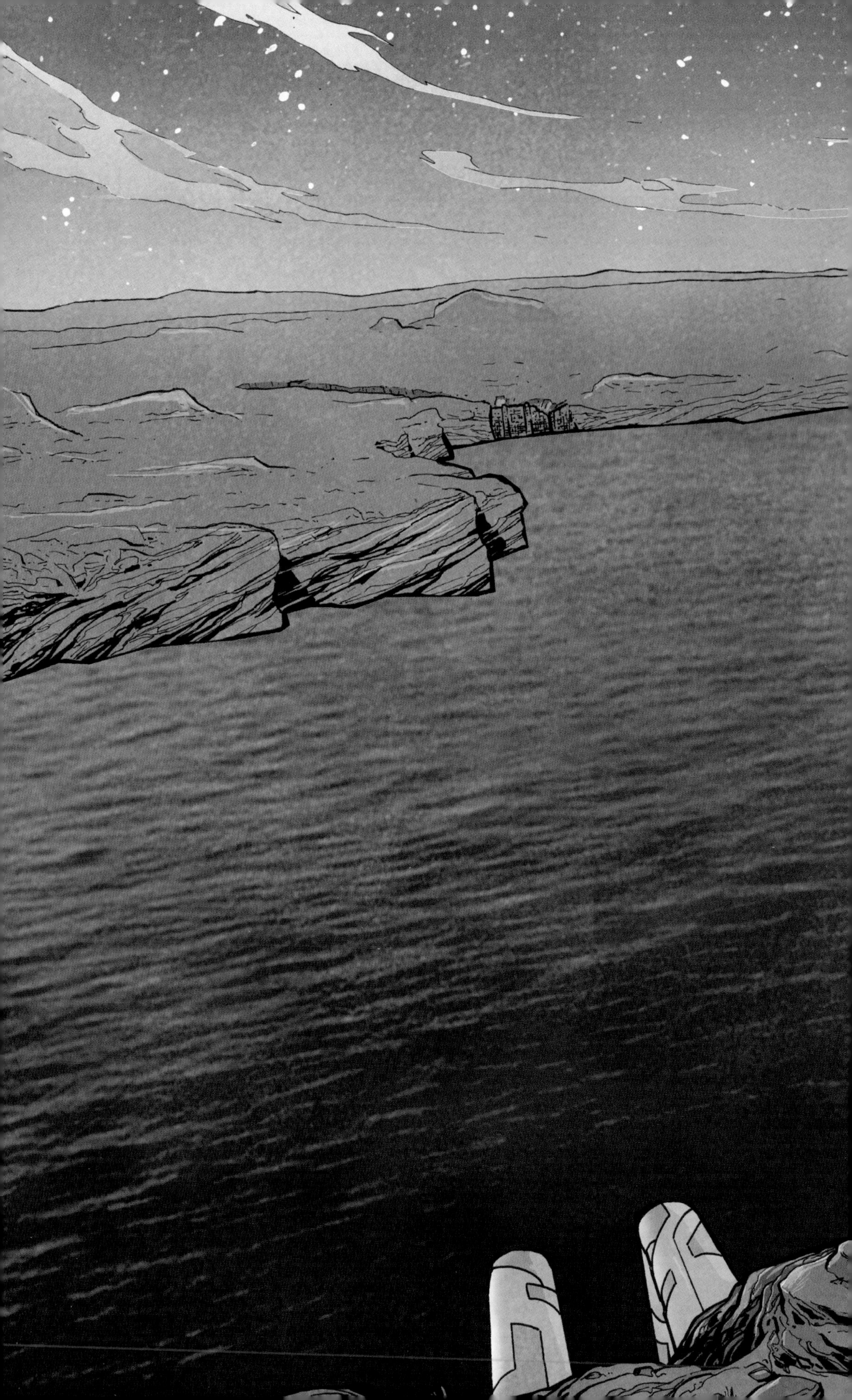

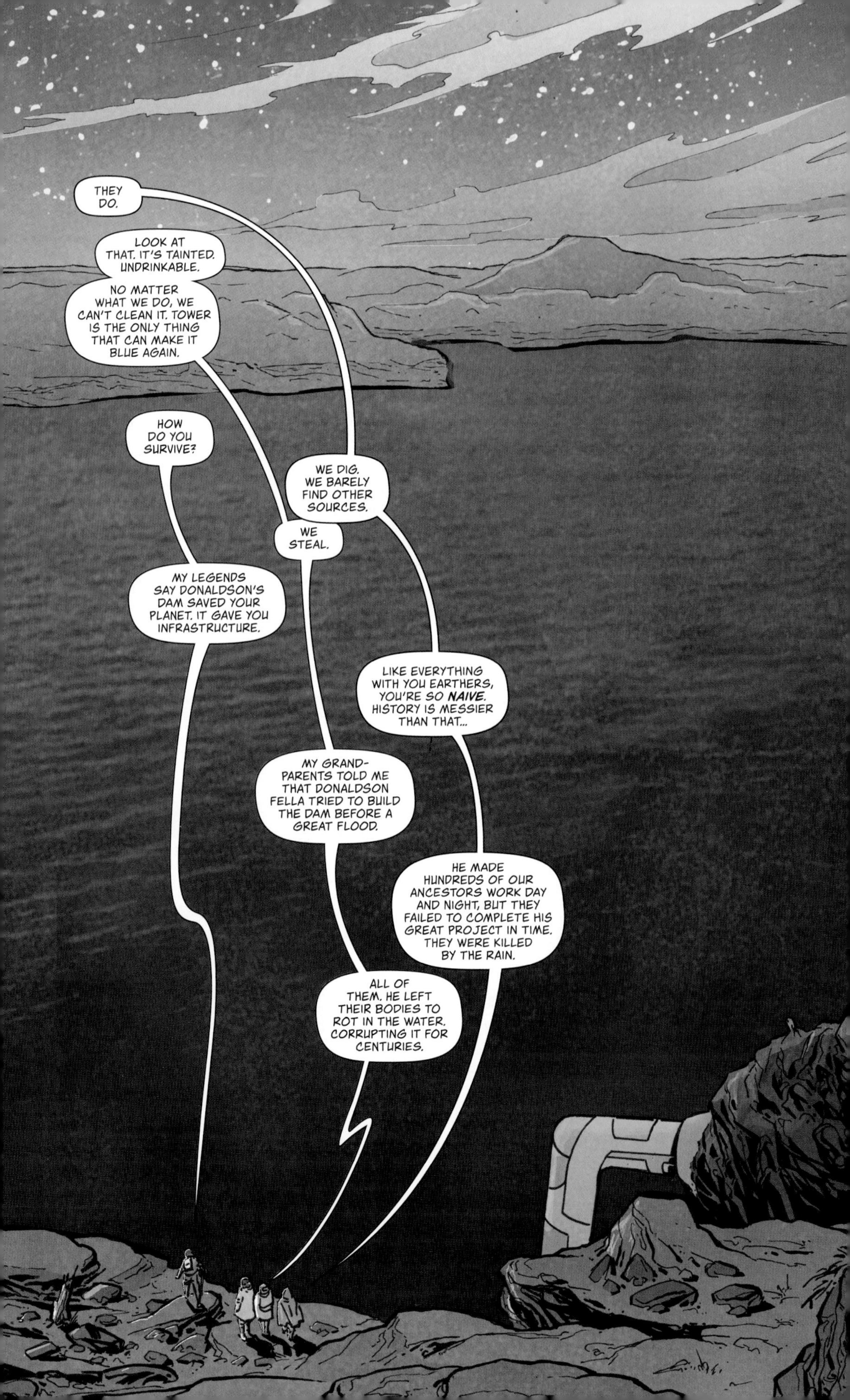
THEY DO.
LOOK AT THAT. IT'S TAINTED. UNDRINKABLE.
NO MATTER WHAT WE DO, WE CAN'T CLEAN IT. TOWER IS THE ONLY THING THAT CAN MAKE IT BLUE AGAIN.
HOW DO YOU SURVIVE?
WE DIG. WE BARELY FIND OTHER SOURCES.
WE STEAL.
MY LEGENDS SAY DONALDSON'S DAM SAVED YOUR PLANET. IT GAVE YOU INFRASTRUCTURE.
LIKE EVERYTHING WITH YOU EARTHERS, YOU'RE SO NAIVE. HISTORY IS MESSIER THAN THAT...
MY GRAND-PARENTS TOLD ME THAT DONALDSON FELLA TRIED TO BUILD THE DAM BEFORE A GREAT FLOOD.
HE MADE HUNDREDS OF OUR ANCESTORS WORK DAY AND NIGHT, BUT THEY FAILED TO COMPLETE HIS GREAT PROJECT IN TIME. THEY WERE KILLED BY THE RAIN.
ALL OF THEM. HE LEFT THEIR BODIES TO ROT IN THE WATER. CORRUPTING IT FOR CENTURIES.

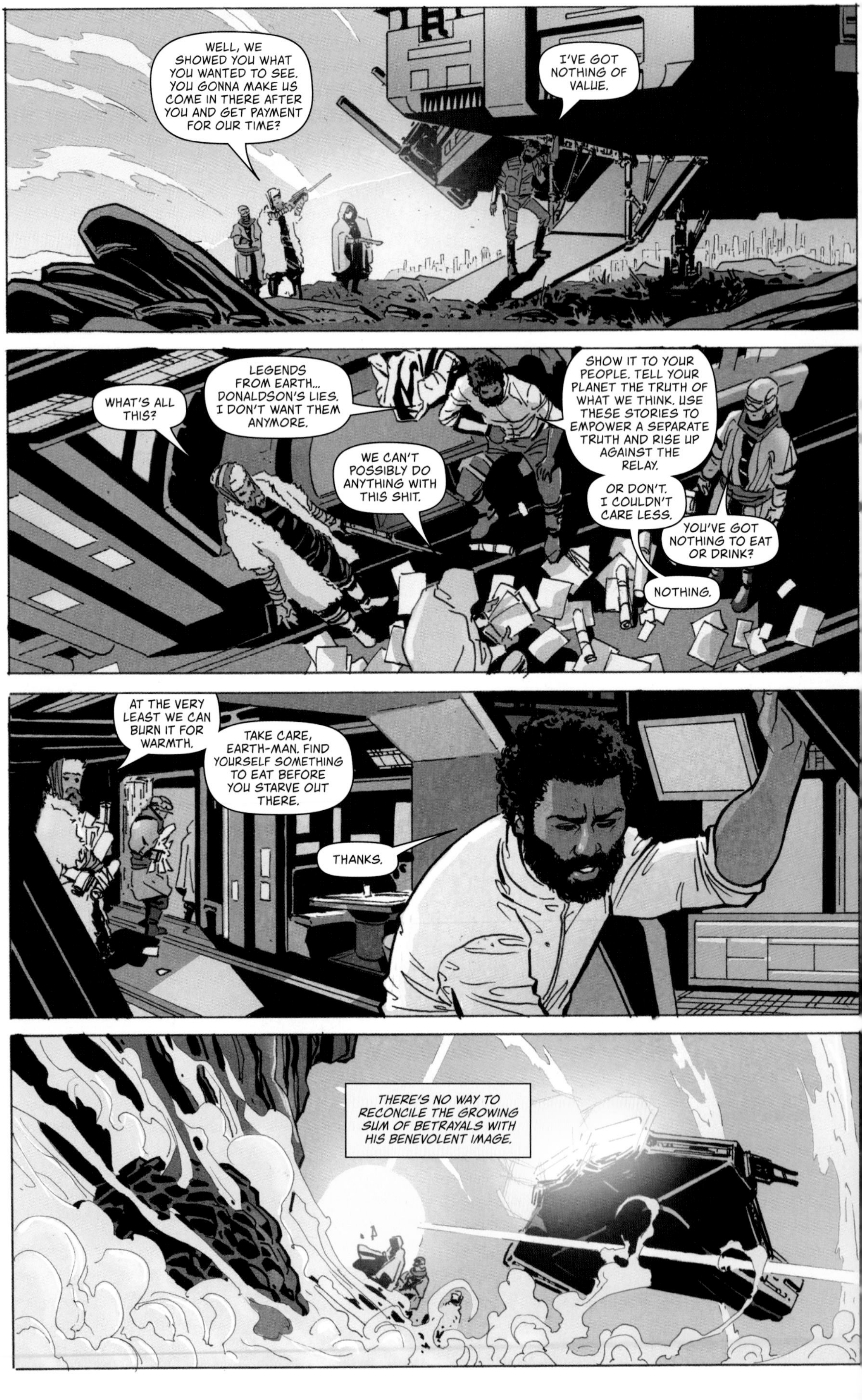
WELL, WE SHOWED YOU WHAT YOU WANTED TO SEE. YOU GONNA MAKE US COME IN THERE AFTER YOU AND GET PAYMENT FOR OUR TIME?
I'VE GOT NOTHING OF VALUE.
WHAT'S ALL THIS?
LEGENDS FROM EARTH... DONALDSON'S LIES. I DON'T WANT THEM ANYMORE.
WE CAN'T POSSIBLY DO ANYTHING WITH THIS SHIT.
SHOW IT TO YOUR PEOPLE. TELL YOUR PLANET THE TRUTH OF WHAT WE THINK. USE THESE STORIES TO EMPOWER A SEPARATE TRUTH AND RISE UP AGAINST THE RELAY.
OR DON'T. I COULDN'T CARE LESS.
YOU'VE GOT NOTHING TO EAT OR DRINK?
NOTHING.
AT THE VERY LEAST WE CAN BURN IT FOR WARMTH.
TAKE CARE, EARTH-MAN. FIND YOURSELF SOMETHING TO EAT BEFORE YOU STARVE OUT THERE.
THANKS.
THERE'S NO WAY TO RECONCILE THE GROWING SUM OF BETRAYALS WITH HIS BENEVOLENT IMAGE.

THE FIRST WORLD REMAINS. THE EDICT IS A LIE.

BUT THE PLANET IS BROKEN. UNBALANCED. THE LEGENDS ARE ALSO A LIE.

THE PEOPLE OF ZALIS RESENT HIM. FOR HE IS SHATTERED VISAGE.

AND YET I SEE HIM IN MYSELF. IN MY MIND'S EYE HE'S MY YOUTHFUL PROCLAMATION OF BETTER THINGS.

IS HE A SUBSTITUTION FOR MEANING IN THE UNIVERSE?

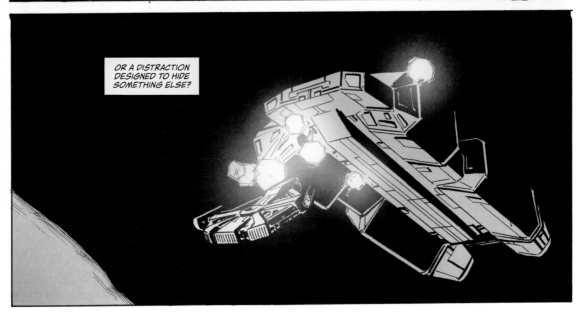

OR A DISTRACTION DESIGNED TO HIDE SOMETHING ELSE?

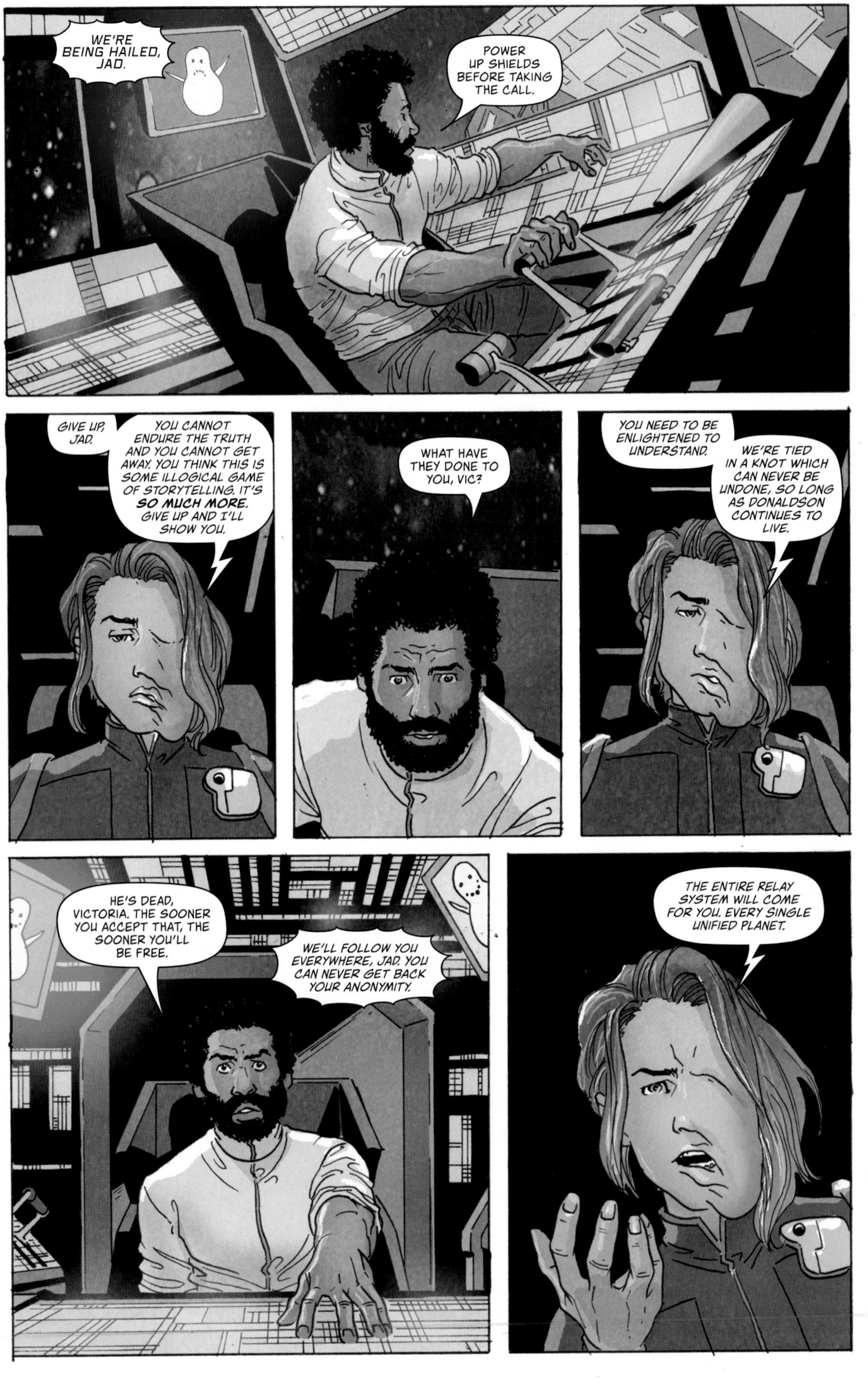
WE'RE BEING HAILED, JAD.
POWER UP SHIELDS BEFORE TAKING THE CALL.
GIVE UP, JAD.
YOU CANNOT ENDURE THE TRUTH AND YOU CANNOT GET AWAY. YOU THINK THIS IS SOME ILLOGICAL GAME OF STORYTELLING. IT'S **SO MUCH MORE.** GIVE UP AND I'LL SHOW YOU.
WHAT HAVE THEY DONE TO YOU, VIC?
YOU NEED TO BE ENLIGHTENED TO UNDERSTAND.
WE'RE TIED IN A KNOT WHICH CAN NEVER BE UNDONE, SO LONG AS DONALDSON CONTINUES TO LIVE.
HE'S DEAD, VICTORIA. THE SOONER YOU ACCEPT THAT, THE SOONER YOU'LL BE FREE.
WE'LL FOLLOW YOU EVERYWHERE, JAD. YOU CAN NEVER GET BACK YOUR ANONYMITY.
THE ENTIRE RELAY SYSTEM WILL COME FOR YOU. EVERY SINGLE UNIFIED PLANET.

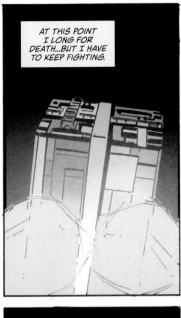

AT THIS POINT I LONG FOR DEATH...BUT I HAVE TO KEEP FIGHTING.

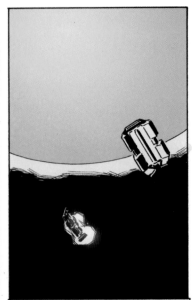

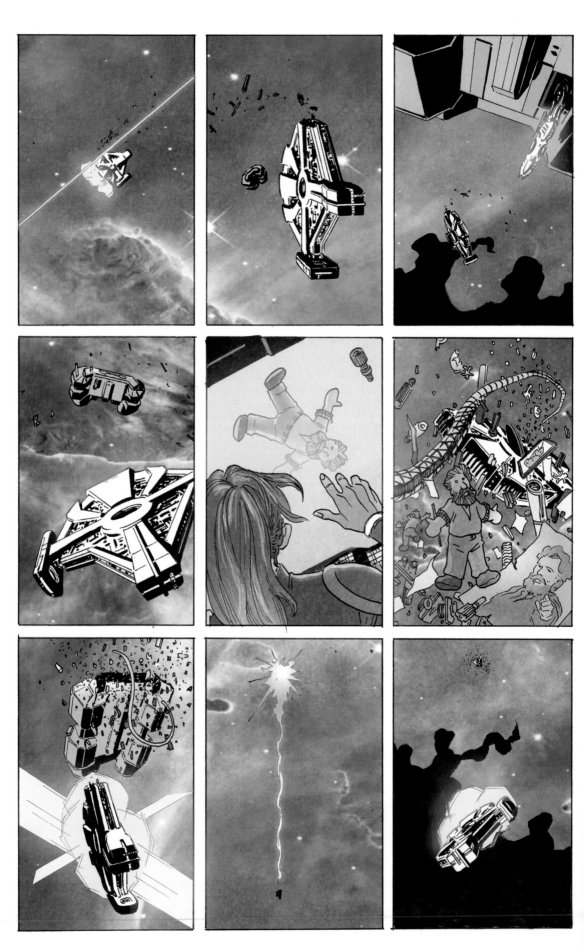

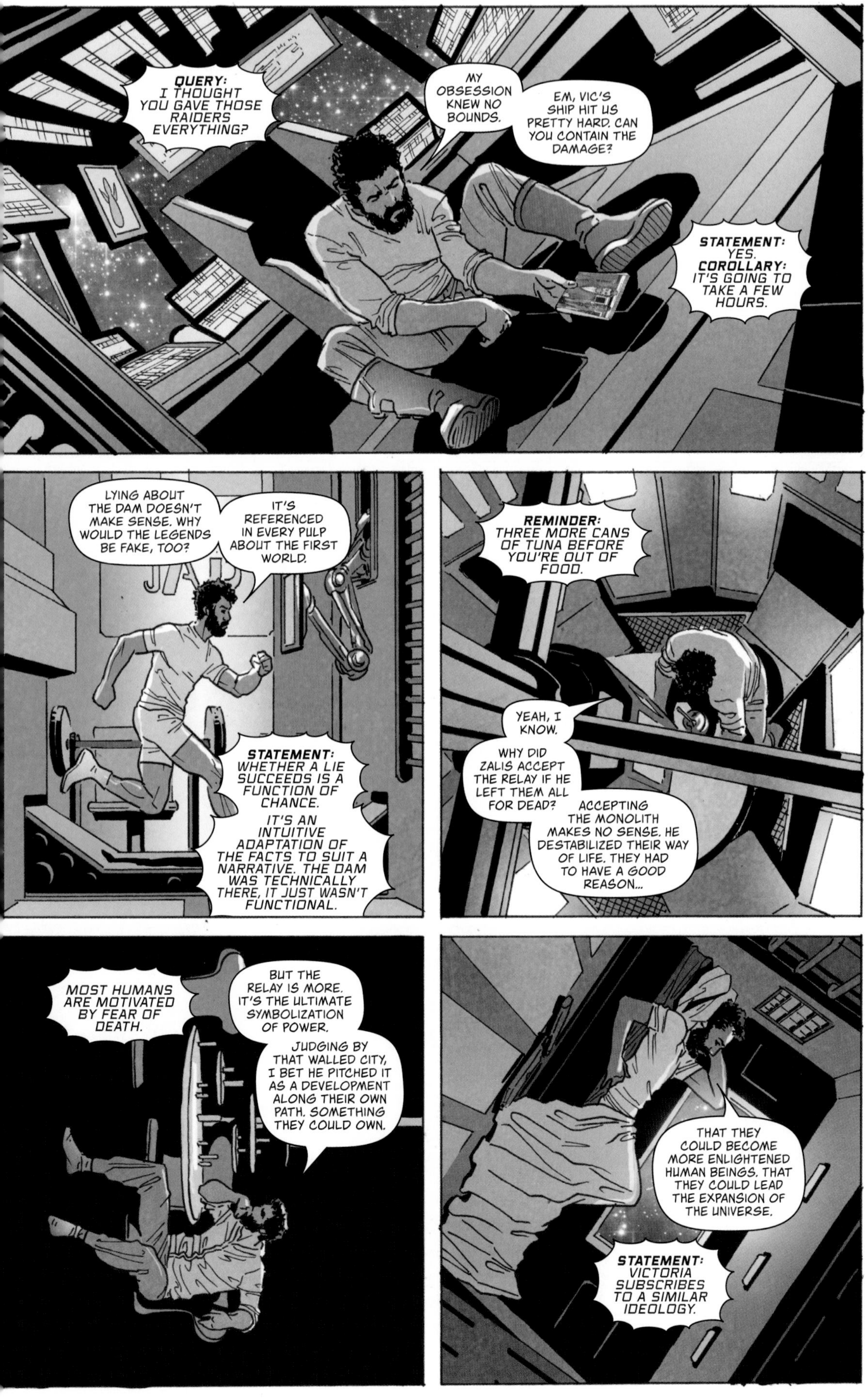
QUERY: I THOUGHT YOU GAVE THOSE RAIDERS EVERYTHING?
MY OBSESSION KNEW NO BOUNDS.
EM, VIC'S SHIP HIT US PRETTY HARD. CAN YOU CONTAIN THE DAMAGE?
STATEMENT: YES. COROLLARY: IT'S GOING TO TAKE A FEW HOURS.
LYING ABOUT THE DAM DOESN'T MAKE SENSE. WHY WOULD THE LEGENDS BE FAKE, TOO?
IT'S REFERENCED IN EVERY PULP ABOUT THE FIRST WORLD.
STATEMENT: WHETHER A LIE SUCCEEDS IS A FUNCTION OF CHANCE.
IT'S AN INTUITIVE ADAPTATION OF THE FACTS TO SUIT A NARRATIVE. THE DAM WAS TECHNICALLY THERE, IT JUST WASN'T FUNCTIONAL.
REMINDER: THREE MORE CANS OF TUNA BEFORE YOU'RE OUT OF FOOD.
YEAH, I KNOW.
WHY DID ZALIS ACCEPT THE RELAY IF HE LEFT THEM ALL FOR DEAD?
ACCEPTING THE MONOLITH MAKES NO SENSE. HE DESTABILIZED THEIR WAY OF LIFE. THEY HAD TO HAVE A GOOD REASON...
MOST HUMANS ARE MOTIVATED BY FEAR OF DEATH.
BUT THE RELAY IS MORE. IT'S THE ULTIMATE SYMBOLIZATION OF POWER.
JUDGING BY THAT WALLED CITY, I BET HE PITCHED IT AS A DEVELOPMENT ALONG THEIR OWN PATH. SOMETHING THEY COULD OWN.
THAT THEY COULD BECOME MORE ENLIGHTENED HUMAN BEINGS. THAT THEY COULD LEAD THE EXPANSION OF THE UNIVERSE.
STATEMENT: VICTORIA SUBSCRIBES TO A SIMILAR IDEOLOGY.

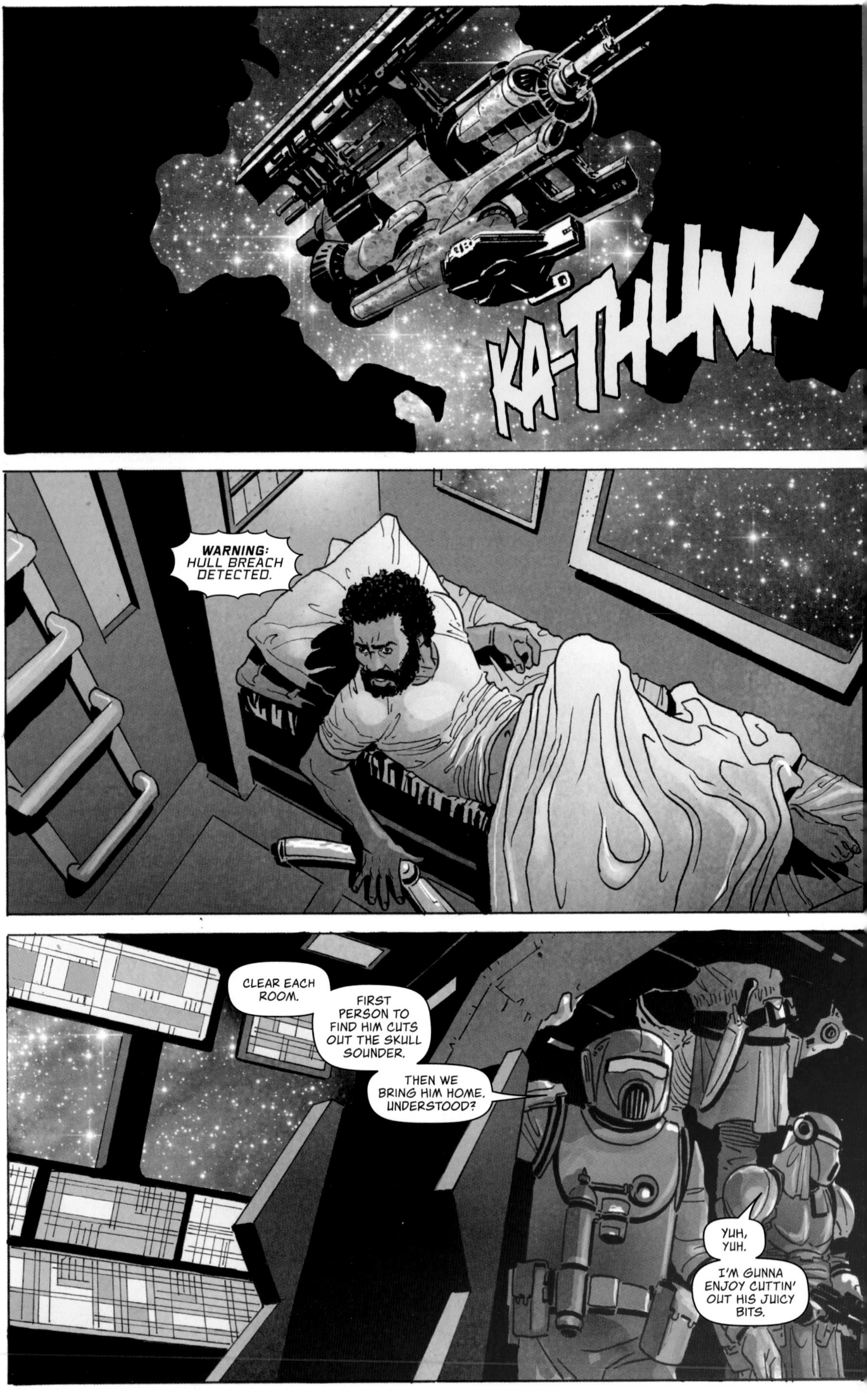
KA-THUNK
WARNING: HULL BREACH DETECTED.
CLEAR EACH ROOM.
FIRST PERSON TO FIND HIM CUTS OUT THE SKULL SOUNDER.
THEN WE BRING HIM HOME. UNDERSTOOD?
YUH, YUH.
I'M GUNNA ENJOY CUTTIN' OUT HIS JUICY BITS.

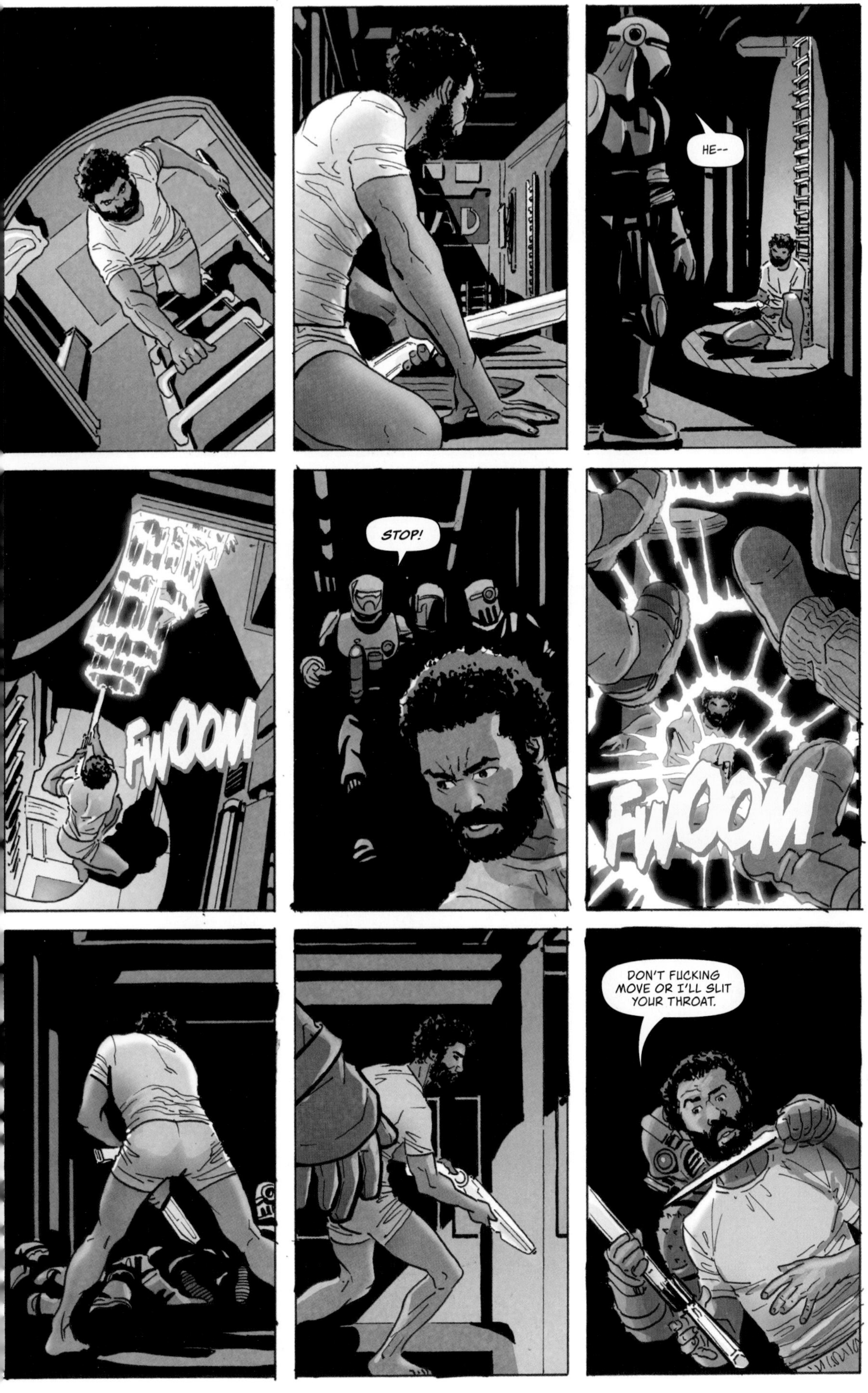
HE--
FWOOM
STOP!
FWOOM
DON'T FUCKING MOVE OR I'LL SLIT YOUR THROAT.

HOLD HIM DOWN.
I'M GOING TO DO IT.
GET OFF OF ME!
YOU'VE GOT SOMETHING IN YOUR SKULL. AND WE NEED IT.
IF YOU'RE GOING TO KILL ME...GET IT OVER WITH.
ACK!
GOT THE SOUNDER.

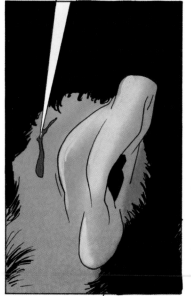

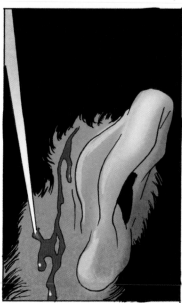

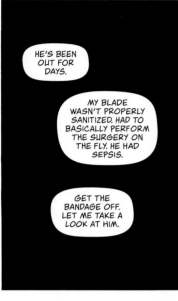

HE'S BEEN OUT FOR DAYS.

MY BLADE WASN'T PROPERLY SANITIZED. HAD TO BASICALLY PERFORM THE SURGERY ON THE FLY. HE HAD SEPSIS.

GET THE BANDAGE OFF. LET ME TAKE A LOOK AT HIM.

WHERE AM I?

WHAT HAPPENED TO MY SHIP?

YOU'RE EXPERIENCING SOME ACUTE HYSTERIA. JUST CALM DOWN. ALL WILL BE CLEAR.

YOU WERE BEING TRACKED.

I'M WILLEM. I KNOW I DON'T LOOK IT, BUT I'M OUR LEAD MEDICAL OFFICER.

WE HAD TO CUT A RELAY TRACKING DEVICE OUT OF YOUR HEAD. THEY CALL 'EM SKULL SOUNDERS.

YOUR BUDS INSIDE THE MONOLITH PUT A METAL ROD UP YOUR SPINE WHILE YOU WERE SLEEPING.

...ARE YOU?

OUR GREAT LEADER HAD ME TAKE IT OUT BEFORE WE BROUGHT YOU HERE.

I ASSURE YOU...

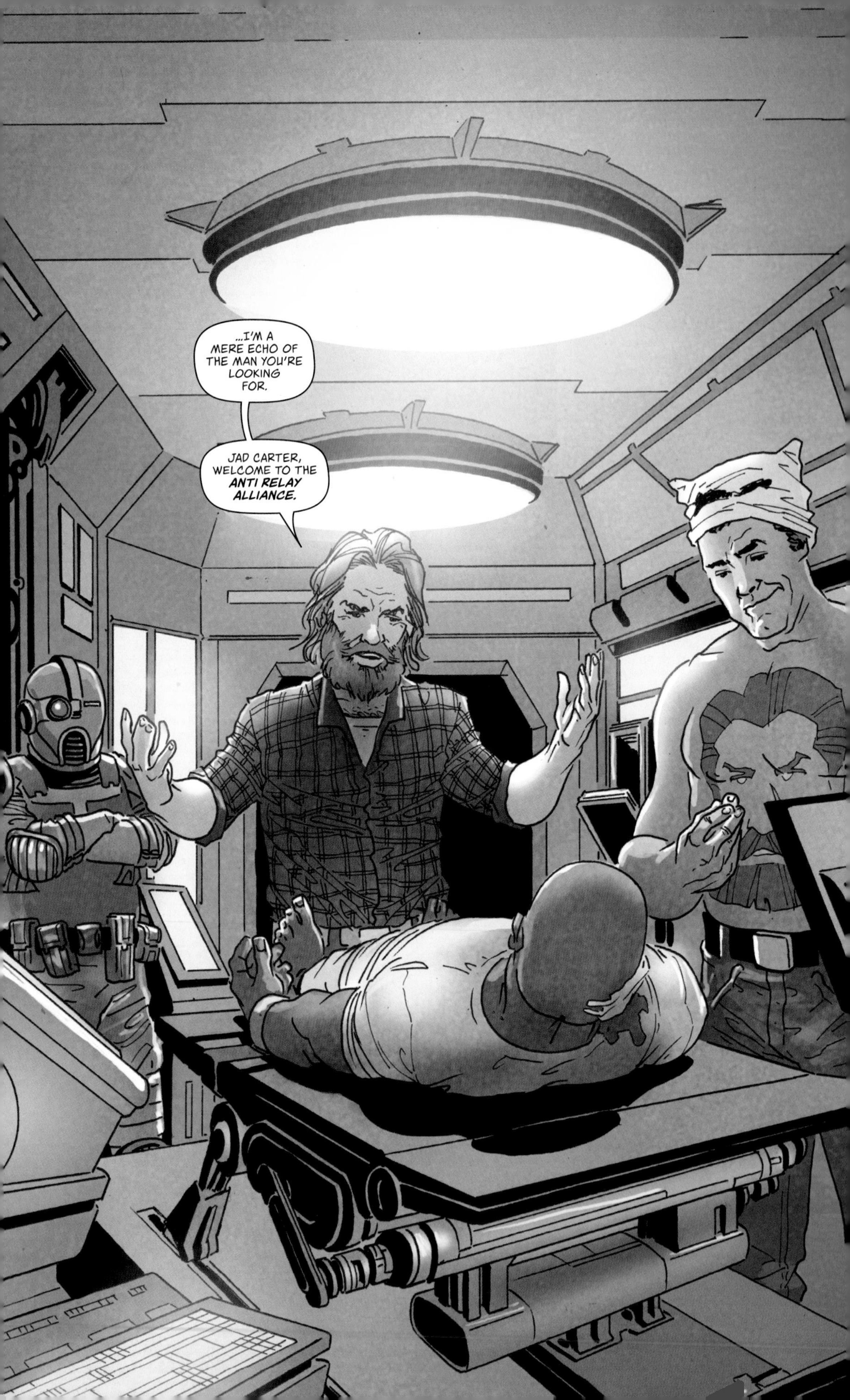
...I'M A MERE ECHO OF THE MAN YOU'RE LOOKING FOR.
JAD CARTER, WELCOME TO THE *ANTI RELAY ALLIANCE.*

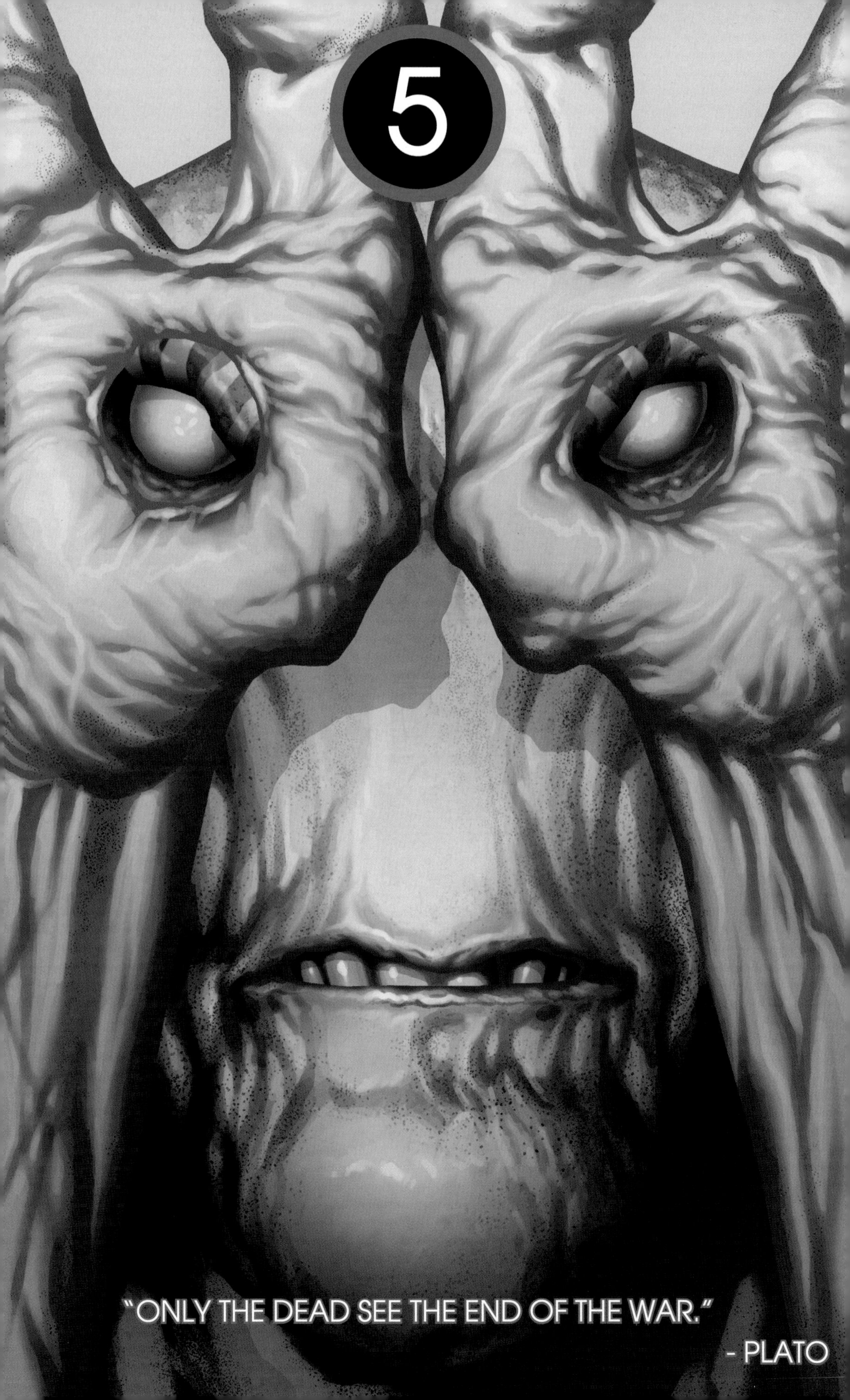

5

"ONLY THE DEAD SEE THE END OF THE WAR."

- PLATO

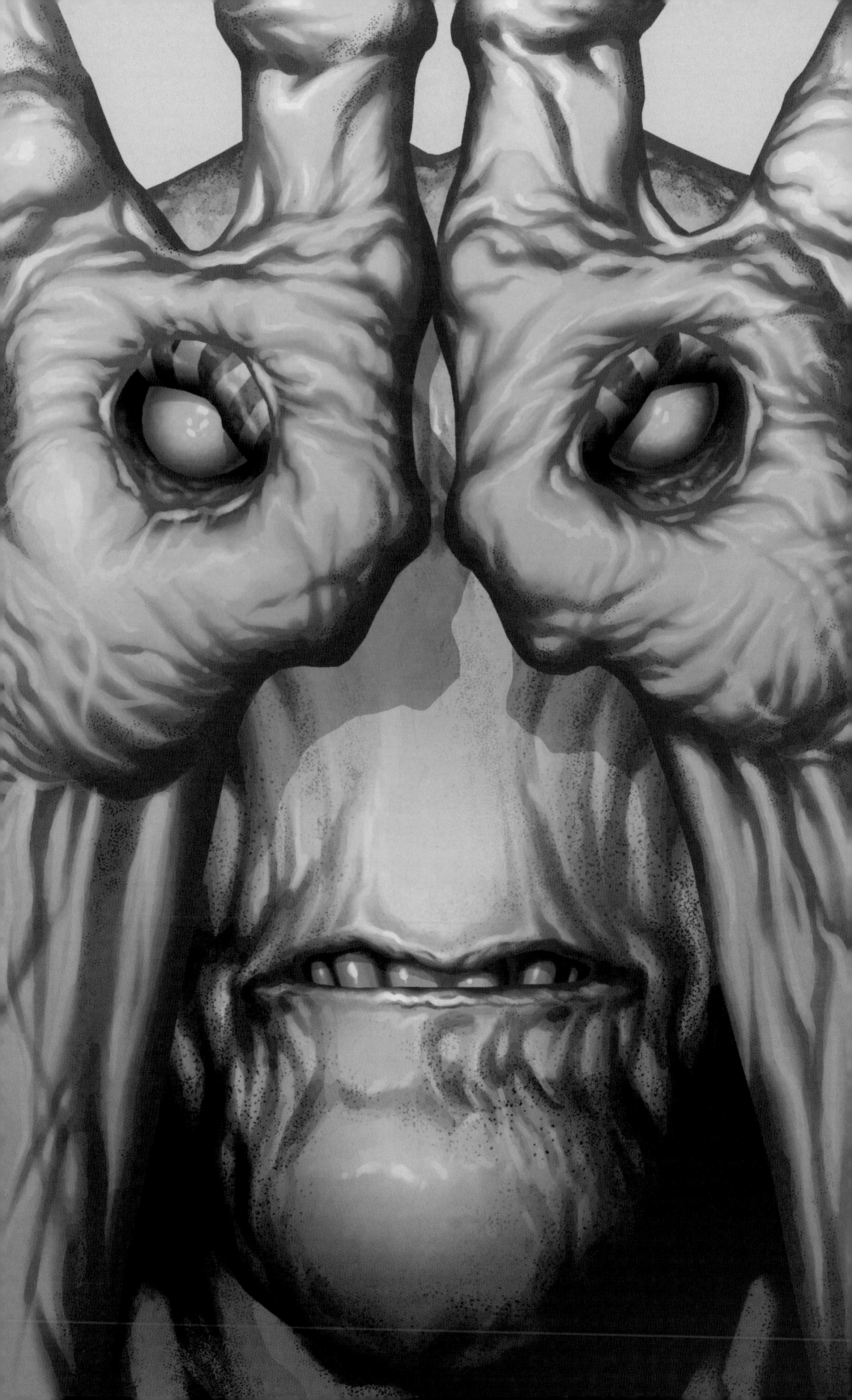

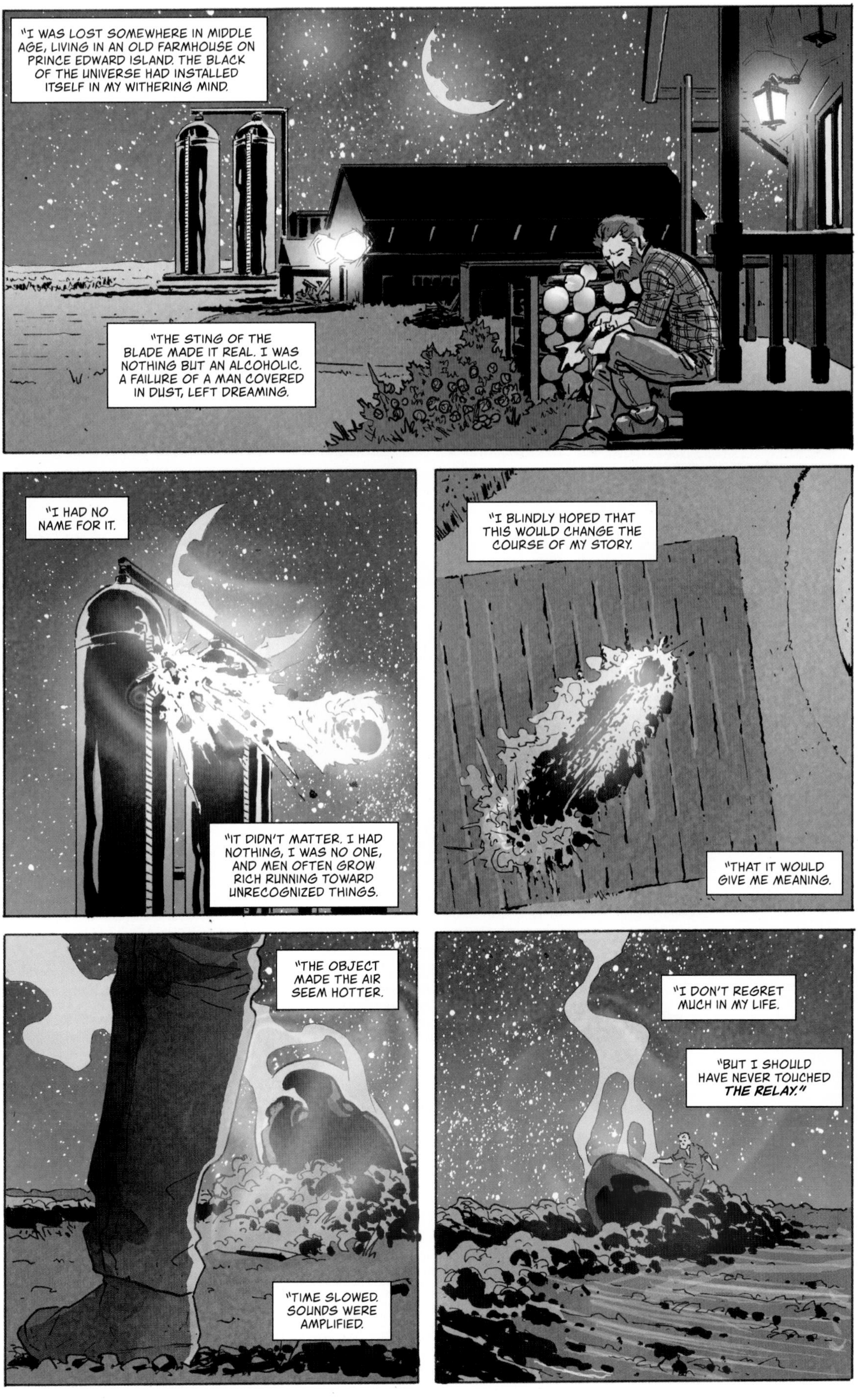
"I WAS LOST SOMEWHERE IN MIDDLE AGE, LIVING IN AN OLD FARMHOUSE ON PRINCE EDWARD ISLAND. THE BLACK OF THE UNIVERSE HAD INSTALLED ITSELF IN MY WITHERING MIND.
"THE STING OF THE BLADE MADE IT REAL. I WAS NOTHING BUT AN ALCOHOLIC. A FAILURE OF A MAN COVERED IN DUST, LEFT DREAMING.
"I HAD NO NAME FOR IT.
"IT DIDN'T MATTER. I HAD NOTHING, I WAS NO ONE, AND MEN OFTEN GROW RICH RUNNING TOWARD UNRECOGNIZED THINGS.
"I BLINDLY HOPED THAT THIS WOULD CHANGE THE COURSE OF MY STORY.
"THAT IT WOULD GIVE ME MEANING.
"THE OBJECT MADE THE AIR SEEM HOTTER.
"TIME SLOWED. SOUNDS WERE AMPLIFIED.
"I DON'T REGRET MUCH IN MY LIFE.
"BUT I SHOULD HAVE NEVER TOUCHED ***THE RELAY."***

"IT WAS AN ERROR IN JUDGMENT.

"I HARDLY RECOGNIZED MYSELF THAT NIGHT.

"SUDDENLY, I'M OUTSIDE MY OWN BODY.

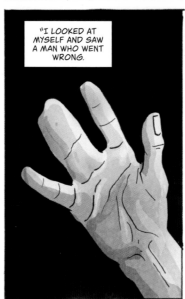

"I LOOKED AT MYSELF AND SAW A MAN WHO WENT WRONG.

"REALITY REWROTE ITSELF IN AN INSTANT.

"I FELT KNOWLEDGE COURSE THROUGH MY VEINS, AND I KNEW...

"...I WAS DEAD.

"MY PARANOIA, MY FEAR, MY PROBLEMS..."

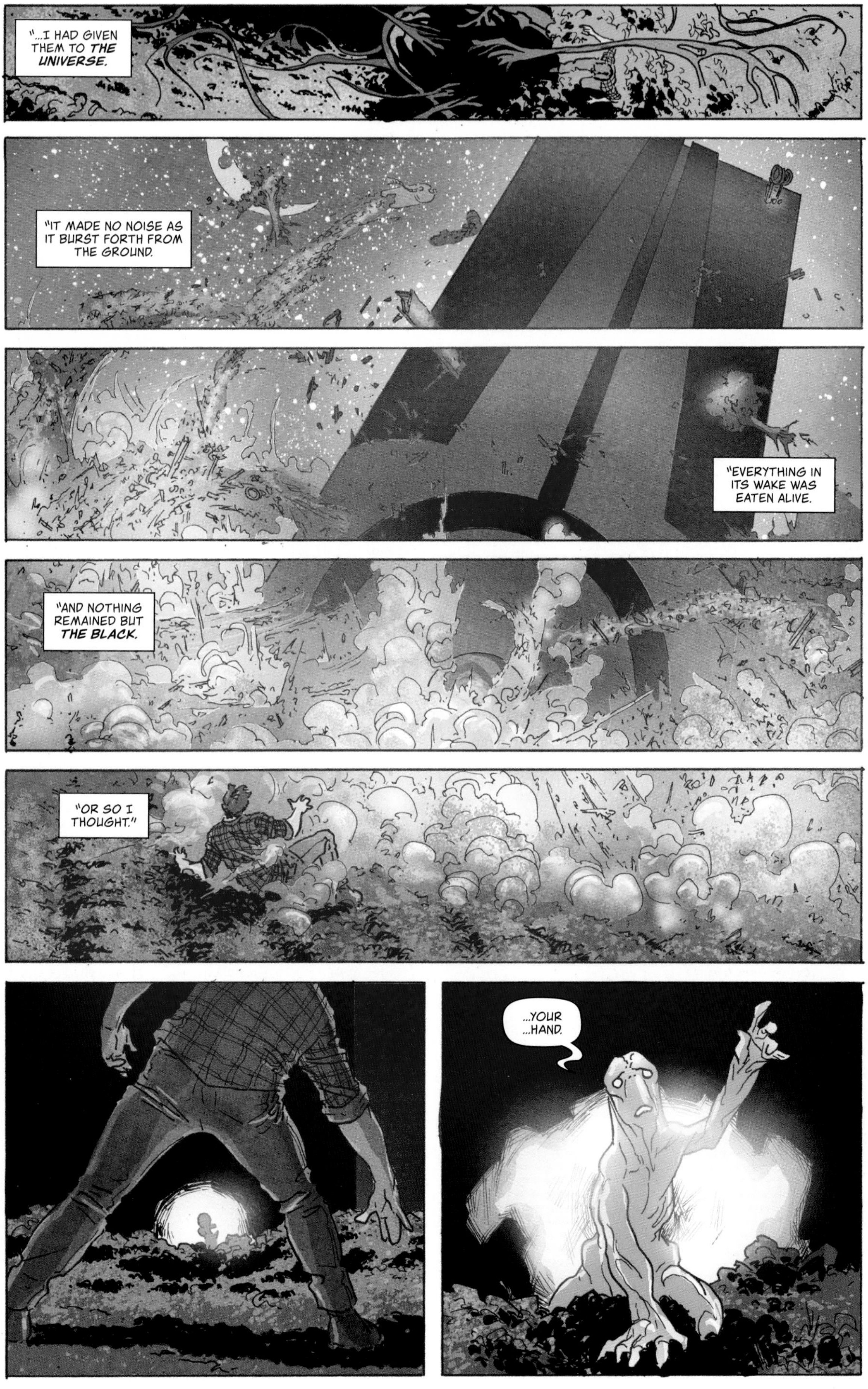
"...I HAD GIVEN THEM TO THE UNIVERSE.
"IT MADE NO NOISE AS IT BURST FORTH FROM THE GROUND.
"EVERYTHING IN ITS WAKE WAS EATEN ALIVE.
"AND NOTHING REMAINED BUT THE BLACK.
"OR SO I THOUGHT."
...YOUR ...HAND.

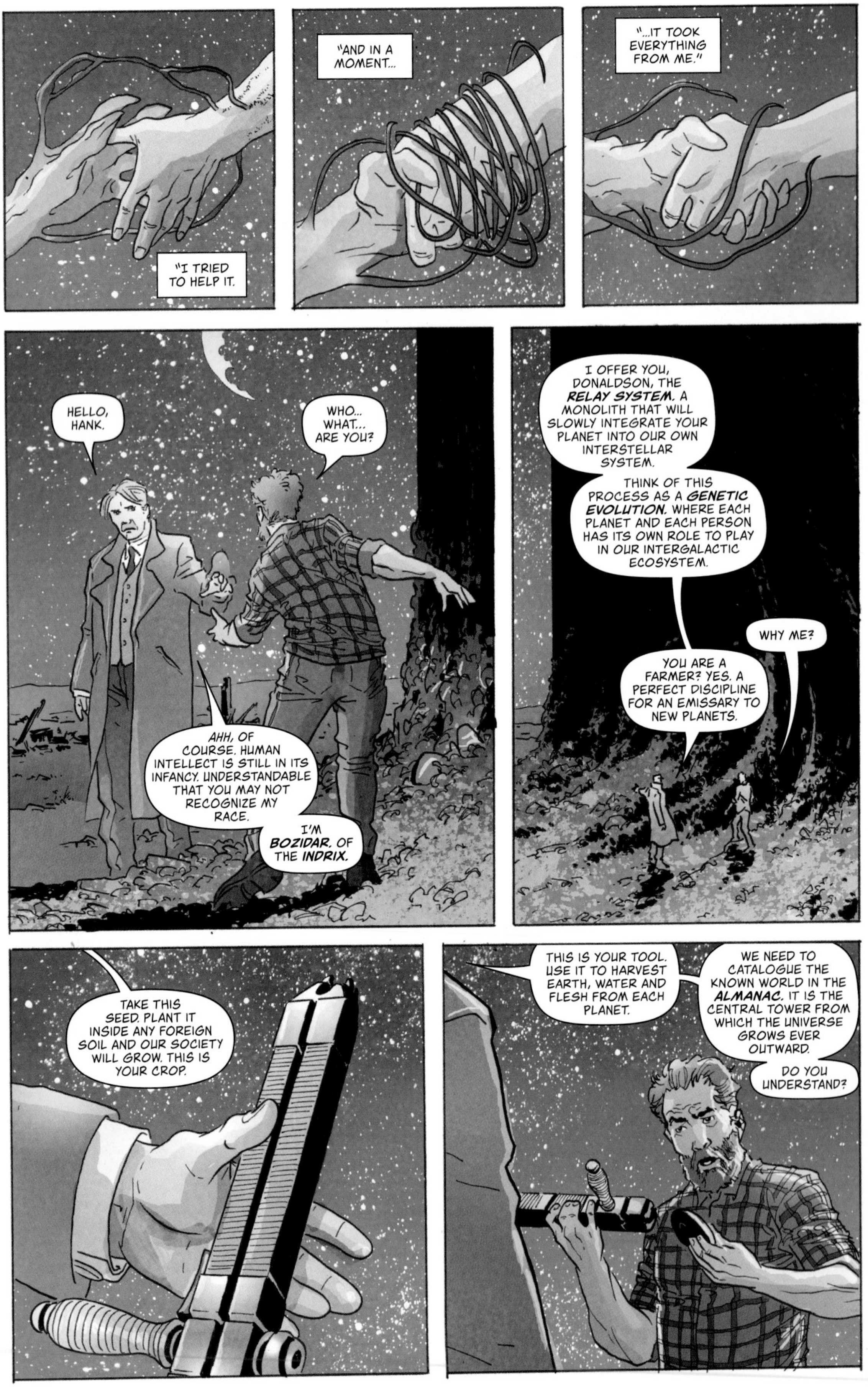
"I TRIED TO HELP IT.
"AND IN A MOMENT...
"...IT TOOK EVERYTHING FROM ME."
HELLO, HANK.
WHO... WHAT... ARE YOU?
AHH, OF COURSE. HUMAN INTELLECT IS STILL IN ITS INFANCY. UNDERSTANDABLE THAT YOU MAY NOT RECOGNIZE MY RACE.
I'M BOZIDAR, OF THE INDRIX.
I OFFER YOU, DONALDSON, THE RELAY SYSTEM. A MONOLITH THAT WILL SLOWLY INTEGRATE YOUR PLANET INTO OUR OWN INTERSTELLAR SYSTEM.
THINK OF THIS PROCESS AS A GENETIC EVOLUTION. WHERE EACH PLANET AND EACH PERSON HAS ITS OWN ROLE TO PLAY IN OUR INTERGALACTIC ECOSYSTEM.
WHY ME?
YOU ARE A FARMER? YES. A PERFECT DISCIPLINE FOR AN EMISSARY TO NEW PLANETS.
TAKE THIS SEED. PLANT IT INSIDE ANY FOREIGN SOIL AND OUR SOCIETY WILL GROW. THIS IS YOUR CROP.
THIS IS YOUR TOOL. USE IT TO HARVEST EARTH, WATER AND FLESH FROM EACH PLANET.
WE NEED TO CATALOGUE THE KNOWN WORLD IN THE ALMANAC. IT IS THE CENTRAL TOWER FROM WHICH THE UNIVERSE GROWS EVER OUTWARD.
DO YOU UNDERSTAND?

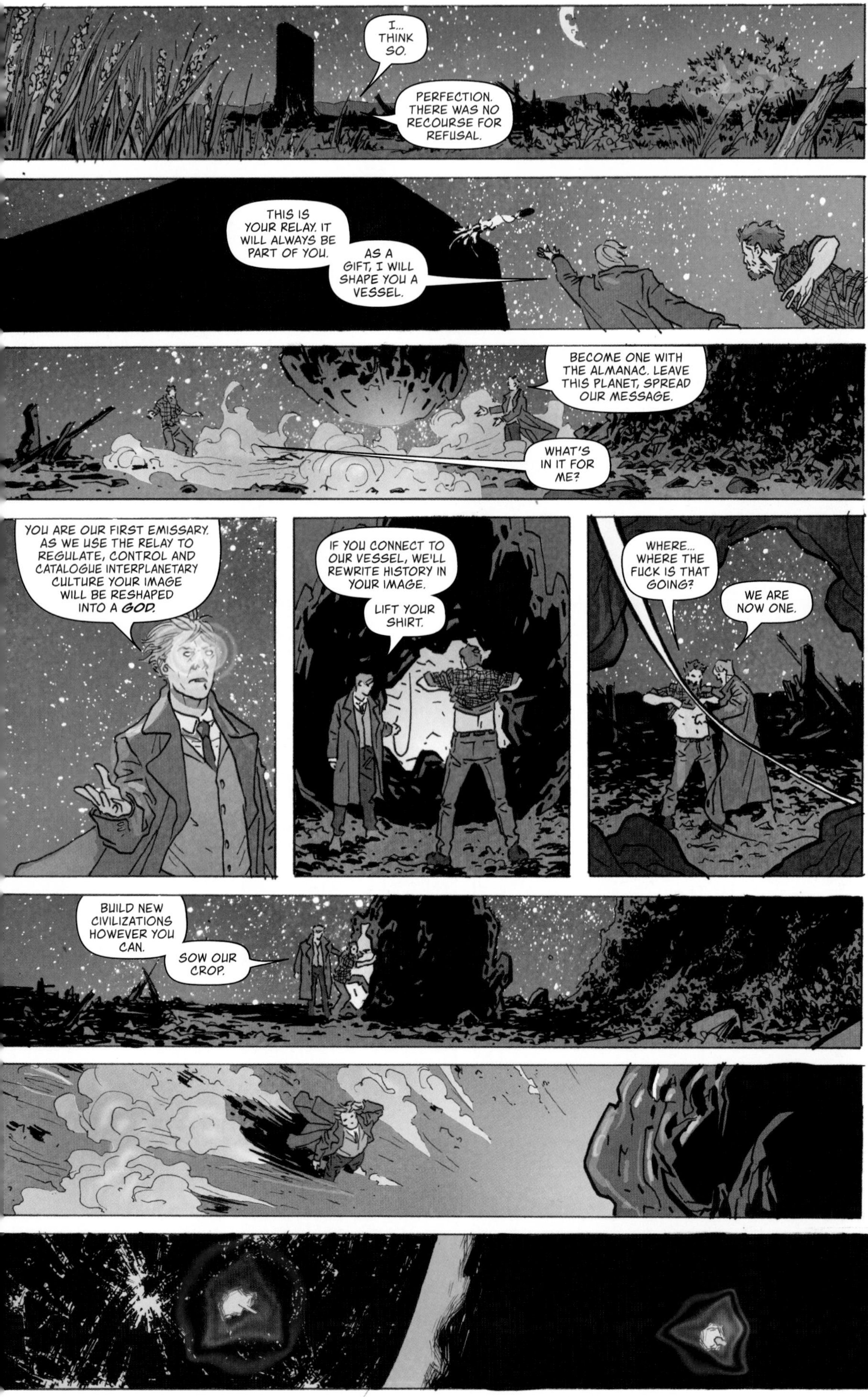

I... THINK SO.
PERFECTION. THERE WAS NO RECOURSE FOR REFUSAL.
THIS IS YOUR RELAY. IT WILL ALWAYS BE PART OF YOU.
AS A GIFT, I WILL SHAPE YOU A VESSEL.
BECOME ONE WITH THE ALMANAC. LEAVE THIS PLANET, SPREAD OUR MESSAGE.
WHAT'S IN IT FOR ME?
YOU ARE OUR FIRST EMISSARY. AS WE USE THE RELAY TO REGULATE, CONTROL AND CATALOGUE INTERPLANETARY CULTURE YOUR IMAGE WILL BE RESHAPED INTO A GOD.
IF YOU CONNECT TO OUR VESSEL, WE'LL REWRITE HISTORY IN YOUR IMAGE.
LIFT YOUR SHIRT.
WHERE... WHERE THE FUCK IS THAT GOING?
WE ARE NOW ONE.
BUILD NEW CIVILIZATIONS HOWEVER YOU CAN.
SOW OUR CROP.

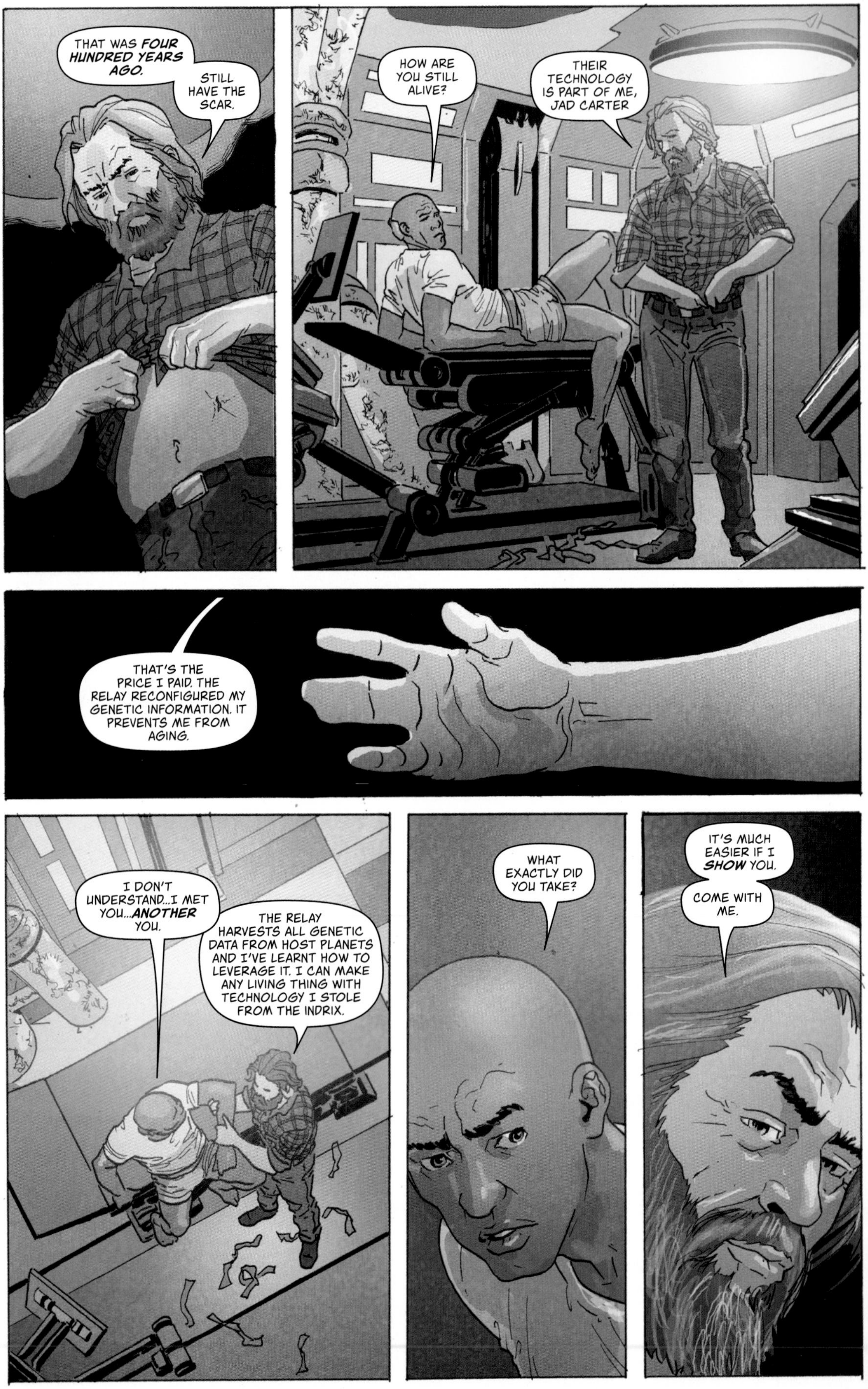
THAT WAS FOUR HUNDRED YEARS AGO.
STILL HAVE THE SCAR.
HOW ARE YOU STILL ALIVE?
THEIR TECHNOLOGY IS PART OF ME, JAD CARTER
THAT'S THE PRICE I PAID. THE RELAY RECONFIGURED MY GENETIC INFORMATION. IT PREVENTS ME FROM AGING.
I DON'T UNDERSTAND...I MET YOU...ANOTHER YOU.
THE RELAY HARVESTS ALL GENETIC DATA FROM HOST PLANETS AND I'VE LEARNT HOW TO LEVERAGE IT. I CAN MAKE ANY LIVING THING WITH TECHNOLOGY I STOLE FROM THE INDRIX.
WHAT EXACTLY DID YOU TAKE?
IT'S MUCH EASIER IF I SHOW YOU.
COME WITH ME.

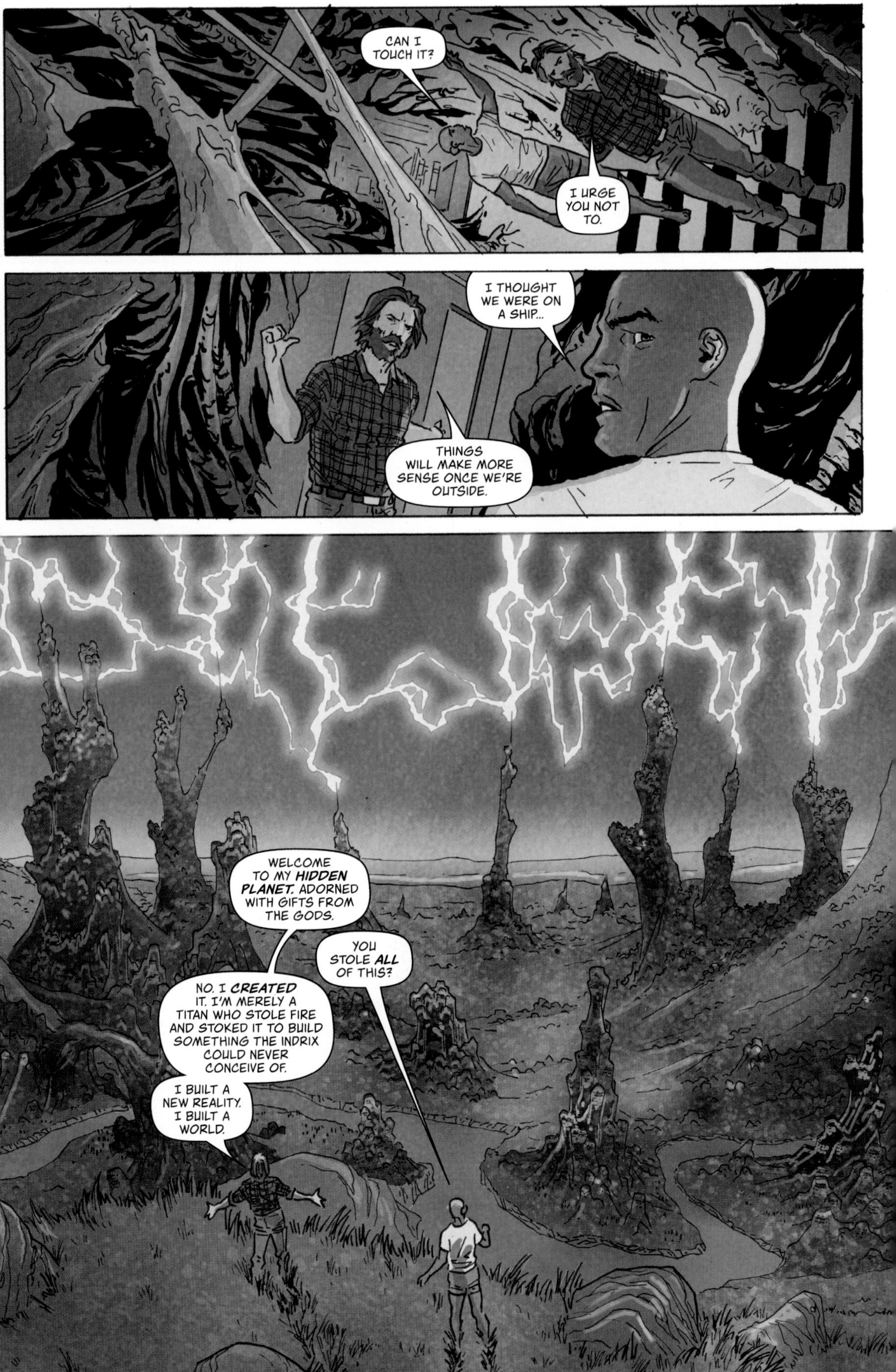
CAN I TOUCH IT?
I URGE YOU NOT TO.
I THOUGHT WE WERE ON A SHIP...
THINGS WILL MAKE MORE SENSE ONCE WE'RE OUTSIDE.
WELCOME TO MY **HIDDEN PLANET.** ADORNED WITH GIFTS FROM THE GODS.
YOU STOLE **ALL** OF THIS?
NO. I **CREATED** IT. I'M MERELY A TITAN WHO STOLE FIRE AND STOKED IT TO BUILD SOMETHING THE INDRIX COULD NEVER CONCEIVE OF.
I BUILT A NEW REALITY. I BUILT A WORLD.

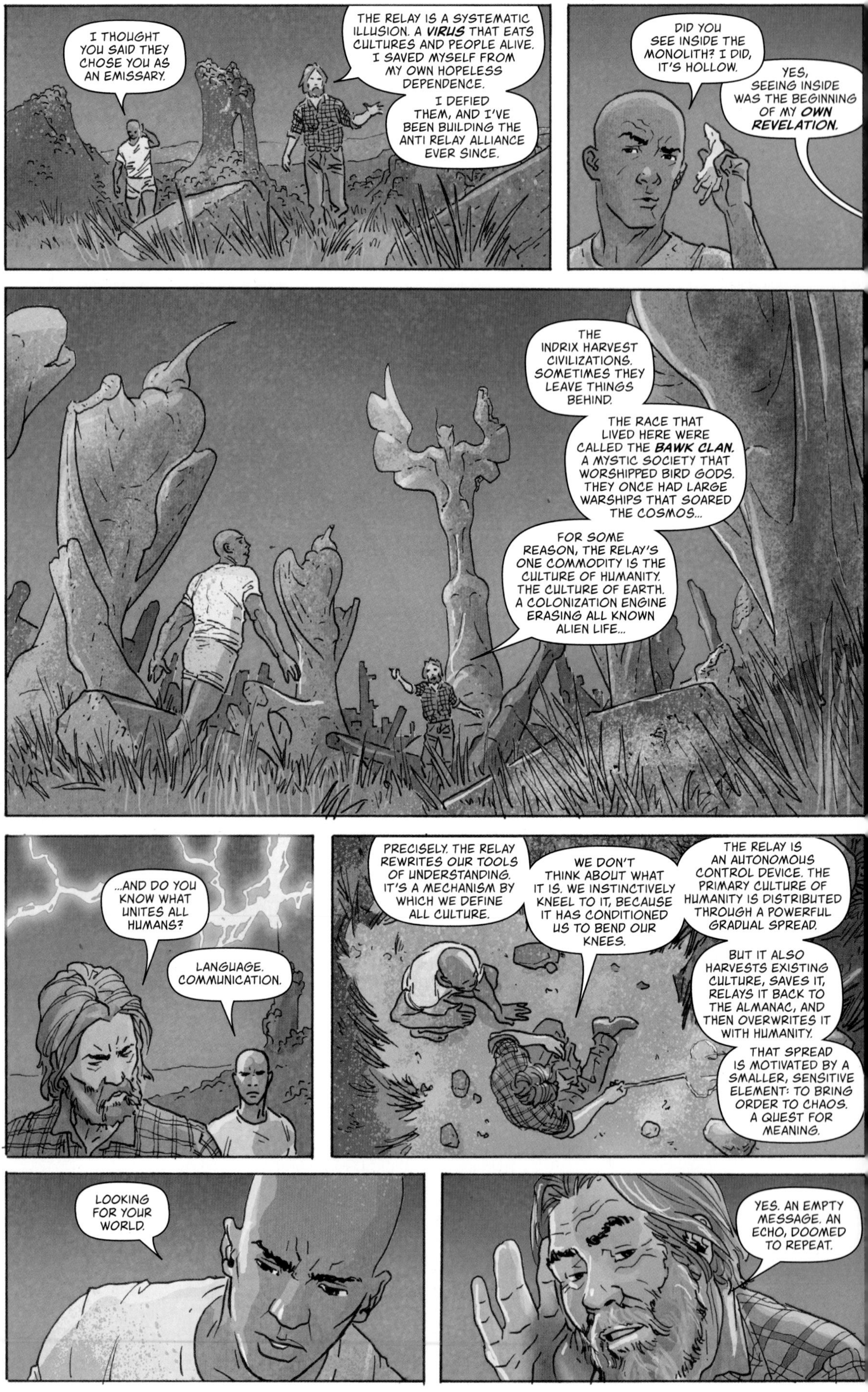

I THOUGHT YOU SAID THEY CHOSE YOU AS AN EMISSARY.
THE RELAY IS A SYSTEMATIC ILLUSION. A VIRUS THAT EATS CULTURES AND PEOPLE ALIVE. I SAVED MYSELF FROM MY OWN HOPELESS DEPENDENCE.
I DEFIED THEM, AND I'VE BEEN BUILDING THE ANTI RELAY ALLIANCE EVER SINCE.
DID YOU SEE INSIDE THE MONOLITH? I DID, IT'S HOLLOW.
YES, SEEING INSIDE WAS THE BEGINNING OF MY OWN REVELATION.
THE INDRIX HARVEST CIVILIZATIONS. SOMETIMES THEY LEAVE THINGS BEHIND.
THE RACE THAT LIVED HERE WERE CALLED THE BAWK CLAN. A MYSTIC SOCIETY THAT WORSHIPPED BIRD GODS. THEY ONCE HAD LARGE WARSHIPS THAT SOARED THE COSMOS...
FOR SOME REASON, THE RELAY'S ONE COMMODITY IS THE CULTURE OF HUMANITY. THE CULTURE OF EARTH. A COLONIZATION ENGINE ERASING ALL KNOWN ALIEN LIFE...
...AND DO YOU KNOW WHAT UNITES ALL HUMANS?
LANGUAGE. COMMUNICATION.
PRECISELY. THE RELAY REWRITES OUR TOOLS OF UNDERSTANDING. IT'S A MECHANISM BY WHICH WE DEFINE ALL CULTURE.
WE DON'T THINK ABOUT WHAT IT IS. WE INSTINCTIVELY KNEEL TO IT, BECAUSE IT HAS CONDITIONED US TO BEND OUR KNEES.
THE RELAY IS AN AUTONOMOUS CONTROL DEVICE. THE PRIMARY CULTURE OF HUMANITY IS DISTRIBUTED THROUGH A POWERFUL GRADUAL SPREAD.
BUT IT ALSO HARVESTS EXISTING CULTURE, SAVES IT, RELAYS IT BACK TO THE ALMANAC, AND THEN OVERWRITES IT WITH HUMANITY.
THAT SPREAD IS MOTIVATED BY A SMALLER, SENSITIVE ELEMENT: TO BRING ORDER TO CHAOS. A QUEST FOR MEANING.
LOOKING FOR YOUR WORLD.
YES. AN EMPTY MESSAGE. AN ECHO, DOOMED TO REPEAT.

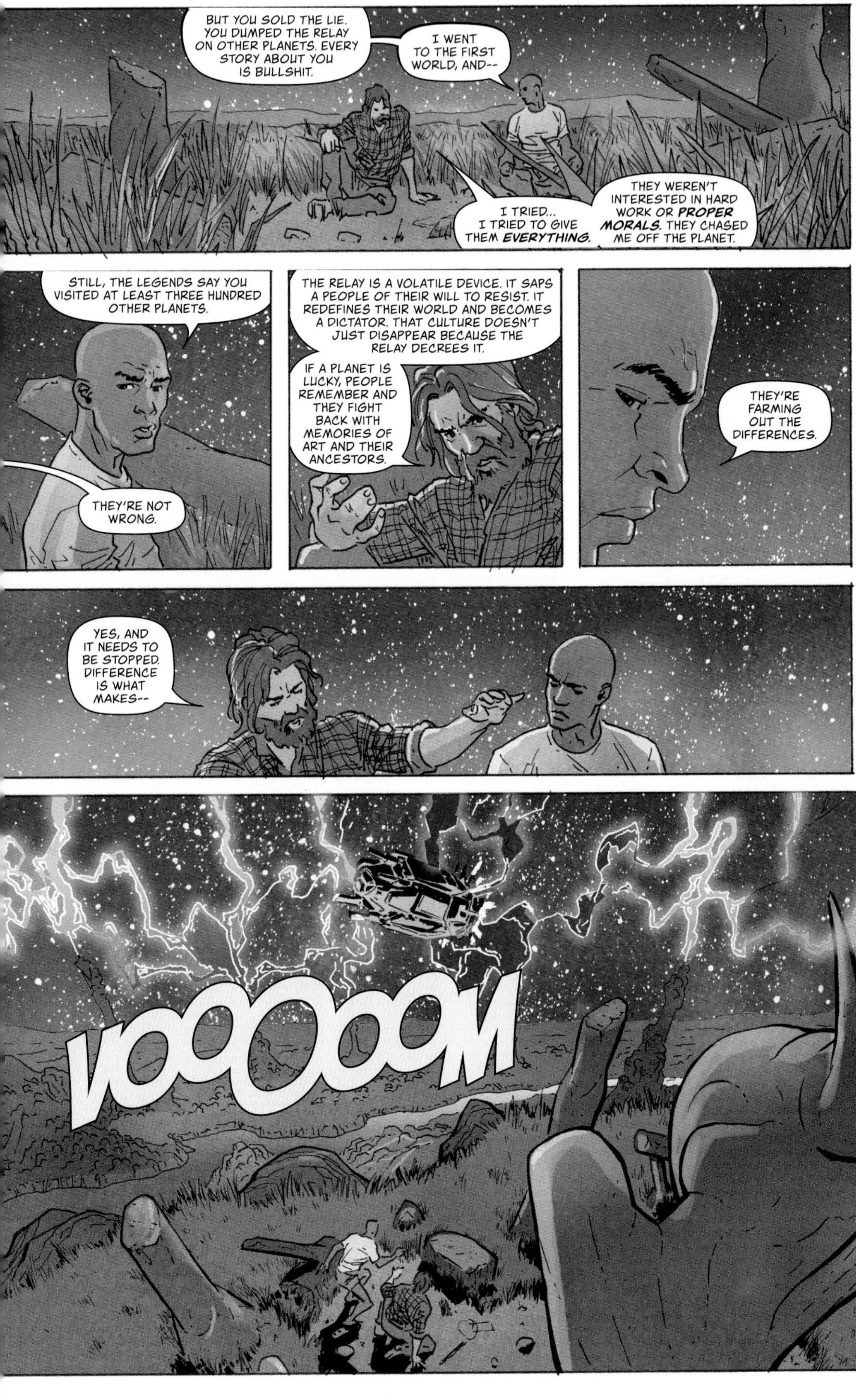
BUT YOU SOLD THE LIE. YOU DUMPED THE RELAY ON OTHER PLANETS. EVERY STORY ABOUT YOU IS BULLSHIT.
I WENT TO THE FIRST WORLD, AND--
I TRIED... I TRIED TO GIVE THEM EVERYTHING.
THEY WEREN'T INTERESTED IN HARD WORK OR PROPER MORALS. THEY CHASED ME OFF THE PLANET.
STILL, THE LEGENDS SAY YOU VISITED AT LEAST THREE HUNDRED OTHER PLANETS.
THEY'RE NOT WRONG.
THE RELAY IS A VOLATILE DEVICE. IT SAPS A PEOPLE OF THEIR WILL TO RESIST. IT REDEFINES THEIR WORLD AND BECOMES A DICTATOR. THAT CULTURE DOESN'T JUST DISAPPEAR BECAUSE THE RELAY DECREES IT.
IF A PLANET IS LUCKY, PEOPLE REMEMBER AND THEY FIGHT BACK WITH MEMORIES OF ART AND THEIR ANCESTORS.
THEY'RE FARMING OUT THE DIFFERENCES.
YES, AND IT NEEDS TO BE STOPPED. DIFFERENCE IS WHAT MAKES--
VOOOOOM

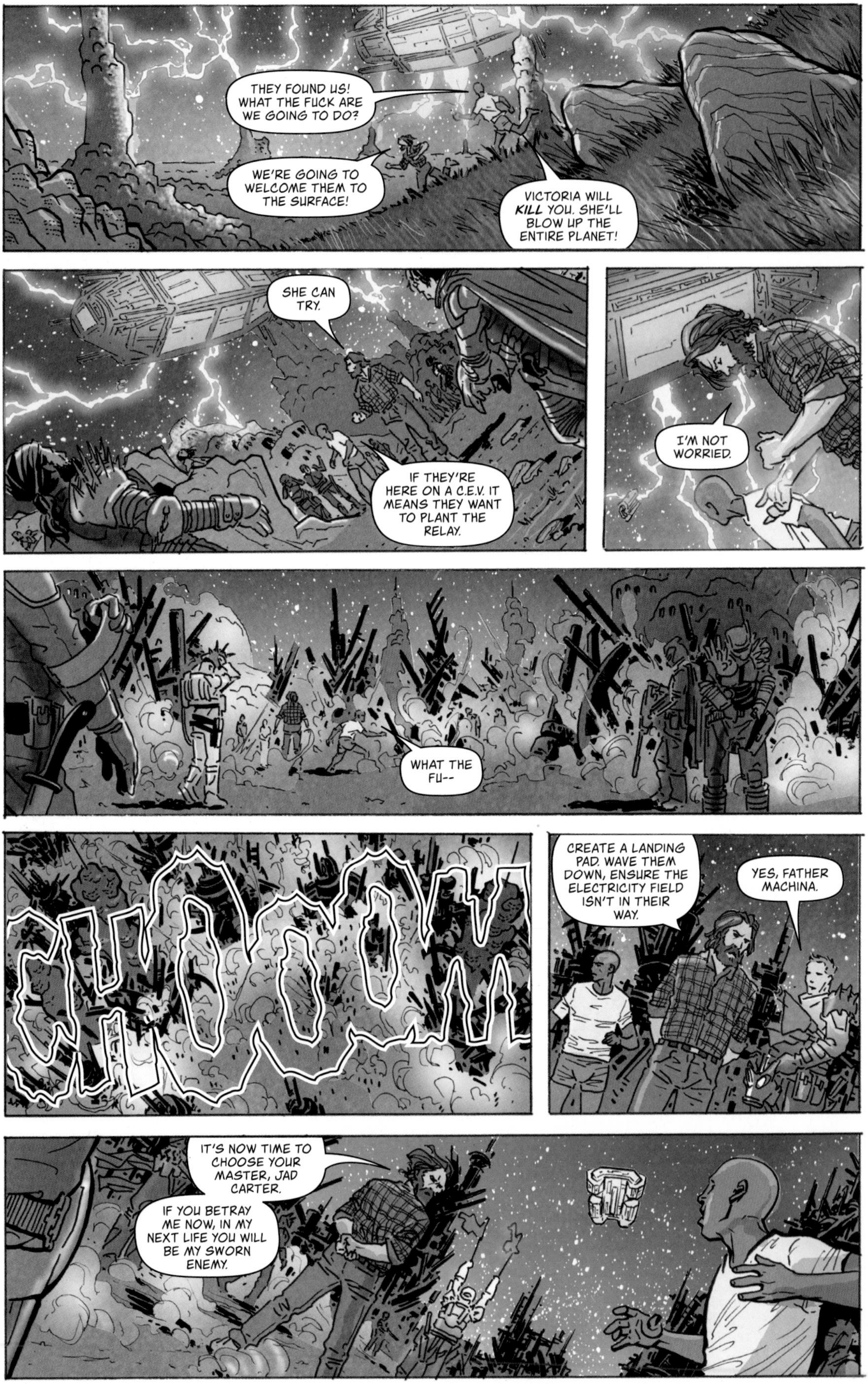
THEY FOUND US! WHAT THE FUCK ARE WE GOING TO DO?
WE'RE GOING TO WELCOME THEM TO THE SURFACE!
VICTORIA WILL KILL YOU. SHE'LL BLOW UP THE ENTIRE PLANET!
SHE CAN TRY.
IF THEY'RE HERE ON A C.E.V. IT MEANS THEY WANT TO PLANT THE RELAY.
I'M NOT WORRIED.
WHAT THE FU--
CHOOOM
CREATE A LANDING PAD. WAVE THEM DOWN, ENSURE THE ELECTRICITY FIELD ISN'T IN THEIR WAY.
YES, FATHER MACHINA.
IT'S NOW TIME TO CHOOSE YOUR MASTER, JAD CARTER.
IF YOU BETRAY ME NOW, IN MY NEXT LIFE YOU WILL BE MY SWORN ENEMY.

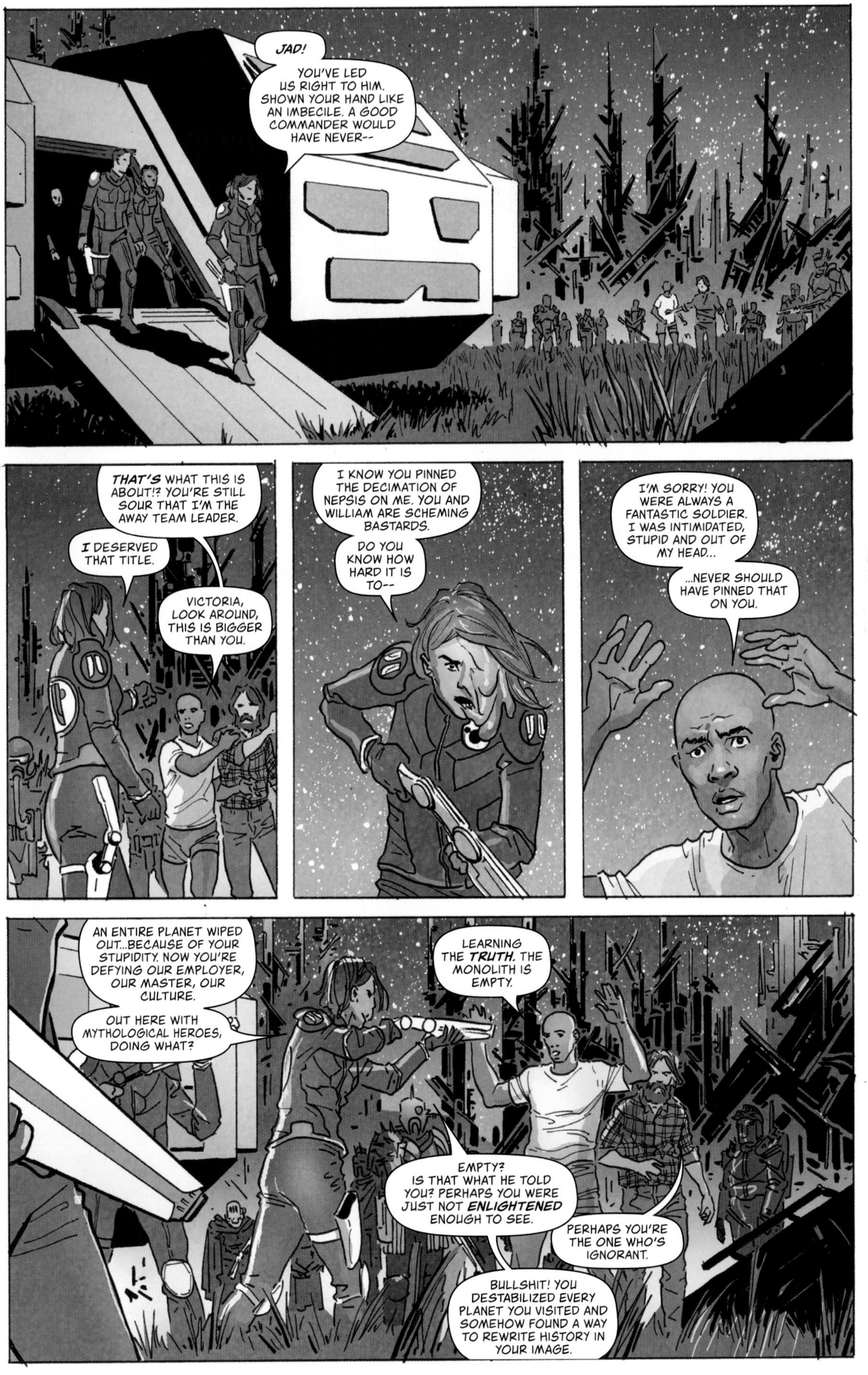

JAD!
YOU'VE LED US RIGHT TO HIM. SHOWN YOUR HAND LIKE AN IMBECILE. A GOOD COMMANDER WOULD HAVE NEVER--
THAT'S WHAT THIS IS ABOUT!? YOU'RE STILL SOUR THAT I'M THE AWAY TEAM LEADER.
I DESERVED THAT TITLE.
VICTORIA, LOOK AROUND, THIS IS BIGGER THAN YOU.
I KNOW YOU PINNED THE DECIMATION OF NEPSIS ON ME. YOU AND WILLIAM ARE SCHEMING BASTARDS.
DO YOU KNOW HOW HARD IT IS TO--
I'M SORRY! YOU WERE ALWAYS A FANTASTIC SOLDIER. I WAS INTIMIDATED, STUPID AND OUT OF MY HEAD...
...NEVER SHOULD HAVE PINNED THAT ON YOU.
AN ENTIRE PLANET WIPED OUT...BECAUSE OF YOUR STUPIDITY. NOW YOU'RE DEFYING OUR EMPLOYER, OUR MASTER, OUR CULTURE.
OUT HERE WITH MYTHOLOGICAL HEROES, DOING WHAT?
LEARNING THE TRUTH. THE MONOLITH IS EMPTY.
EMPTY? IS THAT WHAT HE TOLD YOU? PERHAPS YOU WERE JUST NOT ENLIGHTENED ENOUGH TO SEE.
PERHAPS YOU'RE THE ONE WHO'S IGNORANT.
BULLSHIT! YOU DESTABILIZED EVERY PLANET YOU VISITED AND SOMEHOW FOUND A WAY TO REWRITE HISTORY IN YOUR IMAGE.

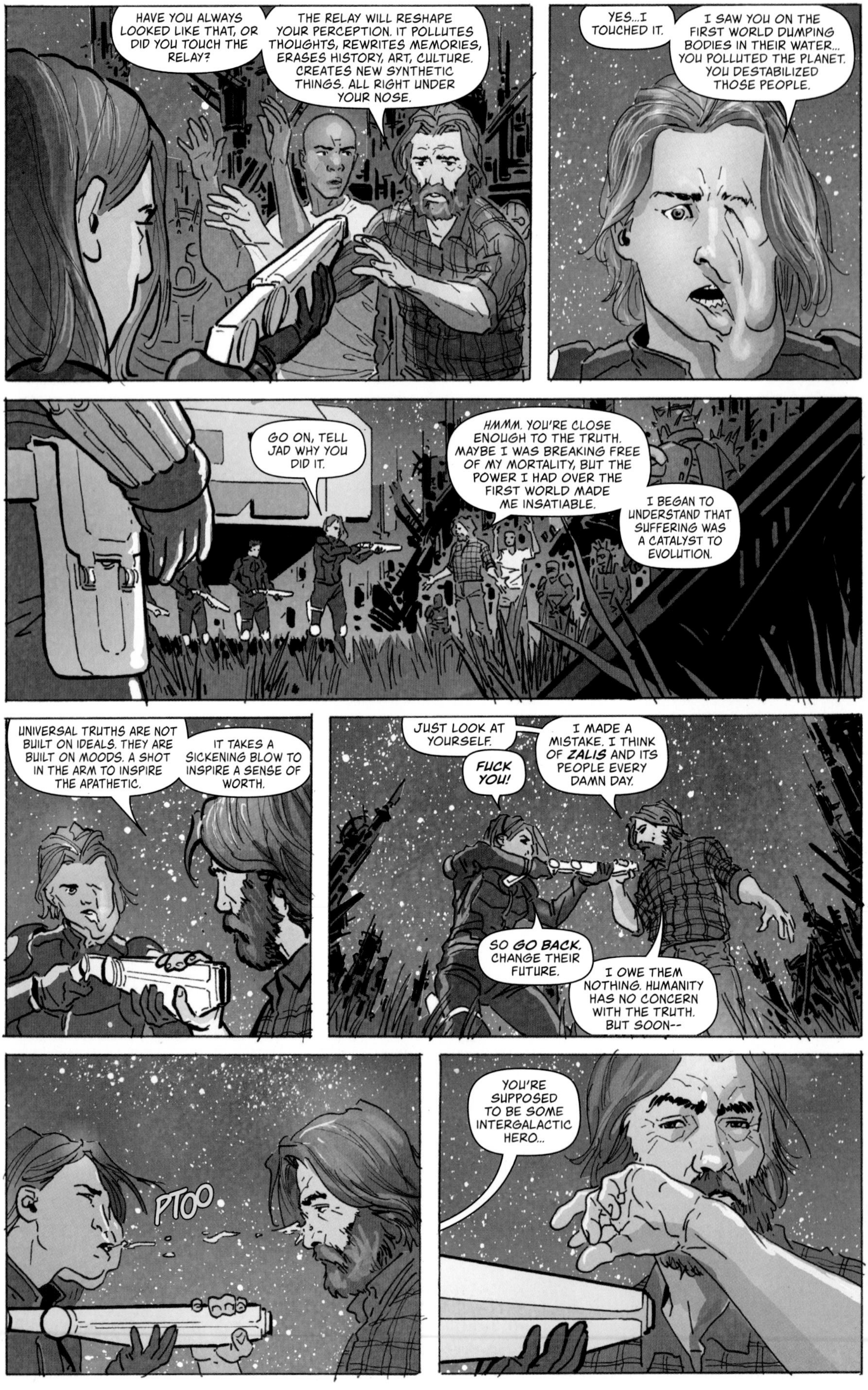
HAVE YOU ALWAYS LOOKED LIKE THAT, OR DID YOU TOUCH THE RELAY?
THE RELAY WILL RESHAPE YOUR PERCEPTION. IT POLLUTES THOUGHTS, REWRITES MEMORIES, ERASES HISTORY, ART, CULTURE. CREATES NEW SYNTHETIC THINGS. ALL RIGHT UNDER YOUR NOSE.
YES...I TOUCHED IT.
I SAW YOU ON THE FIRST WORLD DUMPING BODIES IN THEIR WATER... YOU POLLUTED THE PLANET. YOU DESTABILIZED THOSE PEOPLE.
GO ON, TELL JAD WHY YOU DID IT.
HMMM. YOU'RE CLOSE ENOUGH TO THE TRUTH. MAYBE I WAS BREAKING FREE OF MY MORTALITY, BUT THE POWER I HAD OVER THE FIRST WORLD MADE ME INSATIABLE.
I BEGAN TO UNDERSTAND THAT SUFFERING WAS A CATALYST TO EVOLUTION.
UNIVERSAL TRUTHS ARE NOT BUILT ON IDEALS. THEY ARE BUILT ON MOODS. A SHOT IN THE ARM TO INSPIRE THE APATHETIC.
IT TAKES A SICKENING BLOW TO INSPIRE A SENSE OF WORTH.
JUST LOOK AT YOURSELF.
FUCK YOU!
I MADE A MISTAKE. I THINK OF ZALIS AND ITS PEOPLE EVERY DAMN DAY.
SO GO BACK. CHANGE THEIR FUTURE.
I OWE THEM NOTHING. HUMANITY HAS NO CONCERN WITH THE TRUTH. BUT SOON--
PTOO
YOU'RE SUPPOSED TO BE SOME INTERGALACTIC HERO...

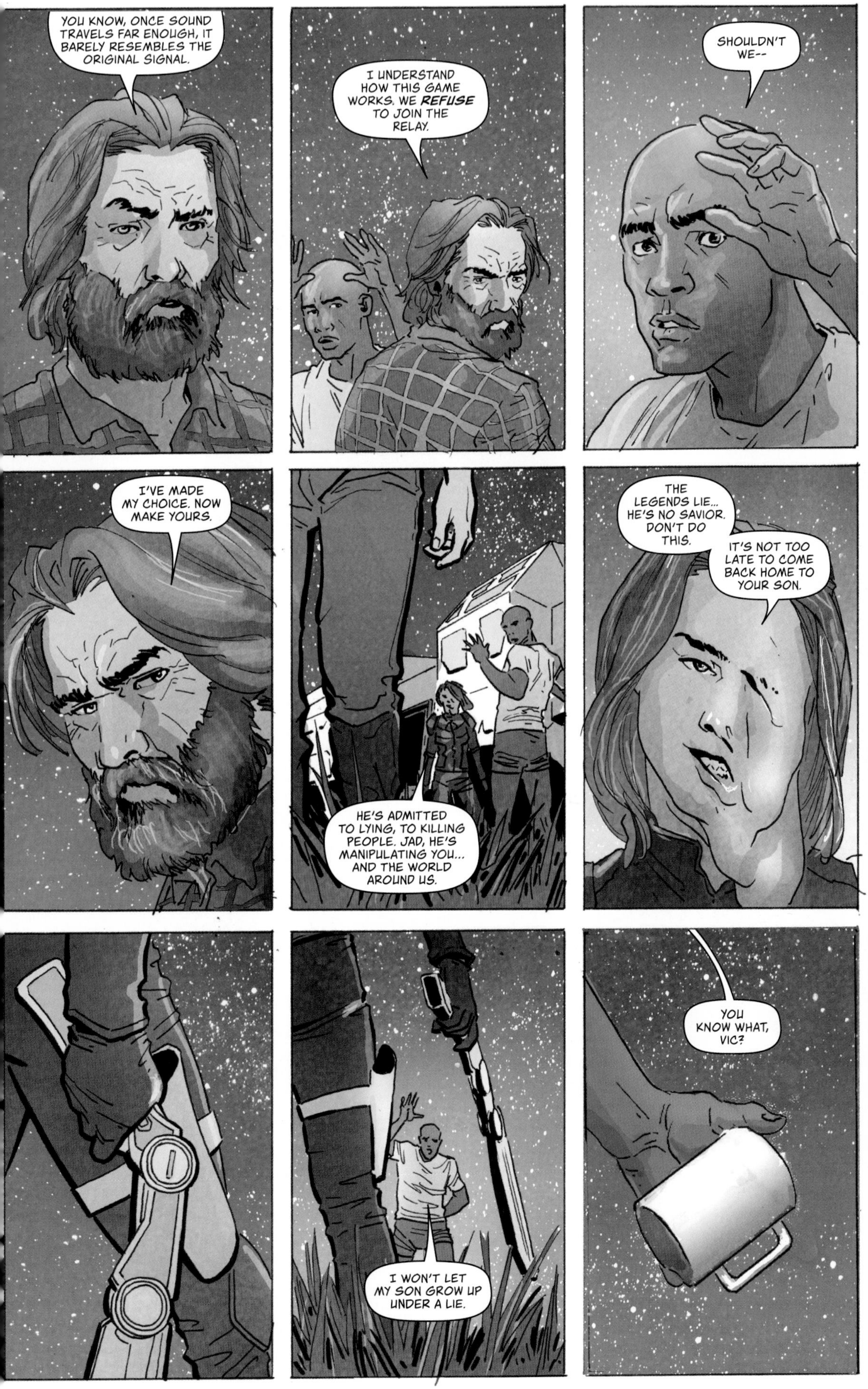
YOU KNOW, ONCE SOUND TRAVELS FAR ENOUGH, IT BARELY RESEMBLES THE ORIGINAL SIGNAL.
I UNDERSTAND HOW THIS GAME WORKS. WE **REFUSE** TO JOIN THE RELAY.
SHOULDN'T WE--
I'VE MADE MY CHOICE. NOW MAKE YOURS.
HE'S ADMITTED TO LYING, TO KILLING PEOPLE. JAD, HE'S MANIPULATING YOU... AND THE WORLD AROUND US.
THE LEGENDS LIE... HE'S NO SAVIOR. DON'T DO THIS.
IT'S NOT TOO LATE TO COME BACK HOME TO YOUR SON.
I WON'T LET MY SON GROW UP UNDER A LIE.
YOU KNOW WHAT, VIC?

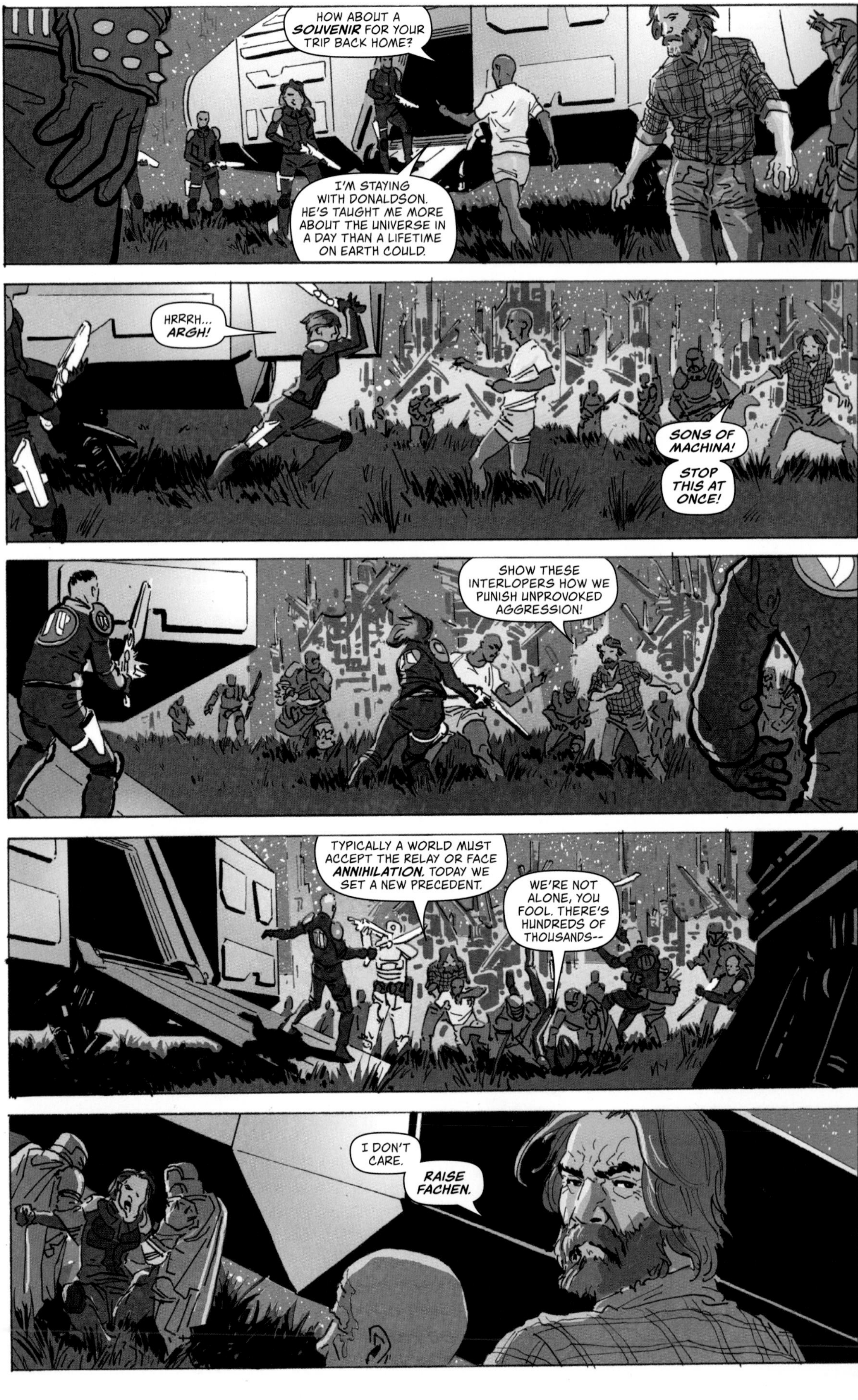
HOW ABOUT A **SOUVENIR** FOR YOUR TRIP BACK HOME?
I'M STAYING WITH DONALDSON. HE'S TAUGHT ME MORE ABOUT THE UNIVERSE IN A DAY THAN A LIFETIME ON EARTH COULD.
HRRRH... **ARGH!**
SONS OF MACHINA!
STOP THIS AT ONCE!
SHOW THESE INTERLOPERS HOW WE PUNISH UNPROVOKED AGGRESSION!
TYPICALLY A WORLD MUST ACCEPT THE RELAY OR FACE **ANNIHILATION.** TODAY WE SET A NEW PRECEDENT.
WE'RE NOT ALONE, YOU FOOL. THERE'S HUNDREDS OF THOUSANDS--
I DON'T CARE.
RAISE FACHEN.

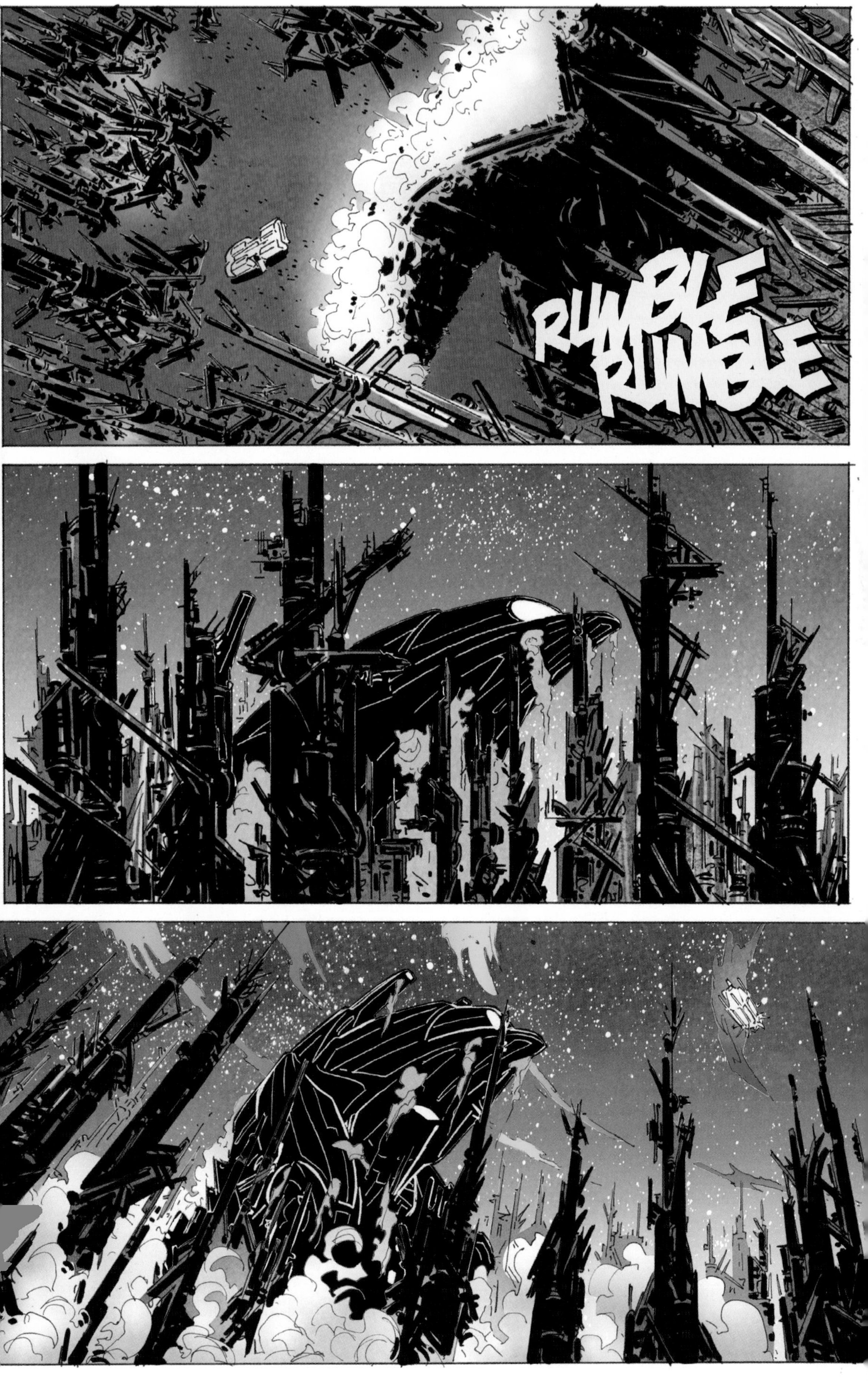
RUMBLE
RUMBLE

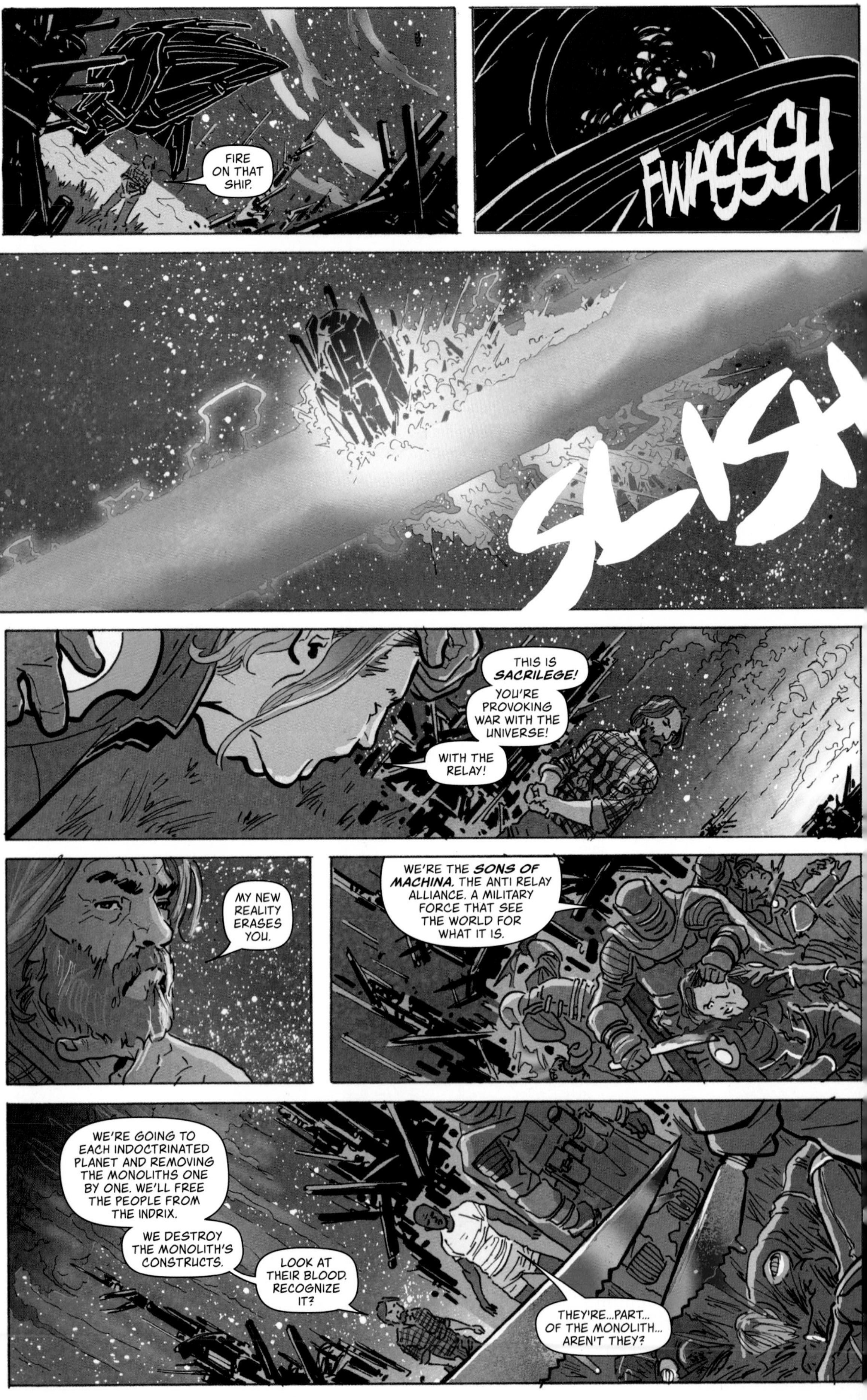
FIRE ON THAT SHIP.
FWASSSH
SLISH
THIS IS SACRILEGE!
YOU'RE PROVOKING WAR WITH THE UNIVERSE!
WITH THE RELAY!
MY NEW REALITY ERASES YOU.
WE'RE THE SONS OF MACHINA. THE ANTI RELAY ALLIANCE. A MILITARY FORCE THAT SEE THE WORLD FOR WHAT IT IS.
WE'RE GOING TO EACH INDOCTRINATED PLANET AND REMOVING THE MONOLITHS ONE BY ONE. WE'LL FREE THE PEOPLE FROM THE INDRIX.
WE DESTROY THE MONOLITH'S CONSTRUCTS.
LOOK AT THEIR BLOOD. RECOGNIZE IT?
THEY'RE...PART... OF THE MONOLITH... AREN'T THEY?

LET'S TAKE ANOTHER WALK.

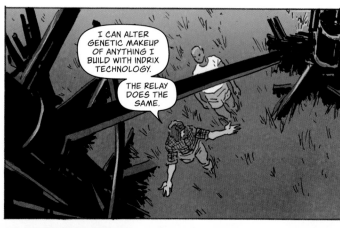

I CAN ALTER GENETIC MAKEUP OF ANYTHING I BUILD WITH INDRIX TECHNOLOGY.

THE RELAY DOES THE SAME.

"IT GATHERS GENETIC INFORMATION, REWRITES IT AND CREATES A NEW SEAMLESS RENDITION OF REALITY.

"THIS IS DONE FOR TOTAL ASSIMILATION, HISTORY CAN BE REWRITTEN IN A DAY AND NO ONE WOULD EVEN BE AWARE OF IT."

SO IT'S ALL AN ILLUSION?

IT'S IMPOSSIBLE TO KNOW WITH ANY DEGREE OF CERTAINTY. BUT THE RELAY BRINGS TOO MUCH CONSTRUCTED ORDER TO CONQUERED PLANETS.

HUMANS WEREN'T MEANT TO LIVE ACROSS THE WHOLE OF THE UNIVERSE.

REALITY IS...MORE COMPLICATED. THE UNIVERSE IS A MESS, NOT A NETWORK.

EXACTLY. I BELIEVE THE INDRIX FARMING AWAY THE CHAOS...THE DIFFERENCES. TAKING IT FOR THEMSELVES. BUT I DON'T KNOW WHAT THEIR END GOAL IS--

THE OLD CULTURE OF EARTH HAS TO BE STORED SOMEWHERE.

I THINK THE INDRIX HOUSE EVERY- THING WITHIN THEIR CENTRAL MONOLITH. THE **ALMANAC** PROCESSES THE SIGNALS FROM ALL THE RELAY PLANETS.

EACH CONQUERED WORLD IS MERELY A CORPUSCLE.

SO WHAT HAPPENS IF WE CUT OFF A TRANSMISSION?

REALITY ON THAT PLANET WILL SHATTER AND THEY'LL COME RUNNING TO FIX THE SIGNAL.

HOP IN.

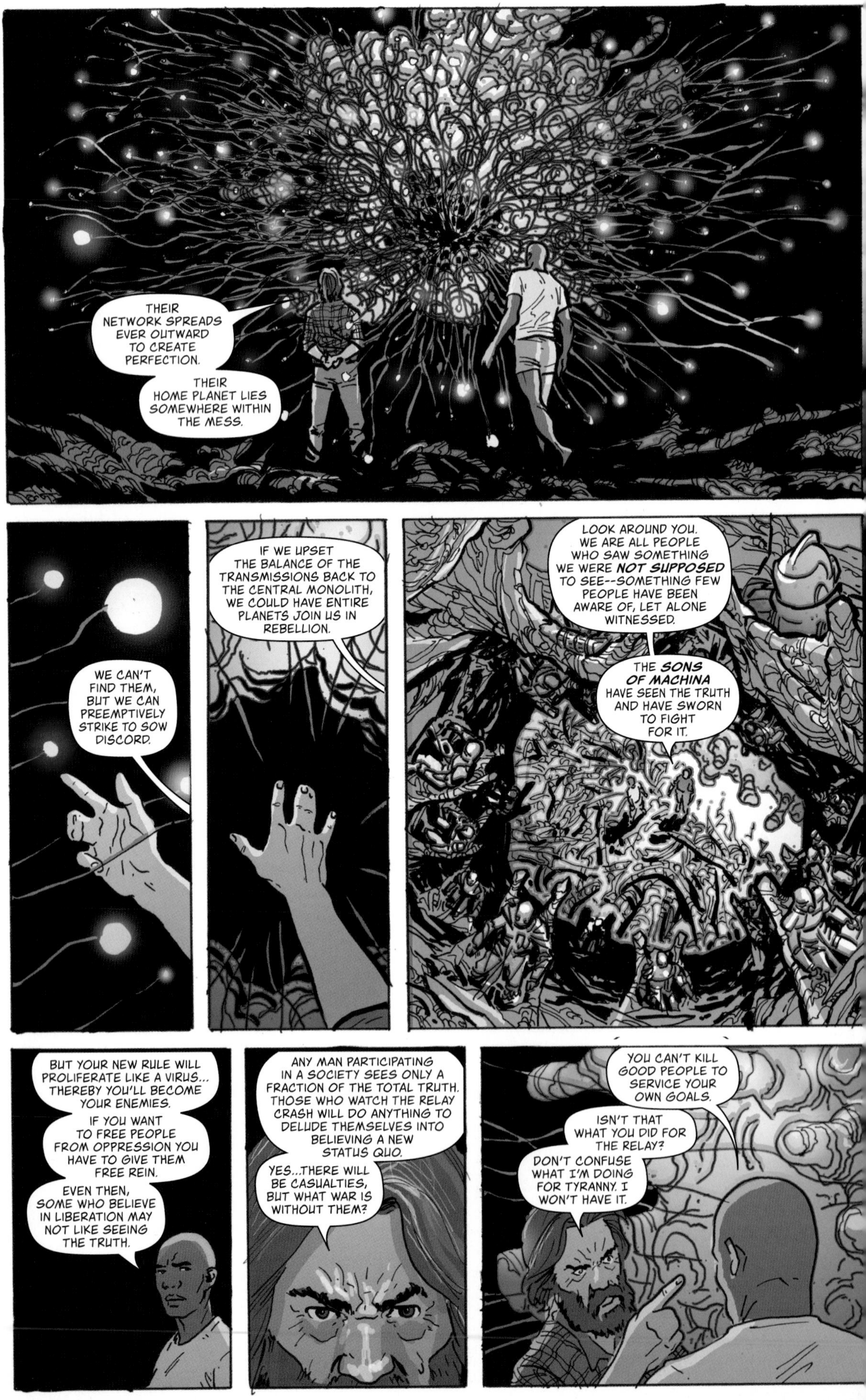
THEIR NETWORK SPREADS EVER OUTWARD TO CREATE PERFECTION.
THEIR HOME PLANET LIES SOMEWHERE WITHIN THE MESS.
WE CAN'T FIND THEM, BUT WE CAN PREEMPTIVELY STRIKE TO SOW DISCORD.
IF WE UPSET THE BALANCE OF THE TRANSMISSIONS BACK TO THE CENTRAL MONOLITH, WE COULD HAVE ENTIRE PLANETS JOIN US IN REBELLION.
LOOK AROUND YOU. WE ARE ALL PEOPLE WHO SAW SOMETHING WE WERE **NOT SUPPOSED** TO SEE--SOMETHING FEW PEOPLE HAVE BEEN AWARE OF, LET ALONE WITNESSED.
THE **SONS OF MACHINA** HAVE SEEN THE TRUTH AND HAVE SWORN TO FIGHT FOR IT.
BUT YOUR NEW RULE WILL PROLIFERATE LIKE A VIRUS... THEREBY YOU'LL BECOME YOUR ENEMIES.
IF YOU WANT TO FREE PEOPLE FROM OPPRESSION YOU HAVE TO GIVE THEM FREE REIN.
EVEN THEN, SOME WHO BELIEVE IN LIBERATION MAY NOT LIKE SEEING THE TRUTH.
ANY MAN PARTICIPATING IN A SOCIETY SEES ONLY A FRACTION OF THE TOTAL TRUTH. THOSE WHO WATCH THE RELAY CRASH WILL DO ANYTHING TO DELUDE THEMSELVES INTO BELIEVING A NEW STATUS QUO.
YES...THERE WILL BE CASUALTIES, BUT WHAT WAR IS WITHOUT THEM?
YOU CAN'T KILL GOOD PEOPLE TO SERVICE YOUR OWN GOALS.
ISN'T THAT WHAT YOU DID FOR THE RELAY?
DON'T CONFUSE WHAT I'M DOING FOR TYRANNY. I WON'T HAVE IT.

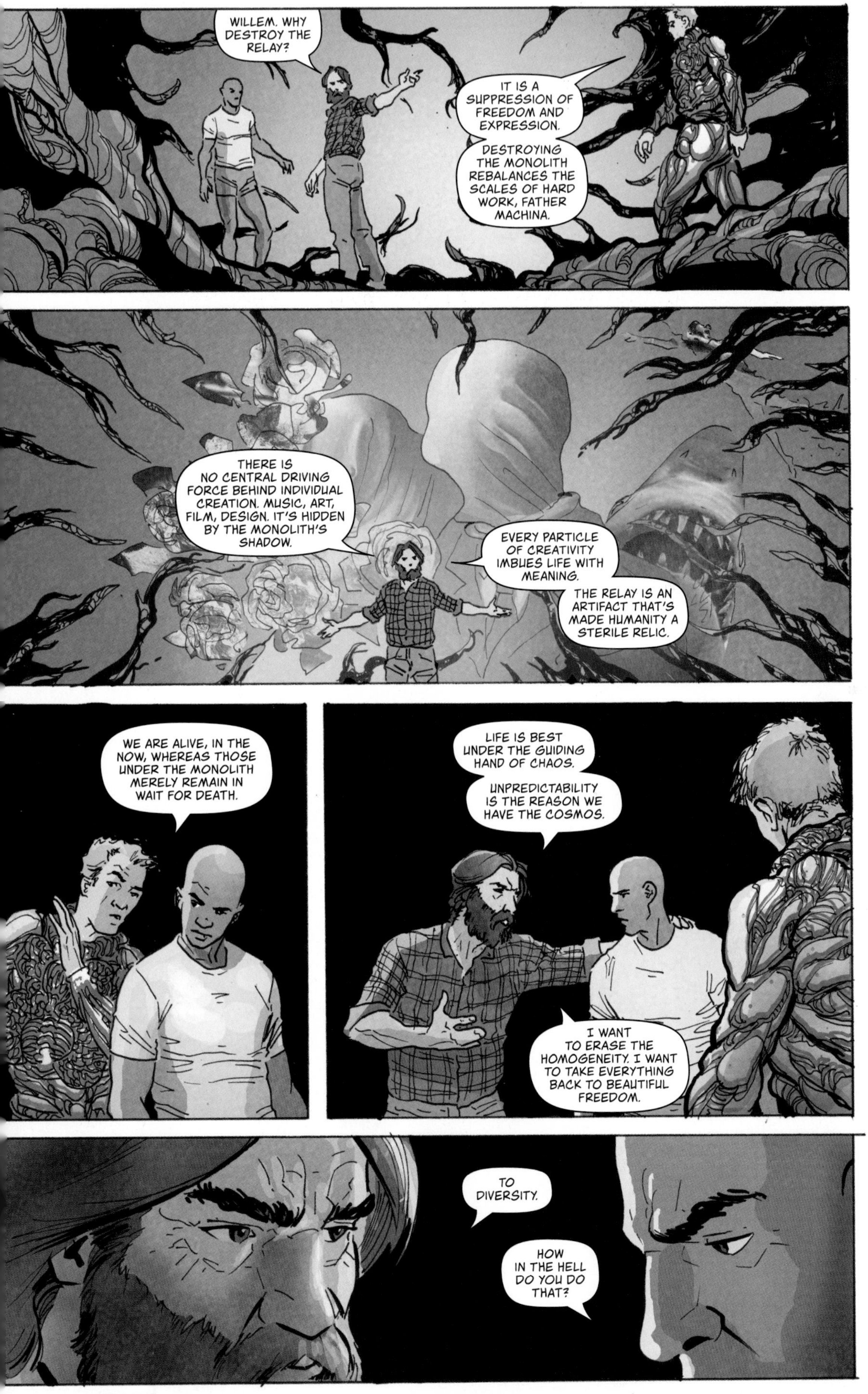
WILLEM. WHY DESTROY THE RELAY?
IT IS A SUPPRESSION OF FREEDOM AND EXPRESSION.
DESTROYING THE MONOLITH REBALANCES THE SCALES OF HARD WORK, FATHER MACHINA.
THERE IS NO CENTRAL DRIVING FORCE BEHIND INDIVIDUAL CREATION. MUSIC, ART, FILM, DESIGN. IT'S HIDDEN BY THE MONOLITH'S SHADOW.
EVERY PARTICLE OF CREATIVITY IMBUES LIFE WITH MEANING.
THE RELAY IS AN ARTIFACT THAT'S MADE HUMANITY A STERILE RELIC.
WE ARE ALIVE, IN THE NOW, WHEREAS THOSE UNDER THE MONOLITH MERELY REMAIN IN WAIT FOR DEATH.
LIFE IS BEST UNDER THE GUIDING HAND OF CHAOS.
UNPREDICTABILITY IS THE REASON WE HAVE THE COSMOS.
I WANT TO ERASE THE HOMOGENEITY. I WANT TO TAKE EVERYTHING BACK TO BEAUTIFUL FREEDOM.
TO DIVERSITY.
HOW IN THE HELL DO YOU DO THAT?

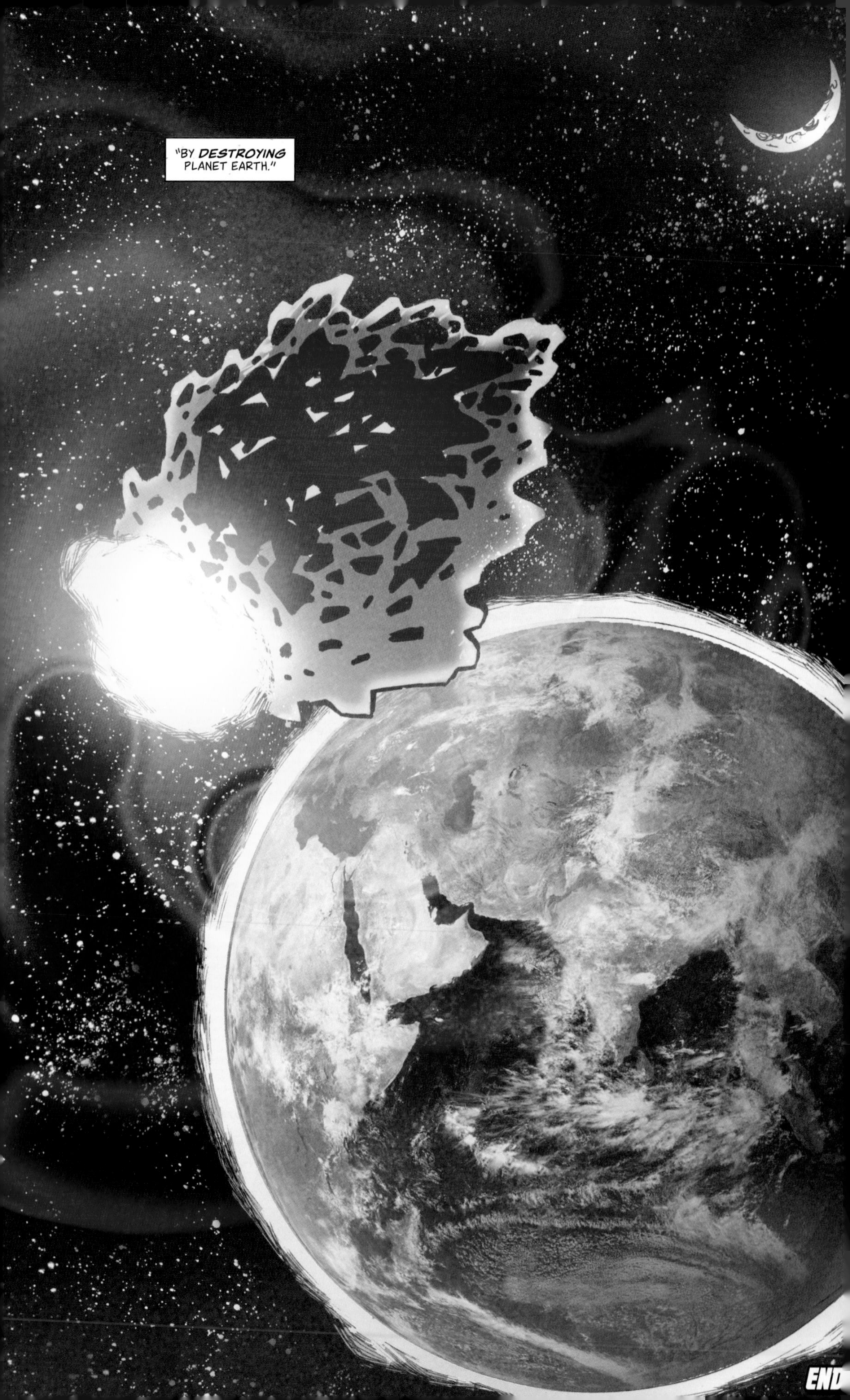
"BY DESTROYING PLANET EARTH."
END

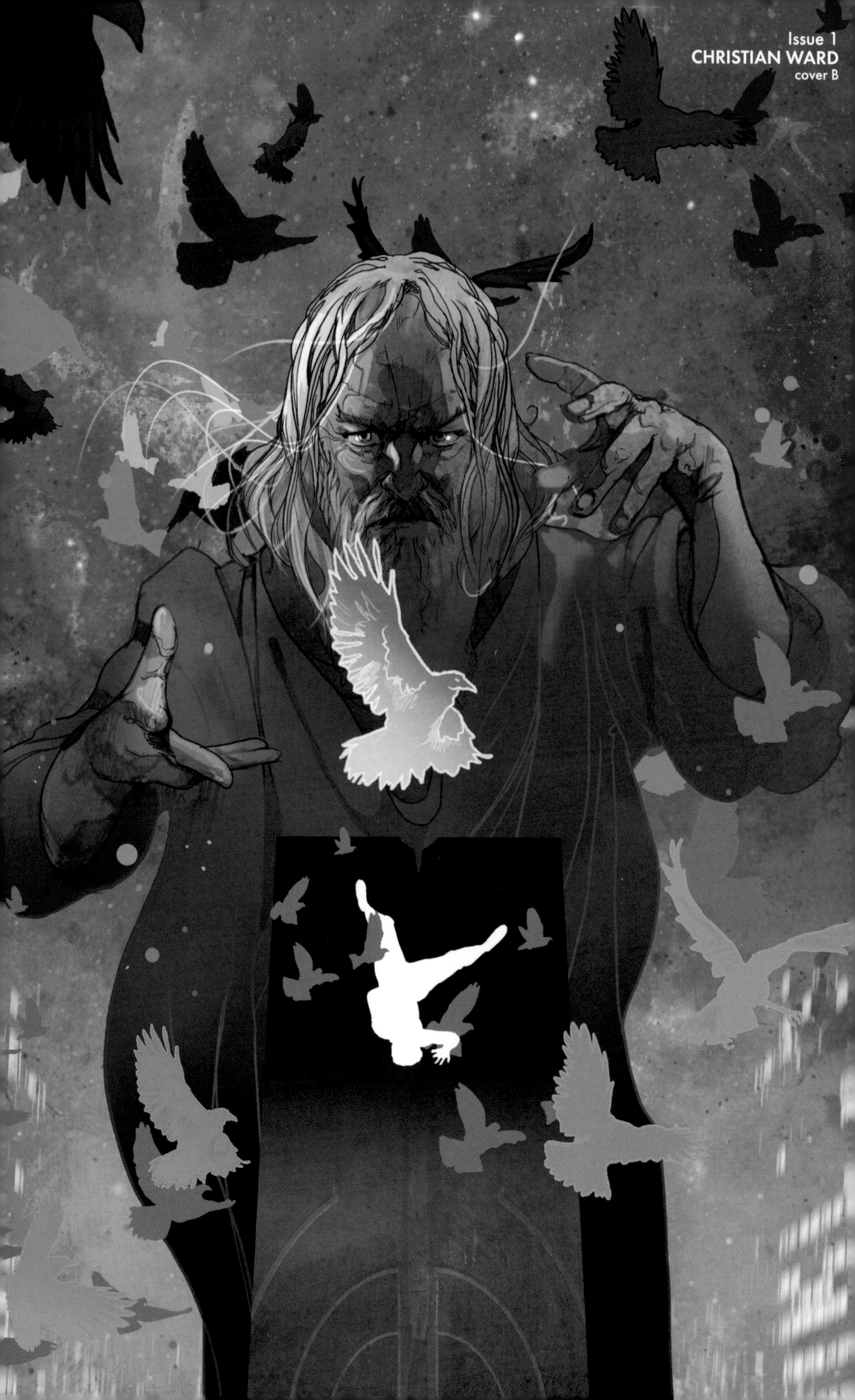

Issue 1
CHRISTIAN WARD
cover B

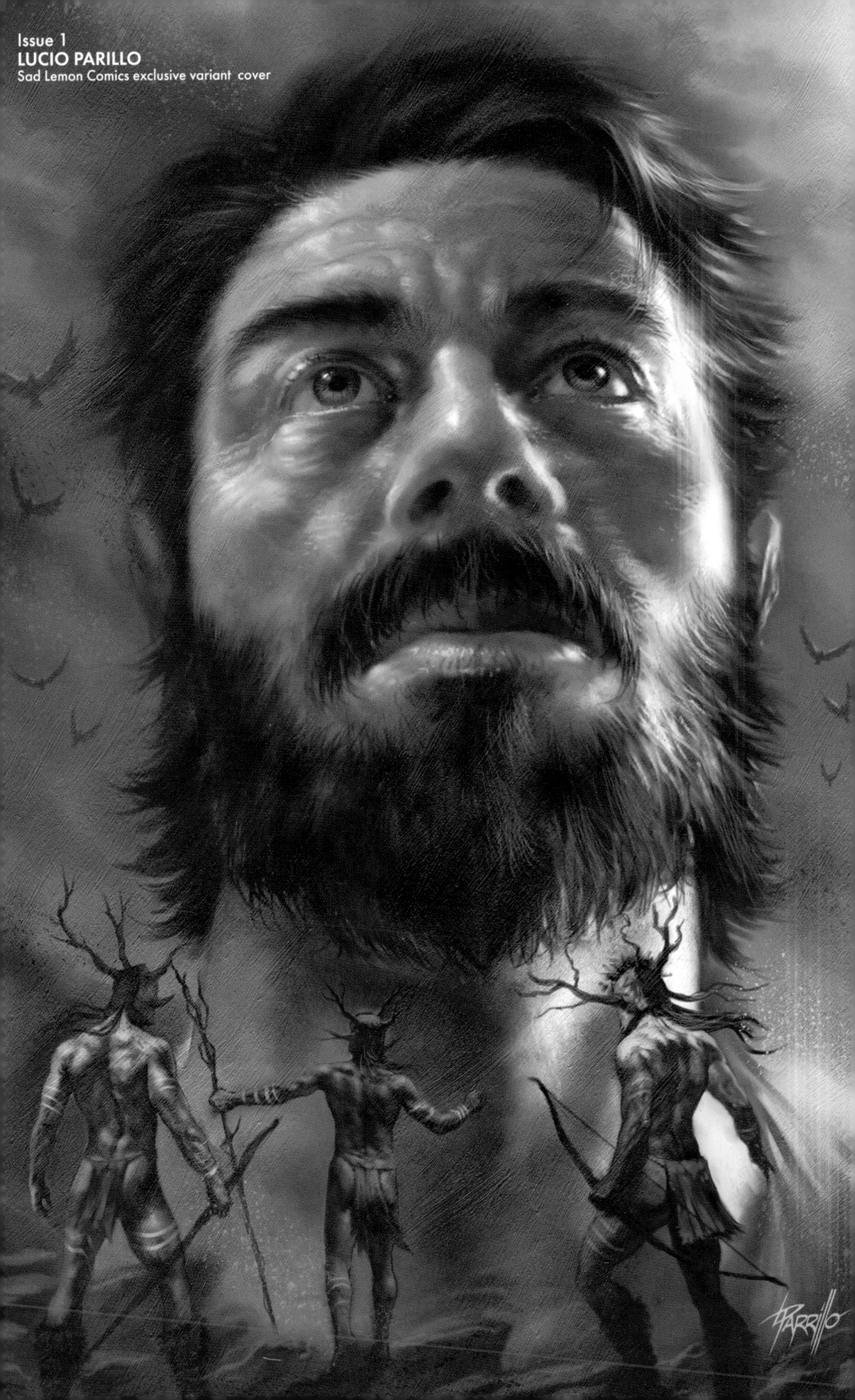

Issue 1
LUCIO PARILLO
Sad Lemon Comics exclusive variant cover

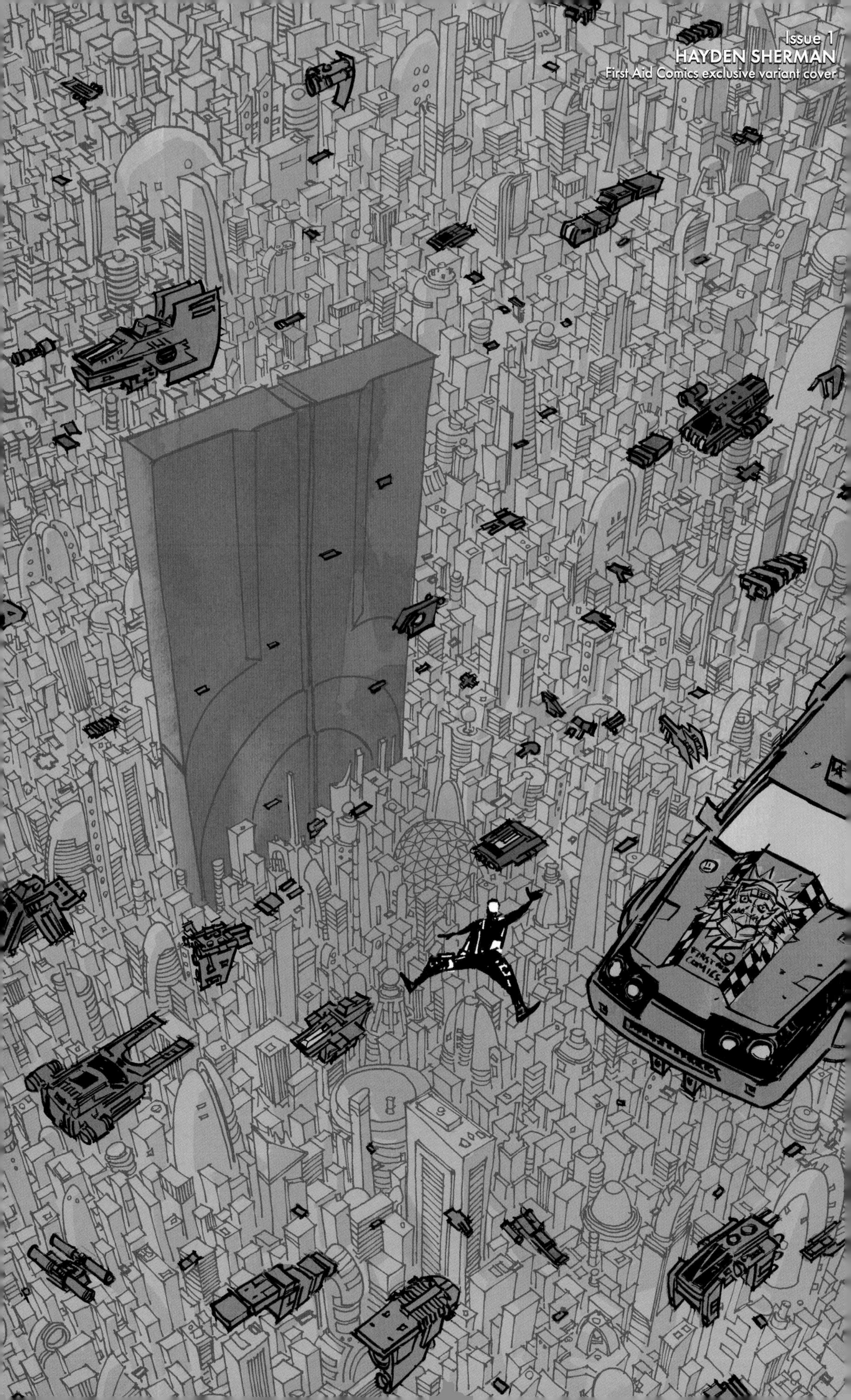
FIRST AID
COMICS

Issue 1
HAYDEN SHERMAN
First Aid Comics exclusive variant cover

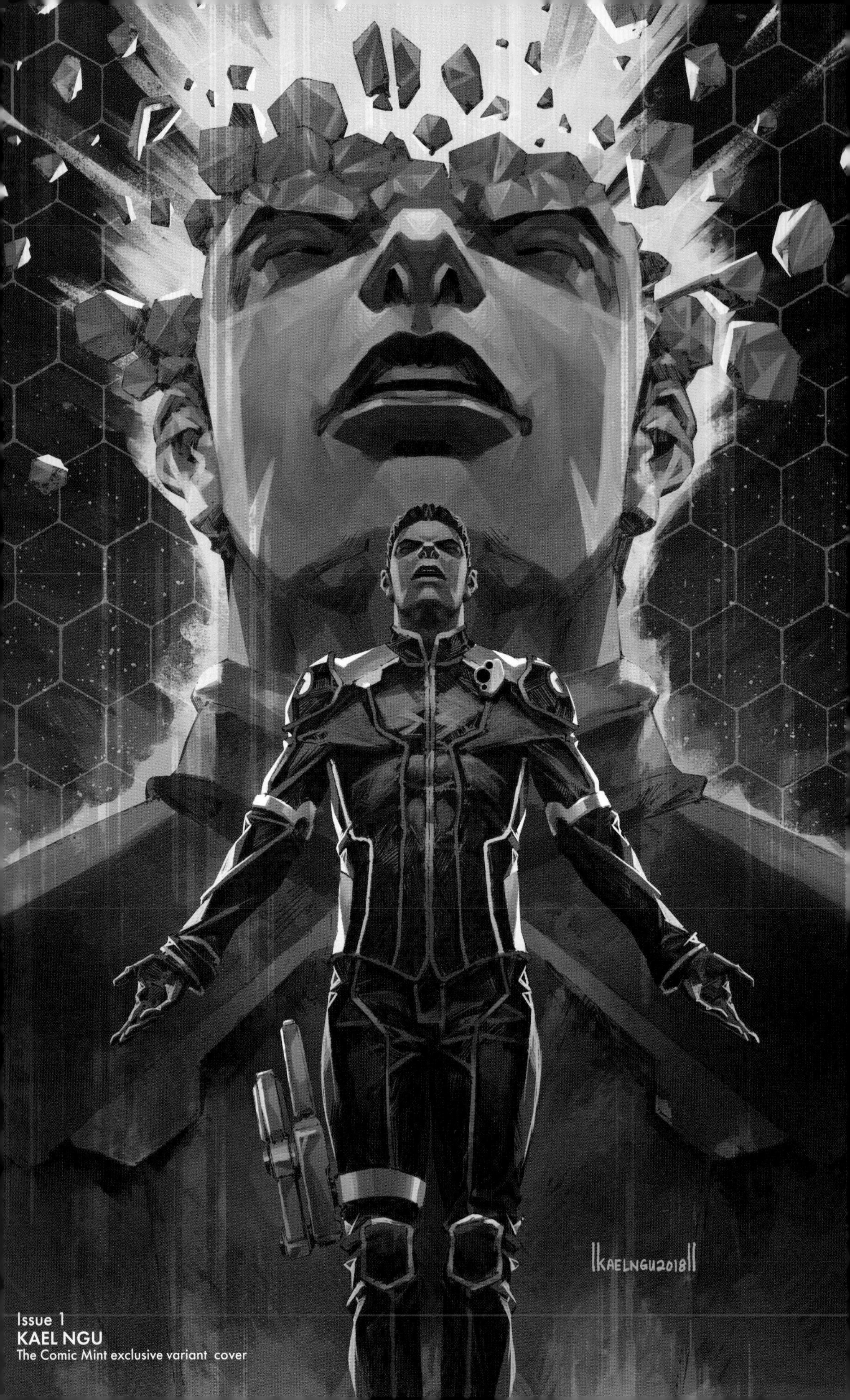
KAELNGU2018

Issue 1
KAEL NGU
The Comic Mint exclusive variant cover

RELAY™

BEHIND THE SCENES

LOGO DESIGNS
By John J. Hill

LETTEREING TESTS
By Charles Pritchett

DIALOGUE 1

TELL ME,
WHAT DO YOU
PLAN TO DO
TO ME?

JAMES, CAN
WE PLEASE THINK
WHAT WE'RE ABOUT
TO DO HERE? I'M
NOT SO SURE...

MRS. JONES,
YOU'RE SUCH A
NICE *LADY*. I'LL
FIND A WAY.

I PLAN ON
MAKING YOU
TALK, THAT'S
WHAT.

DIALOGUE 2

TELL ME,
WHAT DO YOU
PLAN TO DO
TO ME?

JAMES, CAN
WE PLEASE THINK
WHAT WE'RE ABOUT
TO DO HERE? I'M
NOT SO SURE...

MRS. JONES,
YOU'RE SUCH A
NICE *LADY*. I'LL
FIND A WAY.

I PLAN ON
MAKING YOU
TALK, THAT'S
WHAT.

LOCATIONS 1

SOMEWHERE IN SPACE

SECTOR 1138
YESTERDAY.

PLANET EARTH
OCTOBER 22, 1978

LOCATIONS 2

SOMEWHERE IN SPACE

SECTOR 1138
YESTERDAY.

PLANET EARTH
OCTOBER 22, 1978

CAPTIONS 1

"THE THOUGHT OF
DOING ANYTHING
LIKE THAT AGAIN
MAKES ME SICK.

"IT WAS
DISGUSTING,
DUDE."

SHE THOUGHT SHE
COULD GET THE
BEST OF ME. SHE
WAS WRONG.

DEAD
WRONG.

CAPTIONS 1

"THE THOUGHT OF
DOING ANYTHING
LIKE THAT AGAIN
MAKES ME SICK.

"IT WAS
DISGUSTING,
DUDE."

SHE THOUGHT SHE
COULD GET THE
BEST OF ME. SHE
WAS WRONG.

DEAD
WRONG.

BALLOONS

TELL ME,
WHAT DO YOU
PLAN TO DO
TO ME?

MRS. JONES,
YOU'RE SUCH A
NICE LADY. I'LL
FIND A WAY.

I PLAN ON
MAKING YOU
TALK, THAT'S
WHAT.

SPECIAL

MRS. JONES,
YOU'RE SUCH A
NICE *LADY*. I'LL
FIND A WAY.

A

1

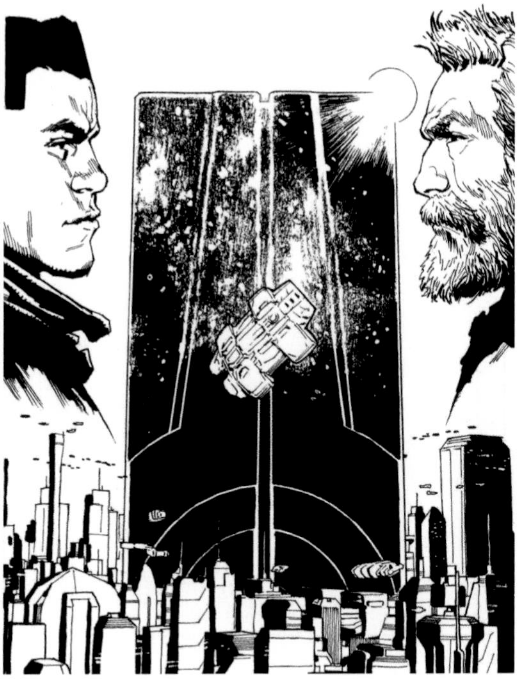

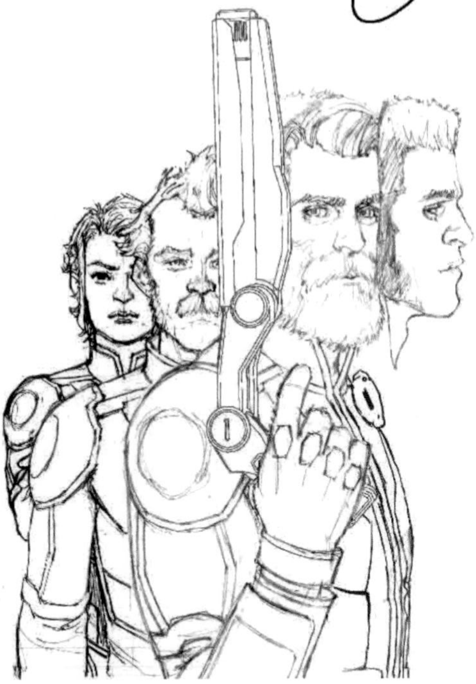

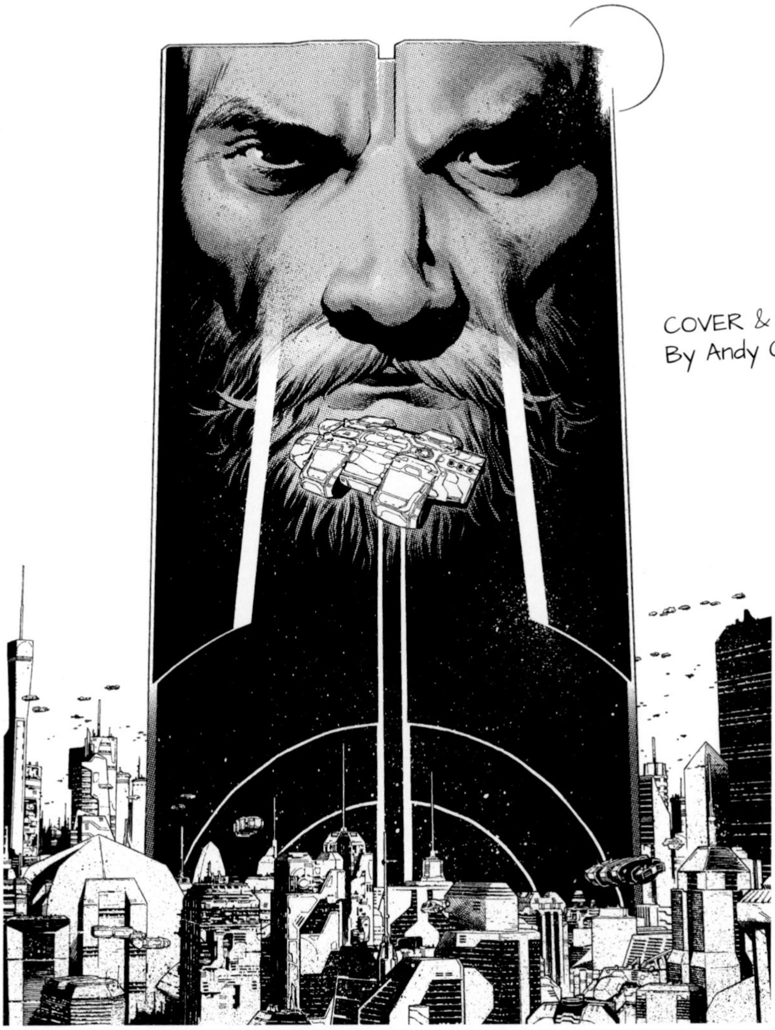

COVER & COVER DESIGNS
By Andy Clarke

ABOUT THE CREATORS OF RELAY™

ZAC THOMPSON writer

🐦 @ZacBeThompson

Zac Thompson is a writer from Prince Edward Island. He is best known for his critically acclaimed comic book series, *The Dregs*, published by Black Mask Studios. His work has also appeared in *IGN*, *Huff Post*, and *VICE*. His debut novel, *Weaponized*, was the winner of the 2016 CryptTV horror fiction contest. Zac is an avid cyclist and overly excitable weirdo who loves his rad cat Pancho more than anything in the world.

ANDY CLARKE artist

Andy began working in comics in 1998 with writer Dan Abnett on *Sinister Dexter* for 2000AD. He has made modest contributions to *Judge Dredd* (including a newspaper strip), worked on *Nikolai Dante and Shimura* with Robbie Morrison and with Kek-W on *Rose O'Rion*. He co-created *Thirteen* with Mike Carey and teamed up with Andy Diggle for *Snow/Tiger*. Since 2005, he has been very fortunate to work with some of the best writers on a small number of titles in the US: *Aquaman*, *R.E.B.E.L.S.* and *Batman* for DC and a *Mystique/Logan Legacy* one-shot for Marvel. He's also done the odd cover here and there.

DALIBOR TALAJIC artist

🐦 @Dalibor410

Dalibor is a professor of clarinet at a music high school...at least he was until Joe Pruett gave him a shot in comics at Desperado Publishing. More recently, his art has been featured in such comic book titles as *The Incredible Hulk*, *X-Men*, *Deadpool Kills the Marvel Universe*, WITCH HAMMER and the AfterShock anthology, SHOCK. His most critically-acclaimed work is *Madaya Mom*.

JOSÉ VILLARRUBIA colorist

Born in Madrid, Spain, and living in Baltimore, José Villarrubia is best known for his collaborations with author Alan Moore: his illustrations for his books *Voice of the Fire* and *The Mirror of Love* and his graphic novel *Promethea*. He has worked extensively for Marvel, DC, Dark Horse, Image, Wildstorm, Vertigo, Valiant, Archie, Legendary and other publishers, doing digitally painted colors. He has been nominated several times for the Eisner Award and won the Harvey Award for *Cuba: My Revolution*.

DAN BROWN colorist

🐦 @danbrowncomics

Hailing from the frozen prairies of central Canada, Dan Brown has been a colorist for every major publisher for the past 23 years. Dan is thrilled to be working with Mike Marts (who gave him his first coloring gig at Marvel, lo those many moons ago) and the rest of the fantastic AfterShock team to bring the next level in comic book entertainment!

CHARLES PRITCHETT letterer

Brought up on the wrong side of the tracks in a bustling metropolis in Newfoundland & Labrador, Canada, Charles is really terrible at writing epic sounding biographies of his life and times. He enjoys a fine stew from time to time and hates to travel. When he's not working with AfterShock Comics, He can be found currently living in Canada's smallest, but nicest province, outnumbered by powerful women in his own household.